THE CRITICS APPLAUD TENNESSEE WILLIAMS:

"He is the greatest U. S. playwright since Eugene O'Neill, and the greatest living playwright anywhere."—TIME

"As a writer of prose drama, Mr. Williams has the genius of a poet."—*Brooks Atkinson,* NEW YORK TIMES

"The foremost American playwright of his time."—SATURDAY REVIEW

"The innocent and the damned, the lonely and the frustrated, the hopeful and the hopeless . . . he brings them into vivid focus with an earthy, irreverently comic passion."
—NEWSWEEK

THREE BY TENNESSEE

Sweet Bird of Youth

The Rose Tattoo

The Night of the Iguana

---

by
Tennessee Williams

A SIGNET CLASSIC

NEW AMERICAN LIBRARY

NEW YORK AND SCARBOROUGH, ONTARIO

SIGNET CLASSIC TRADEMARK REG. U.S. PAT. OFF. AND FOREIGN COUNTRIES
REGISTERED TRADEMARK—MARCA REGISTRADA
HECHO EN WINNIPEG, CANADA

SIGNET, SIGNET CLASSIC, MENTOR, ONYX, PLUME, MERIDIAN AND NAL
BOOKS are published *in the United States* by NAL PENGUIN INC.,
1633 Broadway, New York, New York 10019,
in Canada by The New American Library of Canada Limited,
81 Mack Avenue, Scarborough, Ontario M1L 1M8

FIRST SIGNET CLASSIC PRINTING, NOVEMBER, 1976

6 7 8 9 10 11 12 13 14

PRINTED IN CANADA

Sweet Bird of Youth

———◆———

With a Foreword by the Author

To Cheryl Crawford

Relentless caper for all those who step
The legend of their youth into the noon

HART CRANE

*Foreword**

When I came to my writing desk on a recent morning, I found lying on my desk top an unmailed letter that I had written. I began reading it and found this sentence: "We are all civilized people, which means that we are all savages at heart but observing a few amenities of civilized behavior." Then I went on to say: "I am afraid that I observe fewer of these amenities than you do. Reason? My back is to the wall and has been to the wall for so long that the pressure of my back on the wall has started to crumble the plaster that covers the bricks and mortar."

Isn't it odd that I said the wall was giving way, not my back? I think so. Pursuing this course of free association, I suddenly remembered a dinner date I once had with a distinguished colleague. During the course of this dinner, rather close to the end of it, he broke a long, mournful silence by lifting to me his sympathetic gaze and saying to me, sweetly, "Tennessee, don't you feel that you are blocked as a writer?"

I didn't stop to think of an answer; it came immediately off my tongue without any pause for planning. I said, "Oh, yes, I've always been blocked as a writer but my desire to write has been so strong that it has always broken down the block and gone past it."

Nothing untrue comes off the tongue that quickly. It is planned speeches that contain lies or dissimulations, not what you blurt out so spontaneously in one instant.

It was literally true. At the age of fourteen I discovered writing as an escape from a world of reality in which I felt acutely uncomfortable. It immediately became my place of

* Written prior to the Broadway opening of *Sweet Bird of Youth* and published in the *New York Times* on Sunday, March 8, 1959.

retreat, my cave, my refuge. From what? From being called a sissy by the neighborhood kids, and Miss Nancy by my father, because I would rather read books in my grandfather's large and classical library than play marbles and baseball and other normal kid games, a result of a severe childhood illness and of excessive attachment to the female members of my family, who had coaxed me back into life.

I think no more than a week after I started writing I ran into the first block. It's hard to describe it in a way that will be understandable to anyone who is not a neurotic. I will try. All my life I have been haunted by the obsession that to desire a thing or to love a thing intensely is to place yourself in a vulnerable position, to be a possible, if not a probable, loser of what you most want. Let's leave it like that. That block has always been there and always will be, and my chance of getting, or achieving, anything that I long for will always be gravely reduced by the interminable existence of that block.

I described it once in a poem called "The Marvelous Children."

"He, the demon, set up barricades of gold and purple tinfoil, labeled Fear (and other august titles), which they, the children, would leap lightly over, always tossing backwards their wild laughter."

But having, always, to contend with this adversary of fear, which was sometimes terror, gave me a certain tendency toward an atmosphere of hysteria and violence in my writing, an atmosphere that has existed in it since the beginning.

In my first published work, for which I received the big sum of thirty-five dollars, a story published in the July or August issue of Weird Tales in the year 1928, I drew upon a paragraph in the ancient histories of Herodotus to create a story of how the Egyptian queen, Nitocris, invited all of her enemies to a lavish banquet in a subterranean hall on the shores of the Nile, and how, at the height of this banquet, she excused herself from the table and opened sluice gates admitting the waters of the Nile into the locked banquet hall, drowning her unloved guests like so many rats.

I was sixteen when I wrote this story, but already a confirmed writer, having entered upon this vocation at the age of fourteen, and, if you're well acquainted with my writings since then, I don't have to tell you that it set the keynote for most of the work that has followed.

My first four plays, two of them performed in St. Louis, were correspondingly violent or more so. My first play professionally produced and aimed at Broadway was *Battle of Angels* and it was about as violent as you can get on the stage.

During the nineteen years since then I have only produced five plays that are *not* violent: *The Glass Menagerie, You Touched Me, Summer and Smoke, The Rose Tattoo* and, recently in Florida, a serious comedy called *Period of Adjustment,* which is still being worked on.

What surprises me is the degree to which both critics and audience have accepted this barrage of violence. I think I was surprised, most of all, by the acceptance and praise of *Suddenly Last Summer.* When it was done off Broadway, I thought I would be critically tarred and feathered and ridden on a fence rail out of the New York theatre, with no future haven except in translation for theatres abroad, who might mistakenly construe my work as a castigation of American morals, not understanding that I write about violence in American life only because I am not so well acquainted with the society of other countries.

Last year I thought it might help me as a writer to undertake psychoanalysis and so I did. The analyst, being acquainted with my work and recognizing the psychic wounds expressed in it, asked me, soon after we started, "Why are you so full of hate, anger and envy?"

Hate was the word I contested. After much discussion and argument, we decided that "hate" was just a provisional term and that we would only use it till we had discovered the more precise term. But unfortunately I got restless and started hopping back and forth between the analyst's couch and some Caribbean beaches. I think before we called it quits I had persuaded the doctor that hate was not the right word, that there was some other thing, some other word for it, which we had not yet uncovered, and we left it like that.

Anger, oh yes! And envy, yes! But not hate. I think that hate is a thing, a feeling, that can only exist where there is no understanding. Significantly, good physicians never have it. They never hate their patients, no matter how hateful their patients may seem to be, with their relentless, maniacal concentration on their own tortured egos.

Since I am a member of the human race, when I attack its behavior toward fellow members I am obviously including myself in the attack, unless I regard myself as not human but superior to humanity. I don't. In fact, I can't expose a human weakness on the stage unless I know it through having it myself. I have exposed a good many human weaknesses and brutalities and consequently I have them.

I don't even think that I am more conscious of mine than any of you are of yours. Guilt is universal. I mean a strong sense of guilt. If there exists any area in which a man can rise above his moral condition, imposed upon him at birth and long before birth, by the nature of his breed, then I think it is only a willingness to know it, to face its existence in him, and I think that at least below the conscious level, we all face it. Hence guilty feelings, and hence defiant aggressions, and hence the deep dark of despair that haunts our dreams, our creative work, and makes us distrust each other.

Enough of these philosophical abstractions, for now. To get back to writing for the theatre, if there is any truth in the Aristotelian idea that violence is purged by its poetic representation on a stage, then it may be that my cycle of violent plays have had a moral justification after all. I know that I have felt it. I have always felt a release from the sense of meaninglessness and death when a work of tragic intention has seemed to me to have achieved that intention, even if only approximately, nearly.

I would say that there is something much bigger in life and death than we have become aware of (or adequately recorded) in our living and dying. And, further, to compound this shameless romanticism, I would say that our serious theatre is a search for that something that is not yet successful but is still going on.

Sweet Bird of Youth was presented at the Martin Beck Theatre in New York on March 10, 1959, by Cheryl Crawford. It was directed by Elia Kazan; the stage settings and lighting were by Jo Mielziner, the costumes by Anna Hill Johnstone, and the music by Paul Bowles; production stage manager, David Pardoll. The cast was as follows:

CHANCE WAYNE	PAUL NEWMAN
THE PRINCESS KOSMONOPOLIS	GERALDINE PAGE
FLY	MILTON J. WILLIAMS
MAID	PATRICIA RIPLEY
GEORGE SCUDDER	LOGAN RAMSEY
HATCHER	JOHN NAPIER
BOSS FINLEY	SIDNEY BLACKMER
TOM JUNIOR	RIP TORN
AUNT NONNIE	MARTINE BARTLETT
HEAVENLY FINLEY	DIANA HYLAND
CHARLES	EARL SYDNOR
STUFF	BRUCE DERN
MISS LUCY	MADELEINE SHERWOOD
THE HECKLER	CHARLES TYNER
VIOLET	MONICA MAY
EDNA	HILDA BRAWNER
SCOTTY	CHARLES MC DANIEL
BUD	JIM JETER
MEN IN BAR	DUKE FARLEY, RON HARPER, KENNETH BLAKE
PAGE	GLENN STENSEL

TIME: Modern, an Easter Sunday, from late morning
till late night.

SETTING
and
"SPECIAL
EFFECTS":

The stage is backed by a cyclorama that should
give a poetic unity of mood to the several specific
settings. There are nonrealistic projections on
this "cyc," the most important and constant being
a grove of royal palm trees. There is nearly
always a wind among these very tall palm trees,
sometimes loud, sometimes just a whisper, and
sometimes it blends into a thematic music which
will be identified, when it occurs, as "The
Lament."

During the daytime scenes the cyclorama projection is a poetic abstraction of semitropical sea
and sky in fair spring weather. At night it is the
palm garden with its branches among the stars.

The specific settings should be treated as freely
and sparingly as the sets for *Cat on a Hot Tin
Roof* or *Summer and Smoke*. They'll be described
as you come to them in the script.

act one

scene one

A bedroom of an old-fashioned but still fashionable hotel somewhere along the Gulf Coast in a town called St. Cloud. I think of it as resembling one of those "Grand Hotels" around Sorrento or Monte Carlo, set in a palm garden. The style is vaguely "Moorish." The principal set-piece is a great double bed which should be raked toward the audience. In a sort of Moorish corner backed by shuttered windows, is a wicker tabouret and two wicker stools, over which is suspended a Moorish lamp on a brass chain. The windows are floor length and they open out upon a gallery. There is also a practical door frame, opening onto a corridor: the walls are only suggested.

On the great bed are two figures, a sleeping woman, and a young man awake, sitting up, in the trousers of white silk pajamas. The sleeping woman's face is partly covered by an eyeless black satin domino to protect her from morning glare. She breathes and tosses on the bed as if in the grip of a nightmare. The young man is lighting his first cigarette of the day.

17

Outside the windows there is heard the soft, urgent cries of birds, the sound of their wings. Then a colored waiter, FLY, *appears at door on the corridor, bearing coffee-service for two. He knocks.* CHANCE *rises, pauses a moment at a mirror in the fourth wall to run a comb through his slightly thinning blond hair before he crosses to open the door.*

CHANCE: Aw, good, put it in there.

FLY: Yes, suh.

CHANCE: Give me the Bromo first. You better mix it for me, I'm—

FLY: Hands kind of shaky this mawnin'?

CHANCE [*shuddering after the Bromo*]: Open the shutters a little. Hey, I said a little, not much, not that much!

[*As the shutters are opened we see him clearly for the first time: he's in his late twenties and his face looks slightly older than that; you might describe it as a "ravaged young face" and yet it is still exceptionally good-looking. His body shows no decline, yet it's the kind of a body that white silk pajamas are, or ought to be, made for. A church bell tolls, and from another church, nearer, a choir starts singing The Alleluia Chorus. It draws him to the window, and as he crosses, he says:*]

I didn't know it was—Sunday.

FLY: Yes, suh, it's *Easter* Sunday.

CHANCE [*leans out a moment, hands gripping the shutters*]: Uh-huh. . . .

FLY: That's the Episcopal Church they're singin' in. The bell's from the Catholic Church.

CHANCE: I'll put your tip on the check.

FLY: Thank you, Mr. Wayne.

CHANCE [*as* FLY *starts for the door*]: Hey. How did you know my name?

FLY: I waited tables in the Grand Ballroom when you used to come to the dances on Saturday nights, with that real pretty girl you used to dance so good with, Mr. Boss Finley's daughter?

CHANCE: I'm increasing your tip to five dollars in return for a favor which is not to remember that you have recognized me or anything else at all. Your name is Fly—Shoo, Fly. Close the door with no noise.

VOICE OUTSIDE: Just a minute.

CHANCE: Who's that?

VOICE OUTSIDE: George Scudder.

[*Slight pause.* FLY *exits.*]

CHANCE: How did you know I was here?

[GEORGE SCUDDER *enters: a coolly nice-looking, business-like young man who might be the head of the Junior Chamber of Commerce but is actually a young doctor, about thirty-six or -seven.*]

SCUDDER: The assistant manager that checked you in here last night phoned me this morning that you'd come back to St. Cloud.

CHANCE: So you came right over to welcome me home?

SCUDDER: Your lady friend sounds like she's coming out of ether.

CHANCE: The Princess had a rough night.

SCUDDER: You've latched onto a Princess? [*mockingly*] Gee.

CHANCE: She's traveling incognito.

SCUDDER: Golly, I should think she would, if she's checking in hotels with *you*.

CHANCE: George, you're the only man I know that still says "gee," "golly," and "gosh."

SCUDDER: Well, I'm not the sophisticated type, Chance.

CHANCE: That's for sure. Want some coffee?

SCUDDER: Nope. Just came for a talk. A quick one.

CHANCE: Okay. Start talking, man.

SCUDDER: Why've you come back to St. Cloud?

CHANCE: I've still got a mother and a girl in St. Cloud. How's Heavenly, George?

SCUDDER: We'll get around to that later. [*He glances at his watch.*] I've got to be in surgery at the hospital in twenty-five minutes.

CHANCE: You operate now, do you?

SCUDDER [*opening doctor's bag*]: I'm chief of staff there now.

CHANCE: Man, you've got it made.

SCUDDER: Why have you come back?

CHANCE: I heard that my mother was sick.

SCUDDER: But you said, "How's Heavenly," not "How's my mother," Chance. [CHANCE *sips coffee.*] Your mother died a couple of weeks ago. . . .

[CHANCE *slowly turns his back on the man and crosses to*

the window. Shadows of birds sweep the blind. He lowers it a little before he turns back to SCUDDER.]

CHANCE: Why wasn't I notified?

SCUDDER: You were. A wire was sent you three days before she died at the last address she had for you which was General Delivery, Los Angeles. We got no answer from that and another wire was sent you after she died, the same day of her death and we got no response from that either. Here's the Church Record. The church took up a collection for her hospital and funeral expenses. She was buried nicely in your family plot and the church has also given her a very nice headstone. I'm giving you these details in spite of the fact that I know and everyone here in town knows that you had no interest in her, less than people who knew her only slightly, such as myself.

CHANCE: How did she go?

SCUDDER: She had a long illness, Chance. You know about that.

CHANCE: Yes. She was sick when I left here the last time.

SCUDDER: She was sick at heart as well as sick in her body at that time, Chance. But people were very good to her, especially people who knew her in church, and the Reverend Walker was with her at the end.

[CHANCE *sits down on the bed. He puts out his unfinished cigarette and immediately lights another. His voice becomes thin and strained.*]

CHANCE: She never had any luck.

SCUDDER: Luck? Well, that's all over with now. If you want to know anything more about that, you can get in touch with Reverend Walker about it, although I'm afraid he won't be likely to show much cordiality to you.

CHANCE: She's gone. Why talk about it?

SCUDDER: I hope you haven't forgotten the letter I wrote you soon after you last left town.

CHANCE: No. I got no letter.

SCUDDER: I wrote you in care of an address your mother gave me about a very important private matter.

CHANCE: I've been moving a lot.

SCUDDER: I didn't even mention names in the letter.

CHANCE: What was the letter about?

SCUDDER: Sit over here so I don't have to talk loud about this. Come over here. I can't talk loud about this. [SCUDDER *indicates the chair by the tabouret.* CHANCE *crosses and rests a foot on the chair.*] In this letter I just told you that a certain girl we know had to go through an awful experience, a tragic ordeal, because of past contact with you. I told you that I was only giving you this information so that you would know better than to come back to St. Cloud, but you didn't know better.

CHANCE: I told you I got no letter. Don't tell me about a letter, I didn't get any letter.

SCUDDER: I'm telling you what I told you in this letter.

CHANCE: All right. Tell me what you told me, don't— don't talk to me like a club, a chamber of something. What did you tell me? What ordeal? What girl? Heavenly? Heavenly? George?

SCUDDER: I see it's not going to be possible to talk about this quietly and so I . . .

CHANCE [*rising to block* SCUDDER's *way*]: Heavenly? What ordeal?

SCUDDER: We will not mention names. Chance, I rushed over here this morning as soon as I heard you were back in

St. Cloud, before the girl's father and brother could hear that you were back in St. Cloud, to stop you from trying to get in touch with the girl and to get out of here. That is absolutely all I have to say to you in this room at this moment. . . . But I hope I have said it in a way to impress you with the vital urgency of it, so you will leave. . . .

CHANCE: Jesus! If something's happened to Heavenly, will you please tell me—what?

SCUDDER: I said no names. We are not alone in this room. Now when I go downstairs now, I'll speak to Dan Hatcher, assistant manager here . . . he told me you'd checked in here . . . and tell him you want to check out, so you'd better get Sleeping Beauty and yourself ready to travel, and I suggest that you keep on traveling till you've crossed the State line. . . .

CHANCE: You're not going to leave this room till you've explained to me what you've been hinting at about my girl in St. Cloud.

SCUDDER: There's a lot more to this which we feel ought not to be talked about to anyone, least of all to you, since you have turned into a criminal degenerate, the only right term for you, but, Chance, I think I ought to remind you that once long ago the father of this girl wrote out a prescription for you, a sort of medical prescription, ~~which is castration.~~ You'd better think about that, that would deprive you of all you've got to get by on. [*He moves toward the steps.*]

CHANCE: I'm used to that threat. I'm not going to leave St. Cloud without my girl.

SCUDDER [*on the steps*]: You don't have a girl in St. Cloud. Heavenly and I are going to be married next month. [*He leaves abruptly.*]

[CHANCE, *shaken by what he has heard, turns and picks up phone, and kneels on the floor.*]

CHANCE: Hello? St. Cloud 525. Hello, Aunt Nonnie? This is Chance, yes Chance. I'm staying at the Royal Palms and I . . . what's the matter, has something happened to Heavenly? Why can't you talk now? George Scudder was here and . . . Aunt Nonnie? Aunt Nonnie?

[*The other end hangs up. The sleeping woman suddenly cries out in her sleep.* CHANCE *drops the phone on its cradle and runs to the bed.*]

CHANCE [*bending over her as she struggles out of a nightmare*]: Princess! Princess! Hey, *Princess Kos!* [*He removes her eyemask; she sits up gasping and staring wild-eyed about her.*]

PRINCESS: Who are you? Help!

CHANCE [*on the bed*]: Hush now. . . .

PRINCESS: Oh . . . I . . . had . . . a *terrible* dream.

CHANCE: It's all right. Chance's with you.

PRINCESS: Who?

CHANCE: Me.

PRINCESS: I don't know who you are!

CHANCE: You'll remember soon, Princess.

PRINCESS: I don't know, I don't know. . . .

CHANCE: It'll come back to you soon. What are you reachin' for, honey?

PRINCESS: Oxygen! Mask!

CHANCE: Why? Do you feel short-winded?

PRINCESS: Yes! I have . . . air . . . shortage!

CHANCE [*looking for the correct piece of luggage*]: Which bag is your oxygen in? I can't remember which bag we packed it in. Aw, yeah, the crocodile case, / the one with the combination lock. Wasn't the first number zero . . . [*He comes back to the bed and reaches for a bag under its far side.*]

PRINCESS [*as if with her dying breath*]: Zero, zero. Two zeros to the right and then back around to . . .

CHANCE: Zero, three zeros, two of them to the right and the last one to the left. . . .

PRINCESS: Hurry! I can't breathe, I'm dying!

CHANCE: I'm getting it, Princess.

PRINCESS: HURRY!

CHANCE: Here we are, I've got it. . . .

[*He has extracted from case a small oxygen cylinder and mask. He fits the inhalator over her nose and mouth. She falls back on the pillow. He places the other pillow under her head. After a moment, her panicky breath subsiding, she growls at him.*]

PRINCESS: Why in hell did you lock it up in that case?

CHANCE [*standing at the head of the bed*]: You said to put all your valuables in that case.

PRINCESS: I meant my jewelry, and you know it, you, bastard!

CHANCE: Princess, I didn't think you'd have these attacks any more. I thought that having me with you to protect you would stop these attacks of panic, I . . .

PRINCESS: Give me a pill.

CHANCE: Which pill?

PRINCESS: A pink one, a pinkie, and vodka . . .

[*He puts the tank on the floor, and goes over to the trunk. The phone rings.* CHANCE *gives the* PRINCESS *a pill, picks up the vodka bottle and goes to the phone. He sits down with the bottle between his knees.*]

CHANCE [*pouring a drink, phone held between shoulder and ear*]: Hello? Oh, hello, Mr. Hatcher——Oh? But Mr. Hatcher, when we checked in here last night we weren't told that, and Miss Alexandra Del Lago . . .

PRINCESS [*shouting*]: *Don't use my name!*

CHANCE: . . . is suffering from exhaustion, she's not at all well, Mr. Hatcher, and certainly not in any condition to travel. . . . I'm sure you don't want to take the responsibility for what might happen to Miss Del Lago . . .

PRINCESS [*shouting again*]: *Don't use my name!*

CHANCE: . . . if she attempted to leave here today in the condition she's in . . . do you?

PRINCESS: *Hang up!* [*He does. He comes over with his drink and the bottle to the* PRINCESS.] I want to forget everything, I want to forget who I am. . . .

CHANCE [*handing her the drink*]: He said that . . .

PRINCESS [*drinking*]: Please shut up, I'm *forgetting!*

CHANCE [*taking the glass from her*]: Okay, go on, forget. There's nothing better than that, I wish I could do it. . . .

PRINCESS: I can, I will. I'm forgetting . . . I'm forgetting. . . .

[*She lies down.* CHANCE *moves to the foot of the bed, where he seems to be struck with an idea. He puts the bottle down on the floor, runs to the chaise and picks up a tape recorder.*

Taking it back to the bed, he places the recorder on the floor. As he plugs it in, he coughs.]

What's going on?

CHANCE: Looking for my toothbrush.

PRINCESS [*throwing the oxygen mask on the bed*]: Will you please take that away.

CHANCE: Sure you've had enough of it?

PRINCESS [*laughs breathlessly*]: Yes, for God's sake, take it away. I must look hideous in it.

CHANCE [*taking the mask*]: No, no, you just look exotic, like a Princess from Mars or a big magnified insect.

PRINCESS: Thank you, check the cylinder please.

CHANCE: For what?

PRINCESS: Check the air left in it; there's a gauge on the cylinder that gives the pressure. . . .

CHANCE: You're still breathing like a quarter horse that's been run a full mile. Are you sure you don't want a doctor?

PRINCESS: No, for God's sake . . . no!

CHANCE: Why are you so scared of doctors?

PRINCESS [*hoarsely, quickly*]: I don't need them. What happened is nothing at all. It happens frequently to me. Something disturbs me . . . adrenalin's pumped in my blood and I get short-winded, that's all, that's all there is to it . . . I woke up, I didn't know where I was or who I was with, I got panicky . . . adrenalin was released and I got short-winded. . . .

CHANCE: Are you okay now, Princess? Huh? [*He kneels on the bed, and helps straighten up the pillows.*]

PRINCESS: Not quite yet, but I will be. I will be.

CHANCE: You're full of complexes, plump lady.

PRINCESS: What did you call me?

CHANCE: Plump lady.

PRINCESS: Why do you call me that? Have I let go of my figure?

CHANCE: You put on a good deal of weight after that disappointment you had last month.

PRINCESS [*hitting him with a small pillow*]: What disappointment? I don't remember any.

CHANCE: Can you control your memory like that?

PRINCESS: Yes. I've had to learn to. What is this place, a hospital? And you, what are you, a male nurse?

CHANCE: I take care of you but I'm not your nurse.

PRINCESS: But you're employed by me, aren't you? For some purpose or other?

CHANCE: I'm not on salary with you.

PRINCESS: What are you on? Just expenses?

CHANCE: Yep. You're footing the bills.

PRINCESS: I see. Yes, I see.

CHANCE: Why're you rubbing your eyes?

PRINCESS: My vision's so cloudy! Don't I wear glasses, don't I have any glasses?

CHANCE: You had a little accident with your glasses.

PRINCESS: What was that?

CHANCE: You fell on your face with them on.

PRINCESS: Were they completely demolished?

CHANCE: One lens cracked.

PRINCESS: Well, please give me the remnants. I don't mind waking up in an intimate situation with someone, but I like to see who it's with, so I can make whatever adjustment seems called for. . . .

CHANCE [rises and goes to the trunk, where he lights cigarette]: You know what I look like.

PRINCESS: No, I don't.

CHANCE: You did.

PRINCESS: I tell you I don't remember, it's all gone away!

CHANCE: I don't believe in amnesia.

PRINCESS: Neither do I. But you have to believe a thing that happens to you.

CHANCE: Where did I put your glasses?

PRINCESS: Don't ask me. You say I fell on them. If I was in that condition I wouldn't be likely to know where anything is I had with me. What happened last night?

[He has picked them up but not given them to her.]

CHANCE: You knocked yourself out.

PRINCESS: Did we sleep here together?

CHANCE: Yes, but I didn't molest you.

PRINCESS: Should I thank you for that, or accuse you of cheating? [She laughs sadly.]

CHANCE: I like you, you're a nice monster.

PRINCESS: Your voice sounds young. Are you young?

CHANCE: My age is twenty-nine years.

PRINCESS: That's young for anyone but an Arab. Are you very good-looking?

CHANCE: I used to be the best-looking boy in this town.

PRINCESS: How large is the town?

CHANCE: Fair-sized.

PRINCESS: Well, I like a good mystery novel, I read them to put me to sleep and if they don't put me to sleep, they're good; but this one's a little too good for comfort. I wish you would find me my glasses. . . .

[*He reaches over headboard to hand the glasses to her. She puts them on and looks him over. Then she motions him to come nearer and touches his bare chest with her finger tips.*]

Well, I may have done better, but God knows I've done worse.

CHANCE: What are you doing now, Princess?

PRINCESS: The tactile approach.

CHANCE: You do that like you were feeling a piece of goods to see if it was genuine silk or phony. . . .

PRINCESS: It feels like silk. Genuine! This much I do remember, that I like bodies to be hairless, silky-smooth gold!

CHANCE: Do I meet these requirements?

PRINCESS: You seem to meet those requirements. But I

still have a feeling that something is not satisfied in the relation between us.

CHANCE [*moving away from her*]: You've had your experiences, I've had mine. You can't expect everything to be settled at once. . . . Two different experiences of two different people. Naturally there's some things that have to be settled between them before there's any absolute agreement.

PRINCESS [*throwing the glasses on the bed*]: Take that splintered lens out before it gets in my eye.

CHANCE [*obeying this instruction by knocking the glasses sharply on the bed table*]: You like to give orders, don't you?

PRINCESS: It's something I seem to be used to.

CHANCE: How would you like to *take* them? To be a slave?

PRINCESS: What time is it?

CHANCE: My watch is in hock somewhere. Why don't you look at yours?

PRINCESS: Where's mine?

[*He reaches lazily over to the table, and hands it to her.*]

CHANCE: It's stopped, at five past seven.

PRINCESS: Surely it's later than that, or earlier, that's no hour when I'm . . .

CHANCE: Platinum, is it?

PRINCESS: No, it's only white gold. I never travel with anything very expensive.

CHANCE: Why? Do you get robbed much? Huh? Do you get "rolled" often?

PRINCESS: Get what?

CHANCE: "Rolled." Isn't that expression in your vocabulary?

PRINCESS: Give me the phone.

CHANCE: For what?

PRINCESS: I said give me the phone.

CHANCE: I know. And I said for what?

PRINCESS: I want to enquire where I am and who is with me?

CHANCE: Take it easy.

PRINCESS: Will you give me the phone?

CHANCE: Relax. You're getting short-winded again. . . . [*He takes hold of her shoulders.*]

PRINCESS: Please let go of me.

CHANCE: Don't you feel secure with me? Lean back. Lean back against me.

PRINCESS: Lean back?

CHANCE: This way, this way. There . . .

[*He pulls her into his arms: She rests in them, panting a little like a trapped rabbit.*]

PRINCESS: It gives you an awful trapped feeling this, this memory block. . . . I feel as if someone I loved had died lately, and I don't want to remember who it could be.

CHANCE: Do you remember your name?

PRINCESS: Yes, I do.

CHANCE: What's your name?

PRINCESS: I think there's some reason why I prefer not to tell you.

CHANCE: Well, I happen to know it. You registered under a phony name in Palm Beach but I discovered your real one. And you admitted it to me.

PRINCESS: I'm the Princess Kosmonopolis.

CHANCE: Yes, and you used to be known as . . .

PRINCESS [*sits up sharply*]: No, stop . . . will you let me do it? Quietly, in my own way? The last place I remember . . .

CHANCE: What's the last place you remember?

PRINCESS: A town with the crazy name of Tallahassee.

CHANCE: Yeah. We drove through there. That's where I reminded you that today would be Sunday and we ought to lay in a supply of liquor to get us through it without us being dehydrated too severely, and so we stopped there but it was a college town and we had some trouble locating a package store, open. . . .

PRINCESS: But we did, did we?

CHANCE [*getting up for the bottle and pouring her a drink*]: Oh, sure, we bought three bottles of Vodka. You curled up in the back seat with one of those bottles and when I looked back you were blotto. I intended to stay on the old Spanish Trail straight through to Texas, where you had some oil wells to look at. I didn't stop here . . . I was stopped.

PRINCESS: What by, a cop? Or . . .

CHANCE: No. No cop, but I was arrested by something.

PRINCESS: My car. Where is my car?

CHANCE [*handing her the drink*]: In the hotel parking lot, Princess.

PRINCESS: Oh, then, this is a hotel?

CHANCE: It's the elegant old Royal Palms Hotel in the town of St. Cloud.

[*Gulls fly past window, shadows sweeping the blind: they cry out with soft urgency.*]

PRINCESS: Those pigeons out there sound hoarse. They sound like gulls to me. Of course, they could be pigeons with laryngitis.

[CHANCE *glances at her with his flickering smile and laughs softly.*]

Will you help me please? I'm about to get up.

CHANCE: What do you want? I'll get it.

PRINCESS: I want to go to the window.

CHANCE: What for?

PRINCESS: To look out of it.

CHANCE: I can describe the view to you.

PRINCESS: I'm not sure I'd trust your description. WELL?

CHANCE: Okay, *oopsa-daisy.*

PRINCESS: My God! I said help me up, not . . . toss me onto the carpet! [*Sways dizzily a moment, clutching bed. Then draws a breath and crosses to the window.*]

[*Pauses as she gazes out, squinting into noon's brilliance.*]

CHANCE: Well, what do you see? Give me your description of the view, Princess?

PRINCESS [*faces the audience*]: I see a palm garden.

CHANCE: And a four-lane highway just past it.

PRINCESS [*squinting and shielding her eyes*]: Yes, I see that and a strip of beach with some bathers and then, an infinite stretch of nothing but water and . . . [*She cries out softly and turns away from the window.*]

CHANCE: What? . . .

PRINCESS: Oh God, I remember the thing I wanted not to. The goddam end of my life! [*She draws a deep shuddering breath.*]

CHANCE [*running to her aid*]: What's the matter?

PRINCESS: Help me back to bed. Oh God, no wonder I didn't want to remember, I was no fool!

[*He assists her to the bed. There is an unmistakable sympathy in his manner, however shallow.*]

CHANCE: Oxygen?

PRINCESS [*draws another deep shuddering breath*]: No! Where's the stuff? Did you leave it in the car?

CHANCE: Oh, the stuff? Under the mattress. [*Moving to the other side of the bed, he pulls out a small pouch.*]

PRINCESS: A stupid place to put it.

CHANCE [*sits at the foot of the bed*]: What's wrong with under the mattress?

PRINCESS [*sits up on the edge of the bed*]: There's such a thing as chambermaids in the world, they make up beds, they come across lumps in a mattress.

CHANCE: This isn't pot. What is it?

PRINCESS: Wouldn't that be pretty? A year in jail in one of those model prisons for distinguished addicts. What is it? Don't you know what it is, you beautiful, stupid young man? It's hashish, Moroccan, the finest.

CHANCE: Oh, hash! How'd you get it through customs when you came back for your come-back?

PRINCESS: I didn't get it through customs. The ship's doctor gave me injections while this stuff was winging over the ocean to a shifty young gentleman who thought he could blackmail me for it. [*She puts on her slippers with a vigorous gesture.*]

CHANCE: Couldn't he?

PRINCESS: Of course not. I called his bluff.

CHANCE: You took injections coming over?

PRINCESS: With my neuritis? I had to. Come on give it to me.

CHANCE: Don't you want it packed right?

PRINCESS: You talk too much. You ask too many questions. I need something quick. [*She rises.*]

CHANCE: I'm a new hand at this.

PRINCESS: I'm sure, or you wouldn't discuss it in a hotel room. . . .

[*She turns to the audience, and intermittently changes the focus of her attention.*]

For years they all told me that it was ridiculous of me to feel that I couldn't go back to the screen or the stage as a middle-aged woman. They told me I was an artist, not just a star whose career depended on youth. But I knew in my heart that the legend of Alexandra del Lago couldn't be separated from an appearance of youth. . . .

There's no more valuable knowledge than knowing the right time to go. I knew it. I went at the right time to go. RETIRED! Where to? To what? To that dead planet the moon. . . .

There's nowhere else to retire to when you retire from an art because, believe it or not, I really was once an artist. So I retired to the moon, but the atmosphere of the moon doesn't have any oxygen in it. I began to feel breathless, in that withered, withering country, of time coming after time not meant to come after, and so I discovered . . . Haven't you fixed it yet?

[CHANCE *rises and goes to her with a cigarette he has been preparing.*]

Discovered this!

And other practices like it, to put to sleep the tiger that raged in my nerves. . . . Why the unsatisfied tiger? In the nerves jungle? Why is anything, anywhere, unsatisfied, and raging? . . .

Ask somebody's good doctor. But don't believe his answer because it isn't . . . the answer . . . if I had just been old but you see, I wasn't old. . . .

I just wasn't young, not young, young. I just wasn't young anymore. . . .

CHANCE: Nobody's young anymore. . . .

PRINCESS: But you see, I couldn't get old with that tiger still in me raging.

CHANCE: Nobody can get old. . . .

PRINCESS: Stars in retirement sometimes give acting lessons. Or take up painting, paint flowers on pots, or landscapes. I could have painted the landscapes of the endless, withering country in which I wandered like a lost nomad. If I could paint deserts and nomads, if I could paint . . . hahaha. . . .

CHANCE: SH-Sh-sh-

PRINCESS: Sorry!

CHANCE: Smoke.

PRINCESS: Yes, smoke! And then the young lovers. . . .

CHANCE: Me?

PRINCESS: You? Yes, finally you. But you come after the come-back. Ha . . . Ha . . . The glorious come-back, when I turned fool and came back. . . . The screen's a very clear mirror. There's a thing called a close-up. The camera advances and you stand still and your head, your face, is caught in the frame of the picture with a light blazing on it and all your terrible history screams while you smile. . . .

CHANCE: How do you know? Maybe it wasn't a failure, maybe you were just scared, just chicken, Princess . . . ha-ha-ha. . . .

PRINCESS: Not a failure . . . after that close-up they gasped. . . . People gasped. . . . I heard them whisper, their shocked whispers. Is that her? Is that her? Her? . . . I made the mistake of wearing a very elaborate gown to the *première*, a gown with a train that had to be gathered up as I rose from my seat and began the interminable retreat from the city of flames, up, up, up the unbearably long theatre aisle, gasping for breath and still clutching up the regal white train of my gown, all the way up the forever . . . length of the aisle, and behind me some small unknown man grabbing at me, saying, stay, stay! At last the top of the aisle, I turned and struck him, then let the train fall, forgot it, and tried to run down the marble stairs, tripped of course, fell and, rolled, rolled, like a sailor's drunk whore to the bottom . . . hands, merciful hands without faces, assisted me to get up. After that? Flight, just flight, not interrupted until I woke up this morning. . . . Oh God it's gone out. . . .

CHANCE: Let me fix you another. Huh? Shall I fix you another?

PRINCESS: Let me finish yours. You can't retire with the out-crying heart of an artist still crying out, in your body, in your nerves, in your what? Heart? Oh, no that's gone, that's . . .

CHANCE [*He goes to her, takes the cigarette out of her hand and gives her a fresh one.*] Here, I've fixed you another one . . . Princess, I've fixed you another. . . . [*He sits on the floor, leaning against the foot of the bed.*]

PRINCESS: Well, sooner or later, at some point in your life, the thing that you lived for is lost or abandoned, and then . . . you die, or find something else. This is my something else. . . . [*She approaches the bed.*] And ordinarily I take the most fantastic precautions against . . . detection. . . . [*She sits on the bed, then lies down on her back, her head over the foot, near his.*] I cannot imagine what possessed me to let you know. Knowing so little about you as I seem to know.

CHANCE: I must've inspired a good deal of confidence in you.

PRINCESS: If that's the case, I've gone crazy. Now tell me something. What is that body of water, that sea, out past the palm garden and four-lane highway? I ask you because I remember now that we turned west from the sea when we went onto that highway called the Old Spanish Trail.

CHANCE: We've come back to the sea.

PRINCESS: What sea?

CHANCE: The Gulf.

PRINCESS: The Gulf?

CHANCE: The Gulf of misunderstanding between me and you. . . .

PRINCESS: We don't understand each other? And lie here smoking this stuff?

CHANCE: Princess, don't forget that this stuff is yours, that you provided me with it.

PRINCESS: What are you trying to prove? [*Church bells toll.*] Sundays go on a long time.

CHANCE: You don't deny it was yours.

PRINCESS: What's mine?

CHANCE: You brought it into the country, you smuggled it through customs into the U.S.A. and you had a fair supply of it at that hotel in Palm Beach and were asked to check out before you were ready to do so, because its aroma drifted into the corridor one breezy night.

PRINCESS: What are you trying to prove?

CHANCE: You don't deny that you introduced me to it?

PRINCESS: Boy, I doubt very much that I have any vice that I'd need to introduce to you. . . .

CHANCE: Don't call me "boy."

PRINCESS: Why not?

CHANCE: It sounds condescending. And all my vices were caught from other people.

PRINCESS: What are you trying to prove? My memory's come back now. Excessively clearly. It was this mutual practice that brought us together. When you came in my cabana to give me one of those papaya cream rubs, you sniffed, you grinned and said you'd like a stick too.

CHANCE: That's right. I knew the smell of it.

PRINCESS: What are you trying to prove?

CHANCE: You asked me four or five times what I'm trying

to prove, the answer is nothing. I'm just making sure that your memory's cleared up now. You do remember me coming in your cabana to give you those papaya cream rubs?

PRINCESS: Of course I do, Carl!

CHANCE: My name is not Carl. It's Chance.

PRINCESS: You called yourself Carl.

CHANCE: I always carry an extra name in my pocket.

PRINCESS: You're not a criminal, are you?

CHANCE: No ma'am, not me. You're the one that's committed a federal offense.

[*She stares at him a moment, and then goes to the door leading to the hall, looks out and listens.*]

What did you do that for?

PRINCESS [*closing the door*]: To see if someone was planted outside the door.

CHANCE: You still don't trust me?

PRINCESS: Someone that gives me a false name?

CHANCE: You registered under a phony one in Palm Beach.

PRINCESS: Yes, to avoid getting any reports or condolences on the disaster I ran from. [*She crosses to the window. There is a pause followed by "The Lament."*] And so we've not arrived at any agreement?

CHANCE: No ma'am, not a complete one.

[*She turns her back to the window and gazes at him from there.*]

PRINCESS: What's the gimmick? The hitch?

CHANCE: The usual one.

PRINCESS: What's that?

CHANCE: Doesn't somebody always hold out for something?

PRINCESS: Are you holding out for something?

CHANCE: Uh-huh. . . .

PRINCESS: What?

CHANCE: You said that you had a large block of stock, more than half ownership in a sort of a second-rate Hollywood Studio, and could put me under contract. I doubted your word about that. You're not like any phony I've met before, but phonies come in all types and sizes. So I held out, even after we locked your cabana door for the papaya cream rubs. . . . You wired for some contract papers we signed. It was notarized and witnessed by three strangers found in a bar.

PRINCESS: Then why did you hold out, still?

CHANCE: I didn't have much faith in it. You know, you can buy those things for six bits in novelty stores. I've been conned and tricked too often to put much faith in anything that could still be phony.

PRINCESS: You're wise. However, I have the impression that there's been a certain amount of intimacy between us.

CHANCE: A certain amount. No more. I wanted to hold your interest.

PRINCESS: Well, you miscalculated. My interest always increases with satisfaction.

CHANCE: Then you're unusual in that respect, too.

PRINCESS: In all respects I'm not common.

CHANCE: But I guess the contract we signed is full of loopholes?

PRINCESS: Truthfully, yes, it is. I can get out of it if I wanted to. And so can the studio. Do you have any talent?

CHANCE: For what?

PRINCESS: Acting, baby, ACTING!

CHANCE: I'm not as positive of it as I once was. I've had more chances than I could count on my fingers, and made the grade almost, but not quite, every time. Something always blocks me. . . .

PRINCESS: What? What? Do you *know?* [*He rises. The lamentation is heard very faintly.*] Fear?

CHANCE: No not fear, but terror . . . otherwise would I be your goddam caretaker, hauling you across the country? Picking you up when you fall? Well would I? Except for that block, be anything less than a star?

PRINCESS: CARL!

CHANCE: Chance. . . . Chance Wayne. You're stoned.

PRINCESS: Chance, come back to your youth. Put off this false, ugly hardness and . . .

CHANCE: And be took in by every con-merchant I meet?

PRINCESS: I'm not a phony, believe me.

CHANCE: Well, then, what is it you want? Come on say it, Princess.

PRINCESS: Chance, come here. [*He smiles but doesn't move.*] Come here and let's comfort each other a little.

[*He crouches by the bed; she encircles him with her bare arms.*]

CHANCE: Princess! Do you know something? All this conversation has been recorded on tape?

PRINCESS: What are you talking about?

CHANCE: Listen. I'll play it back to you. [*He uncovers the tape recorder; approaches her with the earpiece.*]

PRINCESS: How did you get that thing?

CHANCE: You bought it for me in Palm Beach. I said that I wanted it to improve my diction. . . .

[*He presses the "play" button on the recorder. The following in the left column can either be on a public address system, or can be cut.*]

(PLAYBACK)

PRINCESS: What is it? Don't you know what it is? You stupid, beautiful young man. It's hashish, Moroccan, the finest.

CHANCE: Oh, hash? How'd you get it through customs when you came back for your "come-back"?

PRINCESS: I didn't get it through customs. The ship's doctor. . . .

PRINCESS: What a smart cookie you are.

CHANCE: How does it feel to be over a great big barrel?

[*He snaps off the recorder and picks up the reels.*]

PRINCESS: This is blackmail is it? Where's my mink stole?

CHANCE: Not stolen.

[*He tosses it to her contemptuously from a chair.*]

PRINCESS: Where is my jewel case?

CHANCE [*picks it up off the floor and throws it on the bed*]: Here.

PRINCESS [*opens it up and starts to put on some jewelry*]: Every piece is insured and described in detail. Lloyd's in London.

CHANCE: *Who's* a smart cookie, Princess? You want your purse now so you can count your money?

PRINCESS: I don't carry currency with me, just travelers' checks.

CHANCE: I noted that fact already. But I got a fountain pen you can sign them with.

PRINCESS: Ho, Ho!

CHANCE: "Ho, ho!" What an insincere laugh, if that's how you fake a laugh, no wonder you didn't make good in your come-back picture. . . .

PRINCESS: Are you serious about this attempt to blackmail me?

CHANCE: You'd better believe it. Your trade's turned dirt on you, Princess. You understand that language.

PRINCESS: The language of the gutter is understood anywhere that anyone ever fell in it.

CHANCE: Aw, then you *do* understand.

PRINCESS: And if I shouldn't comply with this order of yours?

CHANCE: You still got a name, you're still a personage,

Princess. You wouldn't want "Confidential" or "Whisper" or "Hush-Hush" or the narcotics department of the F.B.I. to get hold of one of these tape-records, would you? And I'm going to make lots of copies. Huh? Princess?

PRINCESS: You are trembling and sweating . . . you see this part doesn't suit you, you just don't play it well, Chance. . . . [CHANCE *puts the reels in a suitcase.*] I hate to think of what kind of desperation has made you try to intimidate me, ME? ALEXANDRA DEL LAGO? with that ridiculous threat. Why it's so silly, it's touching, downright endearing, it makes me feel close to you, Chance.

You were well born, weren't you? Born of good Southern stock, in a genteel tradition, with just one disadvantage, a laurel wreath on your forehead, given too early, without enough effort to earn it . . . where's your scrapbook, Chance? [*He crosses to the bed, takes a travelers' checkbook out of her purse, and extends it to her.*] Where's your book full of little theatre notices and stills that show you in the background of . . .

CHANCE: Here! Here! Start signing . . . or . . .

PRINCESS [*pointing to the bathroom*]: Or WHAT? Go take a shower under cold water. I don't like hot sweaty bodies in a tropical climate. Oh, you, I do want and will accept, still . . . under certain conditions which I will make very clear to you.

CHANCE: Here. [*Throws the checkbook toward the bed.*]

PRINCESS: Put this away. And your leaky fountain pen. . . . When monster meets monster, one monster has to give way, AND IT WILL NEVER BE ME. I'm an older hand at it . . . with much more natural aptitude at it than you have. . . . Now then, you put the cart a little in front of the horse. Signed checks are payment, delivery comes first. Certainly I can afford it, I could deduct you, as my caretaker, Chance, remember that I was a star before big taxes . . . and had a husband who was a great merchant prince. He taught me to deal with money. . . . Now, Chance, please pay close attention while I tell you the very special conditions under which I will keep you in my employment . . . after this miscalculation. . . .

Forget the legend that I was and the ruin of that legend.

Whether or not I do have a disease of the heart that places an early terminal date on my life, no mention of that, no reference to it ever. No mention of death, never, never a word on that odious subject. I've been accused of having a death wish but I think it's life that I wish for, terribly, shamelessly, on any terms whatsoever.

When I say now, the answer must not be later. I have only one way to forget these things I don't want to remember and that's through the act of love-making. That's the only dependable distraction so when I say now, because I need that distraction, it has to be now, not later.

[*She crosses to the bed: He rises from the opposite side of the bed and goes to the window: She gazes at his back as he looks out the window. Pause: Lamentation.*]

[PRINCESS, *finally, softly.*]

Chance, I need that distraction. It's time for me to find out if you're able to give it to me. You mustn't hang onto your silly little idea that you can increase your value by turning away and looking out a window when somebody wants you. . . . I want you. . . . I say now and I mean now, then and not until then will I call downstairs and tell the hotel cashier that I'm sending a young man down with some travelers' checks to cash for me. . . .

CHANCE [*turning slowly from the window*]: Aren't you ashamed, a little?

PRINCESS: Of course I am. Aren't you?

CHANCE: More than a little. . . .

PRINCESS: Close the shutters, draw the curtain across them.

[*He obeys these commands.*]

Now get a little sweet music on the radio and come here to me and make me almost believe that we're a pair of young lovers without any shame.

scene two

As the curtain rises, the PRINCESS *has a fountain pen in hand and is signing checks.* CHANCE, *now wearing dark slacks, socks and shoes of the fashionable loafer type, is putting on his shirt and speaks as the curtain opens.*

CHANCE: Keep on writing, has the pen gone dry?

PRINCESS: I started at the back of the book where the big ones are.

CHANCE: Yes, but you stopped too soon.

PRINCESS: All right, one more from the front of the book as a token of some satisfaction. I said some, not complete.

CHANCE [*picking up the phone*]: Operator—Give me the cashier please.

PRINCESS: What are you doing that for?

49

CHANCE: You have to tell the cashier you're sending me down with some travelers' checks to cash for you.

PRINCESS: Have to? Did you say have to?

CHANCE: Cashier? Just a moment. The Princess Kosmonopolis. [*He thrusts the phone at her.*]

PRINCESS [*into the phone*]: Who is this? But I don't want the cashier. My watch has stopped and I want to know the right time . . . five after three? Thank you . . . he says it's five after three. [*She hangs up and smiles at* CHANCE.] I'm not ready to be left alone in this room. Now let's not fight any more over little points like that, let's save our strength for the big ones. I'll have the checks cashed for you as soon as I've put on my face. I just don't want to be left alone in this place till I've put on the face that I face the world with, baby. Maybe after we get to know each other, we won't fight over little points any more, the struggle will stop, maybe we won't even fight over big points, baby. Will you open the shutters a little bit please? [*He doesn't seem to hear her. The lament is heard.*] I won't be able to see my face in the mirror. . . . Open the shutters, I won't be able to see my face in the mirror.

CHANCE: Do you want to?

PRINCESS [*pointing*]: Unfortunately I have to! Open the shutters!

[*He does. He remains by the open shutters, looking out as the lament in the air continues.*]

CHANCE: —I was born in this town. I was born in St. Cloud.

PRINCESS: That's a good way to begin to tell your life story. Tell me your life story. I'm interested in it, I really would like to know it. Let's make it your audition, a sort of screen test for you. I can watch you in the mirror while I put my face on. And tell me your life story, and if you hold my attention with your life story, I'll know you have

talent, I'll wire my studio on the Coast that I'm still alive
and I'm on my way to the Coast with a young man named
Chance Wayne that I think is cut out to be a great young
star.

CHANCE [*moving out on the forestage*]: Here is the town
I was born in, and lived in till ten years ago, in St. Cloud.
I was a twelve-pound baby, normal and healthy, but with
some kind of quantity "X" in my blood, a wish or a need
to be different. . . . The kids that I grew up with are mostly
still here and what they call "settled down," gone into business, married and bringing up children, the little crowd I
was in with, that I used to be the star of, was the snobset, the
ones with the big names and money. I didn't have either . . .
[*The* PRINCESS *utters a soft laugh in her dimmed-out area.*]
What I had was . . . [*The* PRINCESS *half turns, brush poised
in a faint, dusty beam of light.*]

PRINCESS: BEAUTY! Say it! Say it! What you had was
beauty! I had it! I say it, with pride, no matter how sad,
being gone, now.

CHANCE: Yes, well . . . the others . . . [*The* PRINCESS
*resumes brushing hair and the sudden cold beam of light on
her goes out again*] . . . are all now members of the young
social set here. The girls are young matrons, bridge-players,
and the boys belong to the Junior Chamber of Commerce and
some of them, clubs in New Orleans such as Rex and Comus
and ride on the Mardi Gras floats. Wonderful? No boring . . .
I wanted, expected, intended to get, something better. . . . Yes,
and I did, I got it. I did things that fat-headed gang never
dreamed of. Hell when they were still freshmen at Tulane or
LSU or Ole Miss, I sang in the chorus of the biggest show
in New York, in "Oklahoma," and had pictures in LIFE in
a cowboy outfit, tossin' a ten-gallon hat in the air! YIP . . .
EEEEEE! Ha-ha. . . . And at the same time pursued my other
vocation. . . .
   Maybe the only one I was truly meant for, love-making . . .
slept in the social register of New York! Millionaires' widows
and wives and debutante daughters of such famous names
as Vanderbrook and Masters and Halloway and Connaught,

names mentioned daily in columns, whose credit cards are their faces. . . . And . . .

PRINCESS: What did they pay you?

CHANCE: I gave people more than I took. Middle-aged people I gave back a feeling of youth. Lonely girls? Understanding, appreciation! An absolutely convincing show of affection. Sad people, lost people? Something light and uplifting! Eccentrics? Tolerance, even odd things they long for. . . .
But always just at the point when I might get something back that would solve my own need, which was great, to rise to their level, the memory of my girl would pull me back home to her . . . and when I came home for those visits, man oh man how that town buzzed with excitement. I'm telling you, it would blaze with it, and then that thing in Korea came along. I was about to be sucked into the Army so I went into the Navy, because a sailor's uniform suited me better, the uniform was all that suited me, though. . . .

PRINCESS: Ah-ha!

CHANCE [mocking her]: Ah-ha. I wasn't able to stand the goddam routine, discipline. . . .
I kept thinking, this stops everything. I was twenty-three, that was the peak of my youth and I knew my youth wouldn't last long. By the time I got out, Christ knows, I might be nearly thirty! Who would remember Chance Wayne? In a life like mine, you just can't stop, you know, can't take time out between steps, you've got to keep going right on up from one thing to the other, once you drop out, it leaves you and goes on without you and you're washed up.

PRINCESS: I don't think I know what you're talking about.

CHANCE: I'm talking about the parade. THE parade! The parade! the boys that go places that's the parade I'm talking about, not a parade of swabbies on a wet deck. And so I ran my comb through my hair one morning and noticed that eight or ten hairs had come out, a warning signal of a future baldness. My hair was still thick. But would it be five years

from now, or even three? When the war would be over, that
scared me, that speculation. I started to have bad dreams.
Nightmares and cold sweats at night, and I had palpitations,
and on my leaves I got drunk and woke up in strange places
with faces on the next pillow I had never seen before. My
eyes had a wild look in them in the mirror. . . . I got the
idea I wouldn't live through the war, that I wouldn't come
back, that all the excitement and glory of being Chance
Wayne would go up in smoke at the moment of contact
between my brain and a bit of hot steel that happened to be
in the air at the same time and place that my head was . . .
that thought didn't comfort me any. Imagine a whole lifetime
of dreams and ambitions and hopes dissolving away in one
instant, being blacked out like some arithmetic problem
washed off a blackboard by a wet sponge, just by some little
accident like a bullet, not even aimed at you but just shot
off in space, and so I cracked up, my nerves did. I got a
medical discharge out of the service and I came home in
civvies, then it was when I noticed how different it was, the
town and the people in it. Polite? Yes, but not cordial. No
headlines in the papers, just an item that measured one inch
at the bottom of page five saying that Chance Wayne, the
son of Mrs. Emily Wayne of North Front Street had received
an honorable discharge from the Navy as the result of illness
and was home to recover . . . that was when Heavenly became
more important to me than anything else. . . .

PRINCESS: Is Heavenly a girl's name?

CHANCE: Heavenly is the name of my girl in St. Cloud.

PRINCESS: Is Heavenly why we stopped here?

CHANCE: What other reason for stopping here can you
think of?

PRINCESS: So . . . I'm being used. Why not? Even a dead
race horse is used to make glue. Is she pretty?

CHANCE [*handing* PRINCESS *a snapshot*]: This is a flashlight photo I took of her, nude, one night on Diamond Key,
which is a little sandbar about half a mile off shore which is

under water at high tide. This was taken with the tide coming in. The water is just beginning to lap over her body like it desired her like I did and still do and will always, always. [CHANCE *takes back the snapshot.*] Heavenly was her name. You can see that it fits her. This was her at fifteen.

PRINCESS: Did you have her that early?

CHANCE: I was just two years older, we had each other that early.

PRINCESS: Sheer luck!

CHANCE: Princess, the great difference between people in this world is not between the rich and the poor or the good and the evil, the biggest of all differences in this world is between the ones that had or have pleasure in love and those that haven't and hadn't any pleasure in love, but just watched it with envy, sick envy. The spectators and the performers. I don't mean just ordinary pleasure or the kind you can buy, I mean great pleasure, and nothing that's happened to me or to Heavenly since can cancel out the many long nights without sleep when we gave each other such pleasure in love as very few people can look back on in their lives . . .

PRINCESS: No question, go on with your story.

CHANCE: Each time I came back to St. Cloud I had her love to come back to. . . .

PRINCESS: Something permanent in a world of change?

CHANCE: Yes, after each disappointment, each failure at something, I'd come back to her like going to a hospital. . . .

PRINCESS: She put cool bandages on your wounds? Why didn't you marry this Heavenly little physician?

CHANCE: Didn't I tell you that Heavenly is the daughter of Boss Finley, the biggest political wheel in this part of the country? Well, if I didn't I made a serious omission.

PRINCESS: He disapproved?

CHANCE: He figured his daughter rated someone a hundred, a thousand percent better than me, Chance Wayne. . . . The last time I came back here, she phoned me from the drugstore and told me to swim out to Diamond Key, that she would meet me there. I waited a long time, till almost sunset, and the tide started coming in before I heard the put-put of an outboard motor boat coming out to the sandbar. The sun was behind her, I squinted. She had on a silky wet tank suit and fans of water and mist made rainbows about her . . . she stood up in the boat as if she was water-skiing, shouting things at me an' circling around the sandbar, around and around it!

PRINCESS: She didn't come to the sandbar?

CHANCE: No, just circled around it, shouting things at me. I'd swim toward the boat, I would just about reach it and she'd race it away, throwing up misty rainbows, disappearing in rainbows and then circling back and shouting things at me again. . . .

PRINCESS: What things?

CHANCE: Things like, "Chance go away." "Don't come back to St. Cloud." "Chance, you're a liar." "Chance, I'm sick of your lies!" "My father's right about you!" "Chance, you're no good any more." "Chance, stay away from St. Cloud." The last time around the sandbar she shouted nothing, just waved good-by and turned the boat back to shore.

PRINCESS: Is that the end of the story?

CHANCE: Princess, the end of the story is up to you. You want to help me?

PRINCESS: I want to help you. Believe me, not everybody wants to hurt everybody. I don't want to hurt you, can you believe me?

CHANCE: I can if you prove it to me.

PRINCESS: How can I prove it to you?

CHANCE: I have something in mind.

PRINCESS: Yes, what?

CHANCE: Okay, I'll give you a quick outline of this project I have in mind. Soon as I've talked to my girl and shown her my contract, we go on, you and me. Not far, just to New Orleans, Princess. But no more hiding away, we check in at the Hotel Roosevelt there as Alexandra Del Lago and Chance Wayne. Right away the newspapers call you and give a press conference. . . .

PRINCESS: Oh?

CHANCE: Yes! The idea briefly, a local contest of talent to find a pair of young people to star as unknowns in a picture you're planning to make to show your faith in YOUTH, Princess. You stage this contest, you invite other judges, but your decision decides it!

PRINCESS: And you and . . . ?

CHANCE: Yes, Heavenly and I win it. We get her out of St. Cloud, we go to the West Coast together.

PRINCESS: And me?

CHANCE: You?

PRINCESS: Have you forgotten, for instance, that any public attention is what I least want in the world?

CHANCE: What better way can you think of to show the public that you're a person with bigger than personal interest?

PRINCESS: Oh, yes, yes, but not true.

CHANCE: You could pretend it was true.

PRINCESS: If I didn't despise pretending!

CHANCE: I understand. Time does it. Hardens people. Time and the world that you've lived in.

PRINCESS: Which you want for yourself. Isn't that what you want? [*She looks at him then goes to the phone.*] [*in phone*] Cashier?

Hello Cashier? This is the Princess Kosmonopolis speaking. I'm sending down a young man to cash some travelers' checks for me. [*She hangs up.*]

CHANCE: And I want to borrow your Cadillac for a while. . . .

PRINCESS: What for, Chance?

CHANCE [*posturing*]: I'm pretentious. I want to be seen in your car on the streets of St. Cloud. Drive all around town in it, blowing those long silver trumpets and dressed in the fine clothes you bought me. . . . Can I?

PRINCESS: Chance, you're a lost little boy that I really would like to help find himself.

CHANCE: I passed the screen test!

PRINCESS: Come here, kiss me, I love you. [*She faces the audience.*] Did I say that? Did I mean it? [*Then to* CHANCE *with arms outstretched.*] What a child you are. . . . Come here. . . . [*He ducks under her arms, and escapes to the chair.*]

CHANCE: I want this big display. Big phony display in your Cadillac around town. And a wad a dough to flash in their faces and the fine clothes you've bought me, on me.

PRINCESS: Did I buy you fine clothes?

CHANCE [*picking up his jacket from the chair*]: The finest. When you stopped being lonely because of my company at that Palm Beach Hotel, you bought me the finest. That's the deal for tonight, to toot those silver horns and drive slowly around in the Cadillac convertible so everybody that thought I was washed up will see me. And I have taken my false or true contract to flash in the faces of various people that called me washed up. All right that's the deal. Tomorrow you'll get the car back and what's left of your money. Tonight's all that counts.

PRINCESS: How do you know that as soon as you walk out of this room I won't call the police?

CHANCE: You wouldn't do that, Princess. [*He puts on his jacket.*] You'll find the car in back of the hotel parking lot, and the left-over dough will be in the glove compartment of the car.

PRINCESS: Where will you be?

CHANCE: With my girl, or nowhere.

PRINCESS: Chance Wayne! This was not necessary, all this. I'm not a phony and I wanted to be your friend.

CHANCE: Go back to sleep. As far as I know you're not a bad person, but you just got into bad company on this occasion.

PRINCESS: I am your friend and I'm not a phony. [CHANCE *turns and goes to the steps.*] When will I see you?

CHANCE [*at the top of the steps*]: I don't know—maybe never.

PRINCESS: Never is a long time, Chance, I'll wait.

[*She throws him a kiss.*]

CHANCE: So long.

[*The* PRINCESS *stands looking after him as the lights dim and the curtain closes.*]

act two

scene one

The terrace of BOSS FINLEY'S *house, which is a frame house of Victorian Gothic design, suggested by a door frame at the right and a single white column. As in the other scenes, there are no walls, the action occurring against the sky and sea cyclorama.*

The Gulf is suggested by the brightness and the gulls crying as in Act One. There is only essential porch furniture, Victorian wicker but painted bone white. The men should also be wearing white or off-white suits: the tableau is all blue and white, as strict as a canvas of Georgia O'Keeffe's.

At the rise of the curtain, BOSS FINLEY *is standing in the center and* GEORGE SCUDDER *nearby.*

BOSS FINLEY: Chance Wayne had my daughter when she was fifteen.

SCUDDER: That young.

BOSS: When she was fifteen he had her. Know how I

59

know? Some flashlight photos were made of her, naked, on Diamond Key.

SCUDDER: By Chance Wayne?

BOSS: My little girl was fifteen, barely out of her childhood when— [*calling offstage*] Charles—

[CHARLES *enters*]

BOSS: Call Miss Heavenly—

CHARLES [*concurrently*]: Miss Heavenly. Miss Heavenly. Your daddy wants to see you.

[CHARLES *leaves.*]

BOSS [*to* SCUDDER]: By Chance Wayne? Who the hell else do you reckon? I seen them. He had them developed by some studio in Pass Christian that made more copies of them than Chance Wayne ordered and these photos were circulated. I seen them. That was when I first warned the son-of-a-bitch to git out of St. Cloud. But he's back in St. Cloud right now. I tell you—

SCUDDER: Boss, let me make a suggestion. Call off this rally, I mean your appearance at it, and take it easy tonight. Go out on your boat, you and Heavenly take a short cruise on the Starfish. . . .

BOSS: I'm not about to start sparing myself. Oh, I know, I'll have me a coronary and go like that. But not because Chance Wayne had the unbelievable gall to come back to St. Cloud. [*calling offstage*] Tom Junior!

TOM JUNIOR [*offstage*]: Yes, sir!

BOSS: Has he checked out yet?

TOM JUNIOR [*entering*]: Hatcher says he called their room at the Royal Palms, and Chance Wayne answered the phone, and Hatcher says . . .

BOSS: Hatcher says,—who's Hatcher?

TOM JUNIOR: Dan Hatcher.

BOSS: I hate to expose my ignorance like this but the name Dan Hatcher has no more meaning to me than the name of Hatcher, which is none whatsoever.

SCUDDER [*quietly, deferentially*]: Hatcher, Dan Hatcher, is the assistant manager of the Royal Palms Hotel, and the man that informed me this morning that Chance Wayne was back in St. Cloud.

BOSS: Is this Hatcher a talker, or can he keep his mouth shut?

SCUDDER: I think I impressed him how important it is to handle this thing discreetly.

BOSS: Discreetly, like you handled that operation you done on my daughter, so discreetly that a hillbilly heckler is shouting me questions about it wherever I speak?

SCUDDER: I went to fantastic lengths to preserve the secrecy of that operation.

TOM JUNIOR: When Papa's upset he hits out at anyone near him.

BOSS: I just want to know—Has Wayne left?

TOM JUNIOR: Hatcher says that Chance Wayne told him that this old movie star that he's latched on to . . .

SCUDDER: Alexandra Del Lago.

TOM JUNIOR: She's not well enough to travel.

BOSS: Okay, you're a doctor, remove her to a hospital. Call an ambulance and haul her out of the Royal Palms Hotel.

SCUDDER: Without her consent?

BOSS: Say she's got something contagious, typhoid, bubonic plague. Haul her out and slap a quarantine on her hospital door. That way you can separate them. We can remove Chance Wayne from St. Cloud as soon as this Miss Del Lago is removed from Chance Wayne.

SCUDDER: I'm not so sure that's the right way to go about it.

BOSS: Okay, you think of a way. My daughter's no whore, but she had a whore's operation after the last time he had her. I don't want him passin' another night in St. Cloud. Tom Junior.

TOM JUNIOR: Yes, sir.

BOSS: I want him gone by tomorrow—tomorrow commences at midnight.

TOM JUNIOR: I know what to do, Papa. Can I use the boat?

BOSS: Don't ask me, don't tell me nothin'—

TOM JUNIOR: Can I have *The Starfish* tonight?

BOSS: I don't want to know how, just go about it. Where's your sister?

[CHARLES *appears on the gallery, points out* HEAVENLY *lying on the beach to* BOSS *and exits.*]

TOM JUNIOR: She's lyin' out on the beach like a dead body washed up on it.

BOSS [*calling*]: Heavenly!

TOM JUNIOR: Gawge, I want you with me on this boat trip tonight, Gawge.

BOSS [*calling*]: Heavenly!

SCUDDER: I know what you mean, Tom Junior, but I couldn't be involved in it. I can't even know about it.

BOSS [*calling again*]: Heavenly!

TOM JUNIOR: Okay, don't be involved in it. There's a pretty fair doctor that lost his license for helping a girl out of trouble, and he won't be so goddam finicky about doing this absolutely just thing.

SCUDDER: I don't question the moral justification, which is complete without question. . . .

TOM JUNIOR: Yeah, complete without question.

SCUDDER: But I am a reputable doctor, I haven't lost my license. I'm chief of staff at the great hospital put up by your father. . . .

TOM JUNIOR: I said, don't know about it.

SCUDDER: No, sir, I won't know about it . . . [BOSS *starts to cough.*] I can't afford to, and neither can your father. . . . [SCUDDER *goes to gallery writing prescription.*]

BOSS: Heavenly! Come up here, sugar. [*to* SCUDDER] What's that you're writing?

SCUDDER: Prescription for that cough.

BOSS: Tear it up, throw it away. I've hawked and spit all my life, and I'll be hawking and spitting in the hereafter. You all can count on that.

[*Auto horn is heard.*]

TOM JUNIOR [*leaps up on the gallery and starts to leave*]: Papa, he's drivin' back by.

BOSS: Tom Junior.

[TOM JUNIOR *stops.*]

TOM JUNIOR: Is Chance Wayne insane?

SCUDDER: Is a criminal degenerate sane or insane is a question that lots of law courts haven't been able to settle.

BOSS: Take it to the Supreme Court, they'll hand you down a decision on that question. They'll tell you a handsome young criminal degenerate like Chance Wayne is the mental and moral equal of any white man in the country.

TOM JUNIOR: He's stopped at the foot of the drive.

BOSS: Don't move, don't move, Tom Junior.

TOM JUNIOR: I'm not movin', Papa.

CHANCE [*offstage*]: Aunt Nonnie! Hey, Aunt Nonnie!

BOSS: What's he shouting?

TOM JUNIOR: He's shouting at Aunt Nonnie.

BOSS: Where is she?

TOM JUNIOR: Runnin' up the drive like a dog-track rabbit.

BOSS: He ain't followin', is he?

TOM JUNIOR: Nope. He's drove away.

[AUNT NONNIE *appears before the veranda, terribly flustered, rooting in her purse for something, apparently blind to the men on the veranda.*]

BOSS: Whatcha lookin' for, Nonnie?

NONNIE [*stopping short*]: Oh—I didn't notice you, Tom. I was looking for my *door*-key.

BOSS: Door's open, Nonnie, it's wide open, like a church door.

NONNIE [*laughing*]: Oh, ha, ha . . .

BOSS: Why didn't you answer that good-lookin' boy in the Cadillac car that shouted at you, Nonnie?

NONNIE: Oh. I hoped you hadn't seen him. [*Draws a deep breath and comes on to the terrace, closing her white purse.*] That was Chance Wayne. He's back in St. Cloud, he's at the Royal Palms, he's—

BOSS: Why did you snub him like that? After all these years of devotion?

NONNIE: I went to the Royal Palms to warn him not to stay here but—

BOSS: He was out showing off in that big white Cadillac with the trumpet horns on it.

NONNIE: I left a message for him, I—

TOM JUNIOR: What was the message, Aunt Nonnie? Love and kisses?

NONNIE: Just get out of St. Cloud right away, Chance.

TOM JUNIOR: He's gonna git out, but not in that fish-tail Caddy.

NONNIE [*to* TOM JUNIOR]: I hope you don't mean violence— [*turning to* BOSS] does he, Tom? Violence don't solve problems. It never solves young people's problems. If you will leave it to me, I'll get him out of St. Cloud. I can, I will, I promise. I don't think Heavenly knows he's back in St. Cloud. Tom, you know, Heavenly says it wasn't Chance that—She says it wasn't Chance.

BOSS: You're like your dead sister, Nonnie, gullible as my wife was. You don't know a lie if you bump into it on a street in the daytime. Now go out there and tell Heavenly I want to see her.

NONNIE: Tom, she's not well enough to—

BOSS: Nonnie, you got a whole lot to answer for.

NONNIE: Have I?

BOSS: Yes, you sure have, Nonnie. You favored Chance Wayne, encouraged, aided and abetted him in his corruption of Heavenly over a long, long time. You go get her. You sure do have a lot to answer for. You got a helluva lot to answer for.

NONNIE: I remember when Chance was the finest, nicest, sweetest boy in St. Cloud, and he stayed that way till you, till you—

BOSS: Go get her, go get her! [*She leaves by the far side of the terrace. After a moment her voice is heard calling,* "HEAVENLY? HEAVENLY?"] It's a curious thing, a mighty peculiar thing, how often a man that rises to high public office is drug back down by every soul he harbors under his roof. He harbors them under his roof, and they pull the roof down on him. Every last living one of them.

TOM JUNIOR: Does that include me, Papa?

BOSS: If the shoe fits, put it on you.

TOM JUNIOR: How does that shoe fit me?

BOSS: If it pinches your foot, just slit it down the sides a little—it'll feel comfortable on you.

TOM JUNIOR: Papa, you are UNJUST.

BOSS: What do you want credit for?

TOM JUNIOR: I have devoted the past year to organizin' the "Youth for Tom Finley" clubs.

BOSS: I'm carryin' Tom Finley Junior on my ticket.

TOM JUNIOR: You're lucky to have me on it.

BOSS: How do you figure I'm lucky to have you on it?

TOM JUNIOR: I got more newspaper coverage in the last six months than . . .

BOSS: Once for drunk drivin', once for a stag party you thrown in Capitol City that cost me five thousand dollars to hush it up!

TOM JUNIOR: You are so unjust, it . . .

BOSS: And everyone knows you had to be drove through school like a blazeface mule pullin' a plow uphill: flunked out of college with grades that only a moron would have an excuse for.

TOM JUNIOR: I got re-admitted to college.

BOSS: At my insistence. By fake examinations, answers provided beforehand, stuck in your fancy pockets. And your promiscuity. Why, these Youth for Tom Finley clubs are practically nothin' but gangs of juvenile delinquents, wearin' badges with my name and my photograph on them.

TOM JUNIOR: How about your well known promiscuity, Papa? How about your Miss Lucy?

BOSS: Who is Miss Lucy?

TOM JUNIOR [laughing so hard he staggers]: Who is Miss Lucy? You don't even know who she is, this woman you keep in a fifty-dollar a day hotel suite at the Royal Palms, Papa?

BOSS: What're you talkin' about?

TOM JUNIOR: That rides down the Gulf Stream Highway with a motorcycle escort blowin' their sirens like the Queen of Sheba was going into New Orleans for the day. To use her charge accounts there. And you ask who's Miss Lucy?

She don't even talk good of you. She says you're too old for a lover.

BOSS: That is a goddam lie. Who says Miss Lucy says that?

TOM JUNIOR: She wrote it with lipstick on the ladies' room mirror at the Royal Palms.

BOSS: Wrote what?

TOM JUNIOR: I'll quote it to you exactly. "Boss Finley," she wrote, "is too old to cut the mustard."

[*Pause: the two stags, the old and the young one, face each other, panting.* SCUDDER *has discreetly withdrawn to a far end of porch.*]

BOSS: I don't believe this story!

TOM JUNIOR: Don't believe it.

BOSS: I will check on it, however.

TOM JUNIOR: I already checked on it. Papa, why don't you get rid of her, huh, Papa?

[BOSS FINLEY *turns away, wounded, baffled: stares out at the audience with his old, bloodshot eyes as if he thought that someone out there had shouted a question at him which he didn't quite hear.*]

BOSS: Mind your own goddam business. A man with a mission, which he holds sacred, and on the strength of which he rises to high public office—crucified in this way, publicly, by his own offspring. [HEAVENLY *has entered on the gallery.*] Ah, here she is, here's my little girl. [*stopping* HEAVENLY] You stay here, honey. I think you all had better leave me alone with Heavenly now, huh—yeah. . . . [TOM JUNIOR *and* SCUDDER *exit.*] Now, honey, you stay here. I want to have a talk with you.

HEAVENLY: Papa, I can't talk now.

BOSS: It's necessary.

HEAVENLY: I can't, I can't talk now.

BOSS: All right, don't talk, just listen.

[*But she doesn't want to listen, starts away: He would have restrained her forcibly if an old colored manservant, CHARLES, had not, at that moment, come out on the porch. He carries a stick, a hat, a package, wrapped as a present. Puts them on a table.*]

CHARLES: It's five o'clock, Mister Finley.

BOSS: Huh? Oh—thanks . . .

[*CHARLES turns on a coach lamp by the door. This marks a formal division in the scene. The light change is not realistic; the light doesn't seem to come from the coach lamp but from a spectral radiance in the sky, flooding the terrace.*

[*The sea wind sings. HEAVENLY lifts her face to it. Later that night may be stormy, but now there is just a quickness and freshness coming in from the Gulf. HEAVENLY is always looking that way, toward the Gulf, so that the light from Point Lookout catches her face with its repeated soft stroke of clarity.*

[*In her father, a sudden dignity is revived. Looking at his very beautiful daughter, he becomes almost stately. He approaches her, soon as the colored man returns inside, like an aged courtier comes deferentially up to a Crown Princess or Infanta. It's important not to think of his attitude toward her in the terms of crudely conscious incestuous feeling, but just in the natural terms of almost any aging father's feeling for a beautiful young daughter who reminds him of a dead wife that he desired intensely when she was the age of his daughter.*

[*At this point there might be a phrase of stately, Mozartian music, suggesting a court dance. The flagged terrace may suggest the parquet floor of a ballroom and the two players' movements may suggest the stately, formal movements of a court dance of that time; but if this effect is used, it should be just a suggestion. The change toward "stylization" ought to be held in check.]*

BOSS: You're still a beautiful girl.

HEAVENLY: Am I, Papa?

BOSS: Of course you are. Lookin' at you nobody could guess that—

HEAVENLY [*laughs*]: The embalmers must have done a good job on me, Papa. . . .

BOSS: You got to quit talkin' like that. [*then, seeing* CHARLES] Will you get back in the house! [*Phone rings.*]

CHARLES: Yes, sir, I was just—

BOSS: Go on in! If that phone call is for me, I'm in only to the governor of the state and the president of the Tide-water Oil Corporation.

CHARLES [*offstage*]: It's for Miss Heavenly again.

BOSS: Say she ain't in.

CHARLES: Sorry, she ain't in.

[HEAVENLY *has moved upstage to the low parapet or sea wall that separates the courtyard and lawn from the beach. It is early dusk. The coach lamp has cast a strange light on the setting which is neo-romantic:* HEAVENLY *stops by an ornamental urn containing a tall fern that the salty Gulf wind has stripped nearly bare. The* BOSS *follows her, baffled.*]

BOSS: Honey, you say and do things in the presence of people as if you had no regard of the fact that people have ears to hear you and tongues to repeat what they hear. And so you become a issue.

HEAVENLY: Become what, Papa?

BOSS: A issue, a issue, subject of talk, of scandal—which can defeat the mission that—

HEAVENLY: Don't give me your "Voice of God" speech. Papa, there was a time when you could have saved me, by letting me marry a boy that was still young and clean, but instead you drove him away, drove him out of St. Cloud. And when he came back, you took me out of St. Cloud, and tried to force me to marry a fifty-year-old money bag that you wanted something out of—

BOSS: Now, honey—

HEAVENLY:—and then another, another, all of them ones that you wanted something out of. I'd gone, so Chance went away. Tried to compete, make himself big as these big-shots you wanted to use me for a bond with. He went. He tried. The right doors wouldn't open, and so he went in the wrong ones, and—Papa, you married for love, why wouldn't you let me do it, while I was alive, inside, and the boy still clean, still decent?

BOSS: Are you reproaching me for—?

HEAVENLY [*shouting*]: Yes, I am, Papa, I am. You married for love, but you wouldn't let me do it, and even though you'd done it, you broke Mama's heart, Miss Lucy had been your mistress—

BOSS: Who is Miss Lucy?

HEAVENLY: Oh, Papa, she was your mistress long before Mama died. And Mama was just a front for you. Can I go in now, Papa? Can I go in now?

BOSS: No, no, not till I'm through with you. What a terrible, terrible thing for my baby to say . . . [*He takes her in his arms.*] Tomorrow, tomorrow morning, when the big after-Easter sales commence in the stores—I'm gonna send you in town with a motorcycle escort, straight to the Maison

Blanche. When you arrive at the store, I want you to go directly up to the office of Mr. Harvey C. Petrie and tell him to give you unlimited credit there. Then go down and outfit yourself as if you was—buyin' a trousseau to marry the Prince of Monaco. . . . Purchase a full wardrobe, includin' furs. Keep 'em in storage until winter. Gown? Three, four, five, the most lavish. Slippers? Hell, pairs and pairs of 'em. Not one hat—but a dozen. I made a pile of dough on a deal involvin' the sale of rights to oil under water here lately, and baby, I want you to buy a piece of jewelry. Now about that, you better tell Harvey to call me. Or better still, maybe Miss Lucy had better help you select it. She's wise as a backhouse rat when it comes to a stone,—that's for sure. . . . Now where'd I buy that clip that I give your mama? D'you remember the clip I bought your mama? Last thing I give your mama before she died . . . I knowed she was dyin' when I bought her that clip, and I bought that clip for fifteen thousand dollars mainly to make her think she was going to get well. . . . When I pinned it on her on the night-gown she was wearing, that poor thing started crying. She said, for God's sake, Boss, what does a dying woman want with such a big diamond? I said to her, honey, look at the price tag on it. What does the price tag say? See them five figures, that one and that five and them three aughts on there? Now, honey, make sense, I told her. If you was dying, if there was any chance of it, would I invest fifteen grand in a diamond clip to pin on the neck of a shroud? Ha, haha. That made the old lady laugh. And she sat up as bright as a little bird in that bed with the diamond clip on, receiving callers all day, and laughing and chatting with them, with that diamond clip on inside and she died before midnight, with that diamond clip on her. And not till the very last min-ute did she believe that the diamonds wasn't a proof that she wasn't dying. [*He moves to terrace, takes off robe and starts to put on tuxedo coat.*]

HEAVENLY: Did you bury her with it?

BOSS: Bury her with it? <u>Hell, no.</u> I took it back to the jewelry store in the morning.

HEAVENLY: Then it didn't cost you fifteen grand after all.

BOSS: Hell, did I care what it cost me? I'm not a small man. I wouldn't have cared one hoot if it cost me a million . . . if at that time I had that kind of loot in my pockets. It would have been worth that money to see that one little smile your mama bird give me at noon of the day she was dying.

HEAVENLY: I guess that shows, demonstrates very clearly, that you have got a pretty big heart after all.

BOSS: Who doubts it then? Who? Who ever? [*He laughs.*]

[HEAVENLY *starts to laugh and then screams hysterically. She starts going toward the house.*]

[BOSS *throws down his cane and grabs her.*]

Just a minute, Missy. Stop it. Stop it. Listen to me, I'm gonna tell you something. Last week in New Bethesda, when I was speaking on the threat of desegregation to white women's chastity in the South, some heckler in the crowd shouted out, "Hey, Boss Finley, how about your daughter? How about that operation you had done on your daughter at the Thomas J. Finley hospital in St. Cloud? Did she put on black in mourning for her appendix?" Same heckler, same question when I spoke in the Coliseum at the state capitol.

HEAVENLY: What was your answer to him?

BOSS: He was removed from the hall at both places and roughed up a little outside it.

HEAVENLY: Papa, you have got an illusion of power.

BOSS: I have power, which is not an illusion.

HEAVENLY: Papa, I'm sorry my operation has brought this embarrassment on you, but can you imagine it, Papa? I felt worse than embarrassed when I found out that Dr. George Scudder's knife had cut the youth out of my body, made me an old childless woman. Dry, cold, empty, like an old woman. I feel as if I ought to rattle like a dead dried-up vine when the Gulf Wind blows, but, Papa—I won't embarrass you any more. I've made up my mind about something. If they'll let me, accept me, I'm going into a convent.

BOSS [*shouting*]: You ain't going into no convent. This state is a Protestant region and a daughter in a convent would politically ruin me. Oh, I know, you took your mama's religion because in your heart you always wished to defy me. Now, tonight, I'm addressing the Youth for Tom Finley clubs in the ballroom of the Royal Palms Hotel. My speech is going out over a national TV network, and Missy, you're going to march in the ballroom on my arm. You're going to be wearing the stainless white of a virgin, with a Youth for Tom Finley button on one shoulder and a corsage of lilies on the other. You're going to be on the speaker's platform with me, you on one side of me and Tom Junior on the other, to scotch these rumors about your corruption. And you're gonna wear a proud happy smile on your face, you're gonna stare straight out at the crowd in the ballroom with pride and joy in your eyes. Lookin' at you, all in white like a virgin, nobody would dare to speak or believe the ugly stories about you. I'm relying a great deal on this campaign to bring in young voters for the crusade I'm leading. I'm all that stands between the South and the black days of Reconstruction. And you and Tom Junior are going to stand there beside me in the grand crystal ballroom, as shining examples of white Southern youth—in danger.

HEAVENLY [*defiant*]: Papa, I'm not going to do it.

BOSS: I didn't say would you, I said you would, and you will.

HEAVENLY: Suppose I still say I won't.

BOSS: Then you won't, that's all. If you won't, you won't. But there would be consequences you might not like. [*Phone rings.*] Chance Wayne is back in St. Cloud.

CHARLES [*offstage*]: Mr. Finley's residence. Miss Heavenly? Sorry, she's not in.

BOSS: I'm going to remove him, he's going to be removed

from St. Cloud. How do you want him to leave, in that white Cadillac he's riding around in, or in the scow that totes the garbage out to the dumping place in the Gulf?

HEAVENLY: You wouldn't dare?

BOSS: You want to take a chance on it?

CHARLES [*enters*]: That call was for you again, Miss Heavenly.

BOSS: A lot of people approve of taking violent action against corrupters. And on all of them that want to adulterate the pure white blood of the South. Hell, when I was fifteen, I come down barefoot out of the red clay hills as if the Voice of God called me. Which it did, I believe. I firmly believe He called me. And nothing, nobody, nowhere is gonna stop me, never. . . . [*He motions to* CHARLES *for gift.* CHARLES *hands it to him.*] Thank you, Charles. I'm gonna pay me an early call on Miss Lucy.

[*A sad, uncertain note has come into his voice on this final line. He turns and plods wearily, doggedly off at left.*]

THE CURTAIN FALLS

[*House remains dark for short intermission.*]

scene two

*A corner of cocktail lounge and of outside gallery of the
Royal Palms Hotel. This corresponds in style to the bedroom
set: Victorian with Moorish influence. Royal palms are pro-
jected on the cyclorama which is deep violet with dusk.
There are Moorish arches between gallery and interior: over
the single table, inside, is suspended the same lamp, stained
glass and ornately wrought metal, that hung in the bedroom.
Perhaps on the gallery there is a low stone balustrade that
supports, where steps descend into the garden, an electric
light standard with five branches and pear-shaped globes of
a dim pearly luster. Somewhere out of the sight-lines an
entertainer plays a piano or novachord.*

*The interior table is occupied by two couples that repre-
sent society in St. Cloud. They are contemporaries of*
CHANCE'S. *Behind the bar is* STUFF *who feels the dignity of
his recent advancement from drugstore soda-fountain to the
Royal Palms cocktail lounge: he has on a white mess-jacket,
a scarlet cummerbund and light blue trousers, flatteringly
close-fitted.* CHANCE WAYNE *was once barman here:* STUFF

76

moves with an indolent male grace that he may have uncon-
sciously remembered admiring in CHANCE.

BOSS FINLEY'S *mistress,* MISS LUCY, *enters the cocktail
lounge dressed in a ball gown elaborately ruffled and very
bouffant like an antebellum Southern belle's. A single blonde
curl is arranged to switch girlishly at one side of her sharp
little terrier face. She is outraged over something and her
glare is concentrated on* STUFF *who "plays it cool" behind
the bar.*

STUFF: Ev'nin', Miss Lucy.

MISS LUCY: I wasn't allowed to sit at the banquet table.
No. I was put at a little side table, with a couple of state
legislators an' wives. [*She sweeps behind the bar in a pro-
prietary fashion.*] Where's your Grant's twelve-year-old?
Hey! Do you have a big mouth? I used to remember a kid
that jerked sodas at Walgreen's that had a big mouth. . . .
Put some ice in this. . . . Is yours big, huh? I want to tell you
something.

STUFF: What's the matter with your finger?

[*She catches him by his scarlet cummerbund.*]

MISS LUCY: I'm going to tell you just now. The boss came
over to me with a big candy Easter egg for me. The top of
the egg unscrewed. He told me to unscrew it. So I unscrewed
it. Inside was a little blue velvet jewel box, no not little, a
big one, as big as somebody's mouth, too.

STUFF: Whose mouth?

MISS LUCY: The mouth of somebody who's not a hundred
miles from here.

STUFF [*going off at the left*]: I got to set my chairs.
[STUFF *re-enters at once carrying two chairs. Sets them at
tables while* MISS LUCY *talks.*]

MISS LUCY: I open the jewel box an' start to remove the
great big diamond clip in it. I just got my fingers on it, and

start to remove it and the old son of a bitch slams the lid of the box on my fingers. One fingernail is still blue. And the boss says to me, "Now go downstairs to the cocktail lounge and go in the ladies' room and describe this diamond clip with lipstick on the ladies' room mirror down there. Hanh?" —and he put the jewel box in his pocket and slammed the door so hard goin' out of my suite that a picture fell off the wall.

STUFF [*setting the chairs at the table*]: Miss Lucy, you are the one that said, "I wish you would see what's written with lipstick on the ladies' room mirror" las' Saturday night.

MISS LUCY: To you! Because I thought I could trust you.

STUFF: Other people were here an' all of them heard it.

MISS LUCY: Nobody but you at the bar belonged to the Youth for Boss Finley Club.

[*Both stop short. They've noticed a tall man who has entered the cocktail lounge. He has the length and leanness and luminous pallor of a face that El Greco gave to his saints. He has a small bandage near the hairline. His clothes are country.*]

Hey, you.

HECKLER: Evenin', ma'am.

MISS LUCY: You with the Hillbilly Ramblers? You with the band?

HECKLER: I'm a hillbilly, but I'm not with no band.

[*He notices* MISS LUCY'S *steady, interested stare,* STUFF *leaves with a tray of drinks.*]

MISS LUCY: What do you want here?

HECKLER: I come to hear Boss Finley talk. [*His voice is clear but strained. He rubs his large Adam's apple as he speaks.*]

MISS LUCY: You can't get in the ballroom without a jacket and a tie on. . . . I know who you are. You're the heckler, aren't you?

HECKLER: I don't heckle. I just ask questions, one question or two or three questions, depending on how much time it takes them to grab me and throw me out of the hall.

MISS LUCY: Those questions are loaded questions. You gonna repeat them tonight?

HECKLER: Yes, ma'am, if I can get in the ballroom, and make myself heard.

MISS LUCY: What's wrong with your voice?

HECKLER: When I shouted my questions in New Bethesda last week I got hit in the Adam's apple with the butt of a pistol, and that affected my voice. It still ain't good, but it's better. [*Starts to go.*]

MISS LUCY [*goes to back of bar, where she gets jacket, the kind kept in places with dress regulations, and throws it to* HECKLER]: Wait. Here, put this on. The Boss's talking on a national TV hookup tonight. There's a tie in the pocket. You sit perfectly still at the bar till the Boss starts speaking. Keep your face back of this *Evening Banner*. O.K.?

HECKLER [*opening the paper in front of his face*]: I thank you.

MISS LUCY: I thank you, too, and I wish you more luck than you're likely to have.

[STUFF *re-enters and goes to back of the bar.*]

FLY [*entering on the gallery*]: Paging Chance Wayne. [*auto horn offstage*] Mr. Chance Wayne, please. Paging Chance Wayne. [*He leaves.*]

MISS LUCY [*to* STUFF *who has re-entered*]: Is Chance Wayne back in St. Cloud?

STUFF: You remember Alexandra Del Lago?

MISS LUCY: I guess I do. I was president of her local fan club. Why?

CHANCE [*offstage*]: Hey, Boy, park that car up front and don't wrinkle them fenders.

STUFF: She and Chance Wayne checked in here last night.

MISS LUCY: Well I'll be a dawg's mother. I'm going to look into that. [LUCY *exits*.]

CHANCE [*entering and crossing to the bar*]: Hey, Stuff! [*He takes a cocktail off the bar and sips it.*]

STUFF: Put that down. This ain't no cocktail party.

CHANCE: Man, don't you know . . . phew . . . nobody drinks gin martinis with olives. Everybody drinks vodka martinis with lemon twist nowadays, except the squares in St. Cloud. When I had your job, when I was the barman here at the Royal Palms, I created that uniform you've got on. . . . I copied it from an outfit Vic Mature wore in a Foreign Legion picture, and I looked better in it than he did, and almost as good in it as you do, ha, ha. . . .

AUNT NONNIE [*who has entered at the right*]: Chance. Chance . . .

CHANCE: Aunt Nonnie! [*to* STUFF] Hey, I want a tablecloth on that table, and a bucket of champagne . . . Mumm's Cordon Rouge. . . .

AUNT NONNIE: You come out here.

CHANCE: But, I just ordered champagne in here. [*Suddenly his effusive manner collapses, as she stares at him gravely.*]

AUNT NONNIE: I can't be seen talking to you. . . .

[*She leads him to one side of the stage. A light change has*

occurred which has made it a royal palm grove with a bench.
They cross to it solemnly. STUFF *busies himself at the bar,*
which is barely lit. After a moment he exits with a few
drinks to main body of the cocktail lounge off left. Bar music.
Quiereme Mucho.]

CHANCE [*following her*]: Why?

AUNT NONNIE: I've got just one thing to tell you, Chance,
get out of St. Cloud.

CHANCE: Why does everybody treat me like a low criminal
in the town I was born in?

AUNT NONNIE: Ask yourself that question, ask your con-
science that question.

CHANCE: What question?

AUNT NONNIE: You know, and I know you know . . .

CHANCE: Know what?

AUNT NONNIE: I'm not going to talk about it. I just can't
talk about it. Your head and your tongue run wild. You
can't be trusted. We have to live in St. Cloud. . . . Oh, Chance,
why have you changed like you've changed? Why do you
live on nothing but wild dreams now, and have no address
where anybody can reach you in time to—reach you?

CHANCE: Wild dreams! Yes. Isn't life a wild dream? I never
heard a better description of it. . . . [*He takes a pill and a*
swallow from a flask.]

AUNT NONNIE: What did you just take, Chance? You took
something out of your pocket and washed it down with liquor.

CHANCE: Yes, I took a wild dream and—washed it down
with another wild dream, Aunt Nonnie, that's my life now. . . .

AUNT NONNIE: Why, son?

CHANCE: Oh, Aunt Nonnie, for God's sake, have you forgotten what was expected of me?

AUNT NONNIE: People that loved you expected just one thing of you—sweetness and honesty and . . .

[STUFF *leaves with tray.*]

CHANCE [*kneeling at her side*]: No, not after the brilliant beginning I made. Why, at seventeen, I put on, directed, and played the leading role in "The Valiant," that one-act play that won the state drama contest. Heavenly played in it with me, and have you forgotten? You went with us as the girls' chaperone to the national contest held in . . .

AUNT NONNIE: Son, of course I remember.

CHANCE: In the parlor car? How we sang together?

AUNT NONNIE: You were in love even then.

CHANCE: God, yes, we were in love!

[*He sings softly*]

"If you like-a me, like I like-a you,
And we like-a both the same"
TOGETHER:
   "I'd like-a say, this very day,
   I'd like-a change your name."

[CHANCE *laughs softly, wildly, in the cool light of the palm grove.* AUNT NONNIE *rises abruptly.* CHANCE *catches her hands.*]

AUNT NONNIE: You—*Do*—Take unfair advantage. . . .

CHANCE: Aunt Nonnie, we didn't win that lousy national contest, we just placed second.

AUNT NONNIE: Chance, you didn't place second. You got

honorable mention. Fourth place, except it was just called honorable mention.

CHANCE: Just honorable mention. But in a national contest, honorable mention means something. . . . We would have won it, but I blew my lines. Yes, I that put on and produced the damn thing, couldn't even hear the damn lines being hissed at me by that fat girl with the book in the wings. [*He buries his face in his hands.*]

AUNT NONNIE: I loved you for that, son, and so did Heavenly, too.

CHANCE: It was on the way home in the train that she and I—

AUNT NONNIE [*with a flurry of feeling*]: I know, I— I—

CHANCE [*rising*]: I bribed the Pullman Conductor to let us use for an hour a vacant compartment on that sad, home-going train—

AUNT NONNIE: I know, I— I—

CHANCE: Gave him five dollars, but that wasn't enough, and so I gave him my wrist watch, and my collar pin and tie clip and signet ring and my suit, that I'd bought on credit to go to the contest. First suit I'd ever put on that cost more than thirty dollars.

AUNT NONNIE: Don't go back over that.

CHANCE: —To buy the first hour of love that we had together. When she undressed, I saw that her body was just then, barely, beginning to be a woman's and . . .

AUNT NONNIE: Stop, Chance.

CHANCE: I said, oh, Heavenly, no, but she said yes, and I cried in her arms that night, and didn't know that what I was crying for was—youth, that would go.

AUNT NONNIE: It was from that time on, you've changed.

CHANCE: I swore in my heart that I'd never again come in second in any contest, especially not now that Heavenly was my—Aunt Nonnie, look at this contract. [*He snatches out papers and lights lighter.*]

AUNT NONNIE: I don't want to see false papers.

CHANCE: These are genuine papers. Look at the notary's seal and the signatures of the three witnesses on them. Aunt Nonnie, do you know who I'm with? I'm with Alexandra Del Lago, the Princess Kosmonopolis is my—

AUNT NONNIE: Is your what?

CHANCE: Patroness! Agent! Producer! She hasn't been seen much lately, but still has influence, power, and money—money that can open all doors. That I've knocked at all these years till my knuckles are bloody.

AUNT NONNIE: Chance, even now, if you came back here simply saying, "I couldn't remember the lines, I lost the contest, I—failed," but you've come back here again with—

CHANCE: Will you just listen one minute more? Aunt Nonnie, here is the plan. A local-contest-of-Beauty.

AUNT NONNIE: Oh, Chance.

CHANCE: A local contest of talent that she will win.

AUNT NONNIE: Who?

CHANCE: Heavenly.

AUNT NONNIE: No, Chance. She's not young now, she's faded, she's . . .

CHANCE: Nothing goes that quick, not even youth.

AUNT NONNIE: Yes, it does.

CHANCE: It will come back like magic. Soon as I . . .

AUNT NONNIE: For what? For a fake contest?

CHANCE: For love. The moment I hold her.

AUNT NONNIE: Chance.

CHANCE: It's not going to be a local thing, Aunt Nonnie. It's going to get national coverage. The Princess Kosmonopolis's best friend is that sob sister, Sally Powers. Even you know Sally Powers. Most powerful movie columnist in the world. Whose name is law in the motion . . .

AUNT NONNIE: Chance, lower your voice.

CHANCE: I want people to hear me.

AUNT NONNIE: No, you don't, no you don't. Because if your voice gets to Boss Finley, you'll be in great danger, Chance.

CHANCE: I go back to Heavenly, or I don't. I live or die. There's nothing in between for me.

AUNT NONNIE: What you want to go back to is your clean, unashamed youth. And you can't.

CHANCE: You still don't believe me, Aunt Nonnie?

AUNT NONNIE: No, I don't. Please go. Go away from here, Chance.

CHANCE: Please.

AUNT NONNIE: No, no, go away!

CHANCE: Where to? Where can I go? This is the home of my heart. Don't make me homeless.

AUNT NONNIE: Oh, Chance.

CHANCE: Aunt Nonnie. Please.

AUNT NONNIE [*rises and starts to go*]: I'll write to you. Send me an address. I'll write to you.

[*She exits through bar.* STUFF *enters and moves to bar.*]

CHANCE: Aunt Nonnie . . .

[*She's gone.*]

[CHANCE *removes a pint bottle of vodka from his pocket and something else which he washes down with the vodka. He stands back as two couples come up the steps and cross the gallery into the bar: they sit at a table.* CHANCE *takes a deep breath.* FLY *enters lighted area inside, singing out* "Paging MR. CHANCE WAYNE, MR. CHANCE WAYNE, *pagin'* MR. CHANCE WAYNE."—*Turns about smartly and goes back out through lobby. The name has stirred a commotion at the bar and table visible inside.*]

EDNA: Did you hear *that*? Is *Chance Wayne* back in St. Cloud?

[CHANCE *draws a deep breath. Then, he stalks back into the main part of the cocktail lounge like a matador entering a bull ring.*]

VIOLET: My God, yes—there he is.

[CHANCE *reads* FLY'S *message.*]

CHANCE [*to* FLY]: Not now, later, later.

[*The entertainer off left begins to play a piano . . . The* "evening" *in the cocktail lounge is just beginning.*]

[FLY *leaves through the gallery.*]

Well! Same old place, same old gang. Time doesn't pass in St. Cloud. [*To* BUD *and* SCOTTY] Hi!

BUD: How are you . . .

CHANCE [*shouting offstage*]: [FLY *enters and stands on terrace*] Hey, Jackie . . . [*Piano stops.* CHANCE *crosses over to the table that holds the foursome.*] . . . remember my song? Do you—remember my song? . . . You see, he remembers my song. [*The entertainer swings into "It's a Big Wide Wonderful World."*] Now I feel at home. In my home town . . . Come on, everybody—sing!

[*This token of apparent acceptance reassures him. The foursome at the table on stage studiously ignore him. He sings:*]

"When you're in love you're a master
Of all you survey, you're a gay Santa Claus.
There's a great big star-spangled sky up above you,
When you're in love you're a hero . . ."

Come on! Sing, ev'rybody!

[*In the old days they did; now they don't. He goes on, singing a bit; then his voice dies out on a note of embarrassment. Somebody at the bar whispers something and another laughs.* CHANCE *chuckles uneasily and says:*]

What's wrong here? The place is dead.

STUFF: You been away too long, Chance.

CHANCE: Is that the trouble?

STUFF: That's all. . . .

[JACKIE, *off, finishes with an arpeggio. The piano lid slams. There is a curious hush in the bar.* CHANCE *looks at the table.* VIOLET *whispers something to* BUD. *Both girls rise abruptly and cross out of the bar.*]

BUD [*yelling at* STUFF]: Check, Stuff.

CHANCE [*with exaggerated surprise*]: Well, *Bud and Scotty.*

I didn't see you at all. Wasn't that Violet and Edna at your table? [*He sits at the table between* BUD *and* SCOTTY.]

SCOTTY: I guess they didn't recognize you, Chance.

BUD: Violet did.

SCOTTY: Did Violet?

BUD: She said, "My God, Chance Wayne."

SCOTTY: That's recognition and profanity, too.

CHANCE: I don't mind. I've been snubbed by experts, and I've done some snubbing myself. . . . Hey! [MISS LUCY *has entered at left.* CHANCE *sees her and goes toward her.*] —Is that Miss Lucy or is that Scarlett O'Hara?

MISS LUCY: Hello there, Chance Wayne. Somebody said that you were back in St. Cloud, but I didn't believe them. I said I'd have to see it with my own eyes before . . . Usually there's an item in the paper, in Gwen Phillip's column saying "St. Cloud youth home on visit is slated to play featured role in important new picture," and me being a movie fan I'm always thrilled by it. . . . [*She ruffles his hair.*]

CHANCE: Never do that to a man with thinning hair. [CHANCE's *smile is unflinching; it gets harder and brighter.*]

MISS LUCY: Is your hair thinning, baby? Maybe that's the difference I noticed in your appearance. Don't go 'way till I get back with my drink. . . .

[*She goes to back of bar to mix herself a drink. Meanwhile,* CHANCE *combs his hair.*]

SCOTTY [*to* CHANCE]: Don't throw away those golden hairs you combed out, Chance. Save 'em and send 'em each in letters to your fan clubs.

BUD: Does Chance Wayne have a fan club?

SCOTTY: The most patient one in the world. They've been

waiting years for him to show up on the screen for more than five seconds in a crowd scene.

MISS LUCY [*returning to the table*]: Y'know this boy Chance Wayne used to be so attractive I couldn't stand it. But now I can, almost stand it. Every Sunday in summer I used to drive out to the municipal beach and watch him dive off the high tower. I'd take binoculars with me when he put on those free divin' exhibitions. You still dive, Chance? Or have you given that up?

CHANCE [*uneasily*]: I did some diving last Sunday.

MISS LUCY: Good, as ever?

CHANCE: I was a little off form, but the crowd didn't notice. I can still get away with a double back somersault and a—

MISS LUCY: Where was this, in Palm Beach, Florida, Chance?

[HATCHER *enters.*]

CHANCE [*stiffening*]: Why Palm Beach? Why there?

MISS LUCY: Who was it said they seen you last month in Palm Beach? Oh yes, Hatcher—that you had a job as a beach-boy at some big hotel there?

HATCHER [*stops at steps of the terrace, then leaves across the gallery*]: Yeah, that's what I heard.

CHANCE: Had a job—as a beach-boy?

STUFF: Rubbing oil into big fat millionaires.

CHANCE: What joker thought up that one? [*His laugh is a little too loud.*]

SCOTTY: You ought to get their names and sue them for slander.

CHANCE: I long ago gave up tracking down sources of rumors about me. Of course, it's flattering, it's gratifying to know that you're still being talked about in your old home town, even if what they say is completely fantastic. Hahaha.

[*Entertainer returns, sweeps into "Quiereme Mucho."*]

MISS LUCY: Baby, you've changed in some way, but I can't put my finger on it. You all see a change in him, or has he just gotten older? [*She sits down next to* CHANCE.]

CHANCE [*quickly*]: To change is to live, Miss Lucy, to live is to change, and not to change is to die. You know that, don't you? It used to scare me sometimes. I'm not scared of it now. Are you scared of it, Miss Lucy? Does it scare you?

[*Behind* CHANCE's *back one of the girls has appeared and signaled the boys to join them outside.* SCOTTY *nods and holds up two fingers to mean they'll come in a couple of minutes. The girl goes back out with an angry head-toss.*]

SCOTTY: Chance, did you know Boss Finley was holding a Youth for Tom Finley rally upstairs tonight?

CHANCE: I saw the announcements of it all over town.

BUD: He's going to state his position on that emasculation business that's stirred up such a mess in the state. Had you heard about that?

CHANCE: No.

SCOTTY: He must have been up in some earth satellite if he hasn't heard about that.

CHANCE: No, just out of St. Cloud.

SCOTTY: Well, they picked out a nigger at random and castrated the bastard to show they mean business about white women's protection in this state.

BUD: Some people think they went too far about it. There's

been a whole lot of Northern agitation all over the country.

SCOTTY: The Boss is going to state his own position about that thing before the Youth for Boss Finley Rally upstairs in the Crystal Ballroom.

CHANCE: Aw. Tonight?

STUFF: Yeah, t'night.

BUD: They say that Heavenly Finley and Tom Junior are going to be standing on the platform with him.

PAGEBOY [*entering*]: Paging Chance Wayne. Paging . . .

[*He is stopped short by* EDNA.]

CHANCE: I *doubt* that story, somehow I *doubt* that story.

SCOTTY: You doubt they cut that nigger?

CHANCE: Oh, no, that I don't doubt. You know what that is, don't you? Sex-envy is what that is, and the revenge for sex-envy which is a widespread disease that I have run into personally too often for me to doubt its existence or any manifestation. [*The group push back their chairs, snubbing him.* CHANCE *takes the message from the* PAGEBOY, *reads it and throws it on the floor.*] Hey, Stuff—What d'ya have to do, stand on your head to get a drink around here?—Later, tell her.—Miss Lucy, can you get that Walgreen's soda jerk to give me a shot of vodka on the rocks? [*She snaps her fingers at* STUFF. *He shrugs and sloshes some vodka onto ice.*]

MISS LUCY: Chance? You're too loud, baby.

CHANCE: Not loud enough, Miss Lucy. No. What I meant that I doubt is that Heavenly Finley, that only I know in St. Cloud, would stoop to stand on a platform next to her father while he explains and excuses on TV this random emasculation of a young Nigra caught on a street after midnight. [CHANCE *is speaking with an almost incoherent excite-*

ment, one knee resting on the seat of his chair, swaying the chair back and forth. The HECKLER *lowers his newspaper from his face; a slow fierce smile spreads over his face as he leans forward with tensed throat muscles to catch* CHANCE'S *burst of oratory.*] No! That's what I do not believe. If I believed it, oh, I'd give you a diving exhibition. I'd dive off municipal pier and swim straight out to Diamond Key and past it, and keep on swimming till sharks and barracuda took me for live bait, brother. [*His chair topples over backward, and he sprawls to the floor. The* HECKLER *springs up to catch him.* MISS LUCY *springs up too, and sweeps between* CHANCE *and the* HECKLER, *pushing the* HECKLER *back with a quick, warning look or gesture. Nobody notices the* HECKLER. CHANCE *scrambles back to his feet, flushed, laughing.* BUD *and* SCOTTY *outlaugh him.* CHANCE *picks up his chair and continues. The laughter stops.*] Because I have come back to St. Cloud to take her out of St. Cloud. Where I'll take her is not to a place anywhere except to her place in my heart. [*He has removed a pink capsule from his pocket, quickly and furtively, and drunk it down with his vodka.*]

BUD: Chance, what did you swallow just now?

CHANCE: Some hundred-proof vodka.

BUD: You washed something down with it that you took out of your pocket.

SCOTTY: It looked like a little pink pill.

CHANCE: Oh, ha ha. Yes, I washed down a goof-ball. You want one? I got a bunch of them. I always carry them with me. When you're not having fun, it makes you have it. When you're having fun, it makes you have more of it. Have one and see.

SCOTTY: Don't that damage the brain?

CHANCE: No, the contrary. It stimulates the brain cells.

SCOTTY: Don't it make your eyes look different, Chance?

MISS LUCY: Maybe that's what I noticed. [*as if wishing to change the subject*] Chance, I wish you'd settle an argument for me.

CHANCE: What argument, Miss Lucy?

MISS LUCY: About who you're traveling with. I heard you checked in here with a famous old movie star.

[*They all stare at him. . . . In a way he now has what he wants. He's the center of attraction: everybody is looking at him, even though with hostility, suspicion and a cruel sense of sport.*]

CHANCE: Miss Lucy, I'm traveling with the vice-president and major-stockholder of the film studio which just signed me.

MISS LUCY: Wasn't she once in the movies and very well known?

CHANCE: She was and still is and never will cease to be an important, a legendary figure in the picture industry, here and all over the world, and I am now under personal contract to her.

MISS LUCY: What's her name, Chance?

CHANCE: She doesn't want her name known. Like all great figures, world-known, she doesn't want or need and refuses to have the wrong type of attention. Privacy is a luxury to great stars. Don't ask me her name. I respect her too much to speak her name at this table. I'm obligated to her because she has shown faith in me. It took a long hard time to find that sort of faith in my talent that this woman has shown me. And I refuse to betray it at this table. [*His voice rises; he is already "high."*]

MISS LUCY: Baby, why are you sweating and your hands shaking so? You're not sick, are you?

CHANCE: Sick? Who's sick? I'm the least sick one you know.

MISS LUCY: Well, baby, you know you oughtn't to stay in St. Cloud. Y'know that, don't you? I couldn't believe my ears when I heard you were back here. [*to the two boys*] Could you all believe he was back here?

SCOTTY: What did you come back for?

CHANCE: I wish you would give me one reason why I shouldn't come back to visit the grave of my mother and pick out a monument for her, and share my happiness with a girl that I've loved many years. It's her, Heavenly Finley, that I've fought my way up for, and now that I've made it, the glory will be hers, too. And I've just about persuaded the powers to be to let her appear with me in a picture I'm signed for. Because I . . .

BUD: What is the name of this picture?

CHANCE: . . . Name of it? "Youth!"

BUD: Just "Youth?"

CHANCE: Isn't that a great title for a picture introducing young talent? You all look doubtful. If you don't believe me, well, look. Look at this contract. [*Removes it from his pocket.*]

SCOTTY: You carry the contract with you?

CHANCE: I happen to have it in this jacket pocket.

MISS LUCY: Leaving, Scotty? [SCOTTY *has risen from the table.*]

SCOTTY: It's getting too deep at this table.

BUD: The girls are waiting.

CHANCE [*quickly*]: Gee, Bud, that's a clean set of rags you're wearing, but let me give you a tip for your tailor. A guy of medium stature looks better with natural shoulders,

the padding cuts down your height, it broadens your figure
and gives you a sort of squat look.

BUD: Thanks, Chance.

SCOTTY: You got any helpful hints for my tailor, Chance?

CHANCE: Scotty, there's no tailor on earth that can disguise
a sedentary occupation.

MISS LUCY: Chance, Baby . . .

CHANCE: You still work down at the bank? You sit on
your can all day countin' century notes and once every week
they let you slip one in your pockets? That's a fine set-up,
Scotty, if you're satisfied with it but it's starting to give you
a little pot and a can.

VIOLET [appears in the door, angry]: Bud! Scotty! Come
on.

SCOTTY: I don't get by on my looks, but I drive my own
car. It isn't a Caddy, but it's my own car. And if my own
mother died, I'd bury her myself; I wouldn't let a church
take up a collection to do it.

VIOLET [impatiently]: Scotty, if you all don't come now
I'm going home in a taxi.

[The two boys follow her into the Palm Garden. There
they can be seen giving their wives cab money, and indicating
they are staying.]

CHANCE: The squares have left us, Miss Lucy.

MISS LUCY: Yeah.

CHANCE: Well . . . I didn't come back here to fight with
old friends of mine. . . . Well, it's quarter past seven.

MISS LUCY: Is it?

[*There are a number of men, now, sitting around in the darker corners of the bar, looking at him. They are not ominous in their attitudes. They are simply waiting for something, for the meeting to start upstairs, for something. . . .* MISS LUCY *stares at* CHANCE *and the men, then again at* CHANCE, *nearsightedly, her head cocked like a puzzled terrier's.* CHANCE *is discomfited.*]

CHANCE: Yep . . . How is that Hickory Hollow for steaks? Is it still the best place in town for a steak?

STUFF [*answering the phone at the bar*]: Yeah, it's him. He's here. [*Looks at* CHANCE *ever so briefly, hangs up.*]

MISS LUCY: Baby, I'll go to the checkroom and pick up my wrap and call for my car and I'll drive you out to the airport. They've got an air-taxi out there, a whirly-bird taxi, a helicopter, you know, that'll hop you to New Orleans in fifteen minutes.

CHANCE: I'm not leaving St. Cloud. What did I say to make you think I was?

MISS LUCY: I thought you had sense enough to know that you'd better.

CHANCE: Miss Lucy, you've been drinking, it's gone to your sweet little head.

MISS LUCY: Think it over while I'm getting my wrap. You still got a friend in St. Cloud.

CHANCE: I still have a girl in St. Cloud, and I'm not leaving without her.

PAGEBOY [*offstage*]: Paging Chance Wayne, Mr. Chance Wayne, please.

PRINCESS [*entering with* PAGEBOY]: Louder, young man, louder . . . Oh, never mind, here he is!

[*But* CHANCE *has already rushed out onto the gallery. The*

PRINCESS *looks as if she had thrown on her clothes to escape a building on fire. Her blue-sequined gown is unzipped, or partially zipped, her hair is disheveled, her eyes have a dazed, drugged brightness; she is holding up the eyeglasses with the broken lens, shakily, hanging onto her mink stole with the other hand; her movements are unsteady.*]

MISS LUCY: I know who you are. Alexandra Del Lago.

[*Loud whispering. A pause.*]

PRINCESS [*on the step to the gallery*]: What? Chance!

MISS LUCY: Honey, let me fix that zipper for you. Hold still just a second. Honey, let me take you upstairs. You mustn't be seen down here in this condition. . . .

[CHANCE *suddenly rushes in from the gallery: he conducts the* PRINCESS *outside: she is on the verge of panic. The* PRINCESS *rushes half down the steps to the palm garden: leans panting on the stone balustrade under the ornamental light standard with its five great pearls of light. The interior is dimmed as* CHANCE *comes out behind her.*]

PRINCESS: Chance! Chance! Chance! Chance!

CHANCE [*softly*]: If you'd stayed upstairs that wouldn't have happened to you.

PRINCESS: I did, I stayed.

CHANCE: I told you to wait.

PRINCESS: I waited.

CHANCE: Didn't I tell you to wait till I got back?

PRINCESS: I did, I waited forever, I waited forever for you. Then finally I heard those long sad silver trumpets blowing through the palm garden and then—Chance, the most wonderful thing has happened to me. Will you listen to me? Will you let me tell you?

MISS LUCY [*to the group at the bar*]: Shhh!

PRINCESS: Chance, when I saw you driving under the window with your head held high, with that terrible stiff-necked pride of the defeated which I know so well; I knew that your come-back had been a failure like mine. And I felt something in my heart for you. That's a miracle, Chance. That's the wonderful thing that happened to me. I felt something for someone besides myself. That means my heart's still alive, at least some part of it is, not all of my heart is dead yet. Part's alive still. . . . Chance, please listen to me. I'm ashamed of this morning. I'll never degrade you again, I'll never degrade myself, you and me, again by—I wasn't always this monster. Once I wasn't this monster. And what I felt in my heart when I saw you returning, defeated, to this palm garden, Chance, gave me hope that I could stop being a monster. Chance, you've got to help me stop being the monster that I was this morning, and you can do it, can help me. I won't be ungrateful for it. I almost died this morning, suffocated in a panic. But even through my panic, I saw your kindness. I saw a true kindness in you that you have almost destroyed, but that's still there, a little. . . .

CHANCE: What kind thing did I do?

PRINCESS: You gave my oxygen to me.

CHANCE: Anyone would do that.

PRINCESS: It could have taken you longer to give it to me.

CHANCE: I'm not that kind of monster.

PRINCESS: You're no kind of monster. You're just—

CHANCE: What?

PRINCESS: Lost in the beanstalk country, the ogre's country

at the top of the beanstalk, the country of the flesh-hungry, blood-thirsty ogre—

[*Suddenly a voice is heard from off.*]

VOICE: Wayne?

[*The call is distinct but not loud.* CHANCE *hears it, but doesn't turn toward it; he freezes momentarily, like a stag scenting hunters. Among the people gathered inside in the cocktail lounge we see the speaker,* DAN HATCHER. *In appearance, dress and manner he is the apotheosis of the assistant hotel manager, about* CHANCE'S *age, thin, blond-haired, trim blond mustache, suave, boyish, betraying an instinct for murder only by the ruby-glass studs in his matching cuff links and tie clip.*]

HATCHER: Wayne!

[*He steps forward a little and at the same instant* TOM JUNIOR *and* SCOTTY *appear behind him, just in view.* SCOTTY *strikes a match for* TOM JUNIOR'S *cigarette as they wait there.* CHANCE *suddenly gives the* PRINCESS *his complete and tender attention, putting an arm around her and turning her toward the Moorish arch to the bar entrance.*]

CHANCE [*loudly*]: I'll get you a drink, and then I'll take you upstairs. You're not well enough to stay down here.

HATCHER [*crossing quickly to the foot of the stairs*]: Wayne!

[*The call is too loud to ignore:* CHANCE *half turns and calls back.*]

CHANCE: Who's that?

HATCHER: Step down here a minute!

CHANCE: Oh, *Hatcher!* I'll be right with you.

PRINCESS: Chance, don't leave me alone.

[*At this moment the arrival of* BOSS FINLEY *is heralded by the sirens of several squad cars. The forestage is suddenly brightened from off Left, presumably the floodlights of the cars arriving at the entrance to the hotel. This is the signal the men at the bar have been waiting for. Everybody rushes off Left. In the hot light all alone on stage is* CHANCE; *behind him is the* PRINCESS. *And the* HECKLER *is at the bar. The entertainer plays a feverish tango. Now, off Left,* BOSS FINLEY *can be heard, his public personality very much "on." Amid the flash of flash bulbs we hear off:*]

BOSS [*off*]: Hahaha! Little Bit, smile! Go on, smile for the birdie! Ain't she Heavenly, ain't that the right name for her!

HEAVENLY [*off*]: Papa, I want to go in!

[*At this instant she runs in—to face* CHANCE. . . . *The* HECKLER *rises. For a long instant,* CHANCE *and* HEAVENLY *stand there: he on the steps leading to the Palm Garden and gallery; she in the cocktail lounge. They simply look at each other . . . the* HECKLER *between them. Then the* BOSS *comes in and seizes her by the arm. . . . And there he is facing the* HECKLER *and* CHANCE *both. . . . For a split second he faces them, half lifts his cane to strike at them, but doesn't strike . . . then pulls* HEAVENLY *back off Left stage . . . where the photographing and interviews proceed during what follows.* CHANCE *has seen that* HEAVENLY *is going to go on the platform with her father. . . . He stands there stunned. . . .*]

PRINCESS: Chance! Chance? [*He turns to her blindly.*] Call the car and let's go. Everything's packed, even the . . . tape recorder with my shameless voice on it. . . .

[*The* HECKLER *has returned to his position at the bar. Now* HATCHER *and* SCOTTY *and a couple of other of the boys have come out. . . . The* PRINCESS *sees them and is silent. . . . She's never been in anything like this before. . . .*]

HATCHER: Wayne, step down here, will you.

CHANCE: What for, what do you want?

HATCHER: Come down here, I'll tell you.

CHANCE: You come up here and tell me.

TOM JUNIOR: Come on, you chicken-gut bastard.

CHANCE: Why, hello, Tom Junior. Why are you hiding down there?

TOM JUNIOR: You're hiding, not me, chicken-gut.

CHANCE: You're in the dark, not me.

HATCHER: Tom Junior wants to talk to you privately down here.

CHANCE: He can talk to me privately up here.

TOM JUNIOR: Hatcher, tell him I'll talk to him in the washroom on the mezzanine floor.

CHANCE: I don't hold conversations with people in washrooms. . . .

[TOM JUNIOR *infuriated, starts to rush forward. Men restrain him.*]

What is all this anyhow? It's fantastic. You all having a little conference there? I used to leave places when I was told to. Not now. That time's over. Now I leave when I'm ready. Hear that, Tom Junior? Give your father that message. This is my town. I was born in St. Cloud, not him. He was just called here. He was just called down from the hills to preach hate. I was born here to make love. Tell him about that difference between him and me, and ask him which he thinks has more right to stay here. . . . [*He gets no answer from the huddled little group which is restraining* TOM JUNIOR *from perpetrating murder right there in the cocktail lounge. After all, that would be a bad incident to precede the* BOSS'S *all-South-wide TV appearance . . . and they all know it.* CHANCE, *at the same time, continues to taunt them.*] Tom,

Tom Junior! What do you want me for? To pay me back for the ball game and picture show money I gave you when you were cutting your father's yard grass for a dollar on Saturday? Thank me for the times I gave you my motorcycle and got you a girl to ride the buddy seat with you? Come here! I'll give you the keys to my Caddy. I'll give you the price of any whore in St. Cloud. You still got credit with me because you're Heavenly's brother.

TOM JUNIOR [*almost bursting free*]: Don't say the name of my sister!

CHANCE: I said the name of my girl!

TOM JUNIOR [*breaking away from the group*]: I'm all right, I'm all right. Leave us alone, will you. I don't want Chance to feel that he's outnumbered. [*He herds them out.*] O.K.? Come on down here.

PRINCESS [*trying to restrain CHANCE*]: No, Chance, don't.

TOM JUNIOR: Excuse yourself from the lady and come on down here. Don't be scared to. I just want to talk to you quietly. Just talk. Quiet talk.

CHANCE: Tom Junior, I know that since the last time I was here something has happened to Heavenly and I—

TOM JUNIOR: Don't—speak the name of my sister. Just leave her name off your tongue—

CHANCE: Just tell me what happened to her.

TOM JUNIOR: Just keep your ruttin' voice down.

CHANCE: I know I've done many wrong things in my life, many more than I can name or number, but I swear I never hurt Heavenly in my life.

TOM JUNIOR: You mean to say my sister was had by some-body else—diseased by somebody else the last time you were

in St. Cloud? . . . I know, it's possible, it's barely possible
that you didn't know what you done to my little sister the
last time you come to St. Cloud. You remember that time
when you came home broke? My sister had to pick up your
tabs in restaurants and bars, and had to cover bad checks
you wrote on banks where you had no accounts. Until you
met this rich bitch, Minnie, the Texas one with the yacht,
and started spending week ends on her yacht, and coming
back Mondays with money from Minnie to go on with my
sister. I mean, you'd sleep with Minnie, that slept with any
goddam gigolo bastard she could pick up on Bourbon Street
or the docks, and then you would go on sleeping again with
my sister. And sometime, during that time, you got something besides your gigolo fee from Minnie and passed it
onto my sister, my little sister that had hardly even heard
of a thing like that, and didn't know what it was till it had
gone on too long and—

CHANCE: I left town before I found out I—

[*The lamentation music is heard.*]

TOM JUNIOR: You found out! Did you tell my little sister?

CHANCE: I thought if something was wrong she'd write
me or call me—

TOM JUNIOR: How could she write you or call you, there're
no addresses, no phone numbers in gutters. I'm itching to
kill you—here, on this spot! . . . My little sister, Heavenly,
didn't know about the diseases and operations of whores,
till she had to be cleaned and cured—I mean spayed like a
dawg by Dr. George Scudder's knife. That's right—by the
knife! . . . And tonight—if you stay here tonight, if you're
here after this rally, you're gonna get the knife, too. You
know? The knife? That's all. Now go on back to the lady,
I'm going back to my father. [TOM JUNIOR *exits.*]

PRINCESS [*as* CHANCE *returns to her*]: Chance, for God's
sake, let's go now . . .

[*The Lament is in the air. It blends with the wind-blown
sound of the palms.*]

All day I've kept hearing a sort of lament that drifts
through the air of this place. It says, "Lost, lost, never to be
found again." Palm gardens by the sea and olive groves on
Mediterranean islands all have that lament drifting through
them. "Lost, lost". . . . The isle of Cyprus, Monte Carlo, San
Remo, Torremolenas, Tangiers. They're all places of exile
from whatever we loved. Dark glasses, wide-brimmed hats
and whispers, "Is that her?" Shocked whispers. . . . Oh,
Chance, believe me, after failure comes flight. Nothing ever
comes after failure but flight. Face it. Call the car, have
them bring down the luggage and let's go on along the Old
Spanish Trail. [*She tries to hold him.*]

CHANCE: Keep your grabbing hands off me.

[*Marchers offstage start to sing "Bonnie Blue Flag."*]

PRINCESS: There's no one but me to hold you back from
destruction in this place.

CHANCE: I don't want to be held.

PRINCESS: Don't leave me. If you do I'll turn into the
monster again. I'll be the first lady of the Beanstalk Country.

CHANCE: Go back to the room.

PRINCESS: I'm going nowhere alone. I can't.

CHANCE [*in desperation*]: Wheel chair! [*Marchers enter
from the left,* TOM JUNIOR *and* BOSS *with them.*] Wheel
chair! Stuff, get the lady a wheel chair! She's having another
attack!

[STUFF *and a* BELLBOY *catch at her . . . but she pushes*
CHANCE *away and stares at him reproachfully. . . . The* BELL-
BOY *takes her by the arm. She accepts this anonymous arm
and exits.* CHANCE *and the* HECKLER *are alone on stage.*]

CHANCE [*as if reassuring, comforting somebody besides himself*]: It's all right, I'm alone now, nobody's hanging onto me.

[*He is panting. Loosens his tie and collar. Band in the Crystal Ballroom, muted, strikes up a lively but lyrically distorted variation of some such popular tune as the Lichtensteiner Polka.* CHANCE *turns toward the sound. Then, from Left stage, comes a drum majorette, bearing a gold and purple silk banner inscribed, "Youth for Tom Finley," prancing and followed by* BOSS FINLEY, HEAVENLY *and* TOM JUNIOR, *with a tight grip on her arm, as if he were conducting her to a death chamber.*]

TOM JUNIOR: Papa? Papa! Will you tell Sister to march?

BOSS FINLEY: Little Bit, you hold your haid up *high* when we march into that ballroom. [*Music up high . . . They march up the steps and onto the gallery in the rear . . . then start across it. The* BOSS *calling out:*] Now march! [*And they disappear up the stairs.*]

VOICE [*offstage*]: Now let us pray. [*There is a prayer mumbled by many voices.*]

MISS LUCY [*who has remained behind*]: You still want to try it?

HECKLER: I'm going to take a shot at it. How's my voice?

MISS LUCY: Better.

HECKLER: I better wait here till he starts talkin', huh?

MISS LUCY: Wait till they turn down the chandeliers in the ballroom. . . . Why don't you switch to a question that won't hurt his daughter?

HECKLER: I don't want to hurt his daughter. But he's going to hold her up as the fair white virgin exposed to black lust in the South, and that's his build-up, his lead into his Voice of God speech.

MISS LUCY: He honestly believes it.

HECKLER: I don't believe it. I believe that the silence of God, the absolute speechlessness of Him is a long, long and awful thing that the whole world is lost because of. I think it's yet to be broken to any man, living or any yet lived on earth,—no exceptions, and least of all Boss Finley.

[STUFF *enters, goes to table, starts to wipe it. The chandelier lights go down.*]

MISS LUCY [*with admiration*]: It takes a hillbilly to cut down a hillbilly. . . . [*to* STUFF] Turn on the television, baby.

VOICE [*offstage*]: I give you the beloved Thomas J. Finley.

[STUFF *makes a gesture as if to turn on the TV, which we play in the fourth wall. A wavering beam of light, flickering, narrow, intense, comes from the balcony rail.* STUFF *moves his head so that he's in it, looking into it. . . .* CHANCE *walks slowly downstage, his head also in the narrow flickering beam of light. As he walks downstage, there suddenly appears on the big TV screen, which is the whole back wall of the stage, the image of* BOSS FINLEY. *His arm is around* HEAVENLY *and he is speaking. . . . When* CHANCE *sees the* BOSS'S *arm around* HEAVENLY, *he makes a noise in his throat like a hard fist hit him low. . . . Now the sound, which always follows the picture by an instant, comes on . . . loud.*]

BOSS [*on TV screen*]: Thank you, my friends, neighbors, kinfolk, fellow Americans. . . . I have told you before, but I will tell you again. I got a mission that I hold sacred to perform in the Southland. . . . When I was fifteen I came down barefooted out of the red clay hills. . . . Why? Because the Voice of God called me to execute this mission.

MISS LUCY [*to* STUFF]: He's too loud.

HECKLER: Listen!

BOSS: And what is this mission? I have told you before but

I will tell you again. To shield from pollution a blood that I think is not only sacred to me, but sacred to Him.

[*Upstage we see the* HECKLER *step up the last steps and make a gesture as if he were throwing doors open. . . . He advances into the hall, out of our sight.*]

MISS LUCY: Turn it down, Stuff.

STUFF [*motioning to her*]: Shh!

BOSS: Who is the colored man's best friend in the South? That's right . . .

MISS LUCY: Stuff, turn down the volume.

BOSS: It's me, Tom Finley. So recognized by both races.

STUFF [*shouting*]: He's speaking the word. Pour it on!

BOSS: However—I can't and will not accept, tolerate, condone this threat of a blood pollution.

[MISS LUCY *turns down the volume of the TV set.*]

BOSS: As you all know I had no part in a certain operation on a young black gentleman. I call that incident a deplorable thing. That is the one thing about which I am in total agreement with the Northern radical press. It was a deplorable thing. However . . . I understand the emotions that lay behind it. The passion to protect by this violent emotion something that we hold sacred: our purity of our own blood! But I had

CHANCE: Christ! What lies. What a liar!

MISS LUCY: Wait! . . . Chance, you can still go. I can still help you, baby.

CHANCE [*putting hands on* MISS LUCY'S *shoulders*]: Thanks, but no thank you, Miss Lucy. Tonight, God help me, somehow, I don't know how, but somehow I'll take her out of St. Cloud. I'll wake her up in my arms, and I'll give her life back

no part in, and I did not condone the operation performed on the unfortunate colored gentleman caught prowling the midnight streets of our Capitol City. . . .

to her. Yes, somehow, God help me, somehow!

[STUFF *turns up volume of TV set.*]

HECKLER [*as voice on the TV*]: Hey, Boss Finley! [*The TV camera swings to show him at the back of the hall.*] How about your daughter's operation? How about that operation your daughter had done on her at the Thomas J. Finley hospital here in St. Cloud? Did she put on black in mourning for her appendix? . . .

[*We hear a gasp, as if the* HECKLER *had been hit.*]

[*Picture:* HEAVENLY *horrified. Sounds of a disturbance. Then the doors at the top of stairs up Left burst open and the* HECKLER *tumbles down. . . . The picture changes to* BOSS FINLEY. *He is trying to dominate the disturbance in the hall.*]

BOSS: Will you repeat that question. Have that man step forward. I will answer his question. Where is he? Have that man step forward, I will answer his question. . . . Last Friday . . . Last Friday, Good Friday. I said last Friday, Good Friday . . . Quiet, may I have your attention please. . . . Last Friday, Good Friday, I seen a horrible thing on the campus of our great State University, which I built for the State. A hideous straw-stuffed effigy of myself, Tom Finley, was hung and set fire to in the main quadrangle of the college. This outrage was inspired . . . inspired by the Northern radical press. However, that was Good Friday. Today is Easter. I saw that was Good Friday. Today is Easter Sunday and I am in St. Cloud.

[*During this a gruesome, not-lighted, silent struggle has been going on. The* HECKLER *defended himself, but finally has been overwhelmed and rather systematically beaten. . . . The tight intense follow spot beam stayed on* CHANCE. *If he had any impulse to go to the* HECKLER'S *aid, he'd be discouraged by* STUFF *and another man who stand behind him, watching him. . . . At the height of the beating, there are bursts of great applause. . . . At a point during it,* HEAVENLY *is suddenly escorted down the stairs, sobbing, and collapses. . . .*]

CURTAIN

act three

A while later that night: the hotel bedroom. The shutters in the Moorish Corner are thrown open on the Palm Garden: scattered sounds of disturbance are still heard: something burns in the Palm Garden: an effigy, an emblem? Flickering light from it falls on the PRINCESS. Over the interior scene, the constant serene projection of royal palms, branched among stars.

PRINCESS [pacing with the phone]: Operator! What's happened to my driver?

[CHANCE enters on the gallery, sees someone approaching on other side—quickly pulls back and stands in shadows on the gallery.]

You told me you'd get me a driver. . . . Why can't you get me a driver when you said that you would? Somebody in this hotel can surely get me somebody to drive me at any price asked!—out of this infernal . . .

[She turns suddenly as DAN HATCHER knocks at the corridor

111

door. Behind him appear TOM JUNIOR, BUD *and* SCOTTY, *sweaty, disheveled from the riot in the Palm Garden.*]

Who's that?

SCOTTY: She ain't gonna open, break it in.

PRINCESS [*dropping phone*]: What do you want?

HATCHER: Miss Del Lago . . .

BUD: Don't answer till she opens.

PRINCESS: Who's out there! What do you want?

SCOTTY [*to shaky* HATCHER]: Tell her you want her out of the goddamn room.

HATCHER [*with forced note of authority*]: Shut up. Let me handle this . . . Miss Del Lago, your check-out time was three-thirty P.M., and it's now after midnight. . . . I'm sorry but you can't hold this room any longer.

PRINCESS [*throwing open the door*]: What did you say? Will you repeat what you said! [*Her imperious voice, jewels, furs and commanding presence abash them for a moment.*]

HATCHER: Miss Del Lago . . .

TOM JUNIOR [*recovering quickest*]: This is Mr. Hatcher, assistant manager here. You checked in last night with a character not wanted here, and we been informed he's stayin' in your room with you. We brought Mr. Hatcher up here to remind you that the check-out time is long past and—

PRINCESS [*powerfully*]: My check-out time at any hotel in the world is *when I want to check out.* . . .

TOM JUNIOR: This ain't any hotel in the world.

PRINCESS [*making no room for entrance*]: Also, I don't talk to assistant managers of hotels when I have complaints

to make about discourtesies to me, which I do most certainly
have to make about my experiences here. I don't even talk
to managers of hotels, I talk to owners of them. Directly to
hotel owners about discourtesies to me. [*Picks up satin sheets
on bed.*] These sheets are mine, they go with me. And I have
never suffered such dreadful discourtesies to me at any hotel
at any time or place anywhere in the world. Now I have
found out the name of this hotel owner. This is a chain hotel
under the ownership of a personal friend of mine whose
guest I have been in foreign capitals such as . . . [TOM JUNIOR
has pushed past her into the room.] What in hell is he doing
in my room?

TOM JUNIOR: Where is Chance Wayne?

PRINCESS: Is that what you've come here for? You can
go away then. He hasn't been in this room since he left this
morning.

TOM JUNIOR: Scotty, check the bathroom. . . . [*He checks
a closet, stoops to peer under the bed.* SCOTTY *goes off at
right.*] Like I told you before, we know you're Alexandra
Del Lago traveling with a degenerate that I'm sure you don't
know. That's why you can't stay in St. Cloud, especially after
this ruckus that we— [SCOTTY *re-enters from the bathroom
and indicates to* TOM JUNIOR *that* CHANCE *is not there.*]
—Now if you need any help in getting out of St. Cloud,
I'll be—

PRINCESS [*cutting in*]: Yes. I want a driver. Someone to
drive my car. I want to leave here. I'm desperate to leave
here. I'm not able to drive. I have to be driven away!

TOM JUNIOR: Scotty, you and Hatcher wait outside while
I explain something to her. . . . [*They go and wait outside
the door, on the left end of the gallery.*] I'm gonna git you
a driver, Miss Del Lago. I'll get you a state trooper, half a
dozen state troopers if I can't get you no driver. O.K.? Some
time come back to our town n' see us, hear? We'll lay out
a red carpet for you. O.K.? G'night, Miss Del Lago.

[*They disappear down the hall, which is then dimmed out.*

CHANCE *now turns from where he's been waiting at the other end of the corridor and slowly, cautiously, approaches the entrance to the room. Wind sweeps the Palm Garden; it seems to dissolve the walls; the rest of the play is acted against the night sky. The shuttered doors on the veranda open and* CHANCE *enters the room. He has gone a good deal further across the border of reason since we last saw him. The* PRINCESS *isn't aware of his entrance until he slams the shuttered doors. She turns, startled, to face him.*]

PRINCESS: Chance!

CHANCE: You had some company here.

PRINCESS: Some men were here looking for you. They told me I wasn't welcome in this hotel and this town because I had come here with "a criminal degenerate." I asked them to get me a driver so I can go.

CHANCE: I'm your driver. I'm still your driver, Princess.

PRINCESS: You couldn't drive through the palm garden.

CHANCE: I'll be all right in a minute.

PRINCESS: It takes more than a minute, Chance, will you listen to me? Can you listen to me? I listened to you this morning, with understanding and pity, I did, I listened with pity to your story this morning. I felt something in my heart for you which I thought I couldn't feel. I remembered young men who were what you are or what you're hoping to be. I saw them all clearly, all clearly, eyes, voices, smiles, bodies clearly. But their names wouldn't come back to me. I couldn't get their names back without digging into old programs of plays that I starred in at twenty in which they said, "Madam, the Count's waiting for you," or—Chance? They almost made it. Oh, oh, Franz! Yes, Franz . . . what? Albertzart. Franz Albertzart, oh God, God, Franz Albertzart . . . I had to fire him. He held me too tight in the waltz scene, his anxious fingers left bruises once so violent, they, they dislocated a disc in my spine, and—

CHANCE: I'm waiting for you to shut up.

PRINCESS: I saw him in Monte Carlo not too long ago. He was with a woman of seventy, and his eyes looked older than hers. She held him, she led him by an invisible chain through Grand Hotel . . . lobbies and casinos and bars like a blind, dying lap dog; he wasn't much older than you are now. Not long after that he drove his Alfa-Romeo or Ferrari off the Grand Corniche—accidentally?—Broke his skull like an eggshell. I wonder what they found in it? Old, despaired-of ambitions, little treacheries, possibly even little attempts at blackmail that didn't quite come off, and whatever traces are left of really great charm and sweetness. Chance, Franz Albertzart is Chance Wayne. Will you please try to face it so we can go on together?

CHANCE [pulls away from her]: Are you through? Have you finished?

PRINCESS: You didn't listen, did you?

CHANCE [picking up the phone]: I didn't have to. I told you that story this morning—I'm not going to drive off nothing and crack my head like an eggshell.

PRINCESS: No, because you can't drive.

CHANCE: Operator? Long distance.

PRINCESS: You would drive into a palm tree. Franz Albertzart . . .

CHANCE: Where's your address book, your book of telephone numbers?

PRINCESS: I don't know what you think that you are up to, but it's no good. The only hope for you now is to let me lead you by that invisible loving steel chain through Carltons and Ritzes and Grand Hotels and—

CHANCE: Don't you know, I'd die first? I would rather die first . . . [into phone] Operator? This is an urgent person-to-person call from Miss Alexandra Del Lago to Miss Sally Powers in Beverly Hills, California. . . .

PRINCESS: Oh, no! . . . Chance!

CHANCE: Miss Sally Powers, the Hollywood columnist, yes, Sally Powers. Yes, well get information. I'll wait, I'll wait. . . .

PRINCESS: Her number is Coldwater five-nine thousand. . . . [*Her hand goes to her mouth—but too late.*]

CHANCE: In Beverly Hills, California, Coldwater five-nine thousand.

[*The* PRINCESS *moves out onto forestage; surrounding areas dim till nothing is clear behind her but the palm garden.*]

PRINCESS: Why did I give him the number? Well, why not, after all, I'd have to know sooner or later . . . I started to call several times, picked up the phone, put it down again. Well, let him do it for me. Something's happened. I'm breathing freely and deeply as if the panic was over. Maybe it's over. He's doing the dreadful thing for me, asking the answer for me. He doesn't exist for me now except as somebody making this awful call for me, asking the answer for me. The light's on me. He's almost invisible now. What does that mean? Does it mean that I still wasn't ready to be washed up, counted out?

CHANCE: All right, call Chasen's. Try to reach her at Chasen's.

PRINCESS: Well, one thing's sure. It's only this call I care for. I seem to be standing in light with everything else dimmed out. He's in the dimmed out background as if he'd never left the obscurity he was born in. I've taken the light again as a crown on my head to which I am suited by something in the cells of my blood and body from the time of my birth. It's mine, I was born to own it, as he was born to make this phone call for me to Sally Powers, dear faithful custodian of my outlived legend. [*Phone rings in distance.*]

The legend that I've out-lived. . . . Monsters don't die early; they hang on long. Awfully long. Their vanity's infinite, almost as infinite as their disgust with themselves. . . . [*Phone rings louder: it brings the stage light back up on the hotel bedroom. She turns to* CHANCE *and the play returns to a more realistic level.*] The phone's still ringing.

CHANCE: They gave me another number. . . .

PRINCESS: If she isn't there, give my name and ask them where I can reach her.

CHANCE: Princess?

PRINCESS: What?

CHANCE: I have a personal reason for making this phone call.

PRINCESS: I'm quite certain of that.

CHANCE [*into phone*]: I'm calling for Alexandra Del Lago. She wants to speak to Miss Sally Powers—Oh, is there any number where the Princess could reach her?

PRINCESS: It will be a good sign if they give you a number.

CHANCE: Oh?—Good, I'll call that number . . . Operator? Try another number for Miss Sally Powers. It's Canyon seven-five thousand . . . Say it's urgent, it's Princess Kosmonopolis . . .

PRINCESS: Alexandra Del Lago.

CHANCE: Alexandra Del Lago is calling Miss Powers.

PRINCESS [*to herself*]: Oxygen, please, a little. . . .

CHANCE: Is that you, Miss Powers? This is Chance Wayne talking . . . I'm calling for the Princess Kosmonopolis, she wants to speak to you. She'll come to the phone in a minute.

PRINCESS: I can't. . . . Say I've . . .

CHANCE [*stretching phone cord*]: This is as far as I can stretch the cord, Princess, you've got to meet it halfway.

[PRINCESS *hesitates; then advances to the extended phone.*]

PRINCESS [*in a low, strident whisper*]: Sally? Sally? Is it really you, Sally? Yes, it's me, Alexandra. It's what's left of me, Sally. Oh, yes, I was there, but I only stayed a few minutes. Soon as they started laughing in the wrong places, I fled up the aisle and into the street screaming Taxi—and never stopped running till now. No, I've talked to nobody, heard nothing, read nothing . . . just wanted—dark . . . What? You're just being kind.

CHANCE [*as if to himself*]: Tell her that you've discovered a pair of new stars. Two of them.

PRINCESS: One moment, Sally, I'm—breathless!

CHANCE [*gripping her arm*]: And lay it on thick. Tell her to break it tomorrow in her column, in all of her columns, and in her radio talks . . . that you've discovered a pair of young people who are the stars of tomorrow!

PRINCESS [*to* CHANCE]: Go into the bathroom. Stick your head under cold water. . . . Sally . . . Do you really think so? You're not just being nice, Sally, because of old times— Grown, did you say? My talent? In what way, Sally? More depth? More what, did you say? More power!—well, Sally, God bless you, dear Sally.

CHANCE: Cut the chatter. Talk about me and *HEAVENLY!*

PRINCESS: No, of course I didn't read the reviews. I told you I flew, I flew. I flew as fast and fast as I could. Oh. Oh? Oh . . . How very sweet of you, Sally. I don't even care if you're not altogether sincere in that statement, Sally. I think you know what the past fifteen years have been like, because I do have the—"out-crying heart of an—artist." Excuse me,

Sally, I'm crying, and I don't have any Kleenex. Excuse me, Sally, I'm crying. . . .

CHANCE [*hissing behind her*]: Hey. Talk about me! [*She kicks* CHANCE'S *leg.*]

PRINCESS: What's that, Sally? Do you really believe so? Who? For what part? Oh, my God! . . . Oxygen, oxygen, quick!

CHANCE [*seizing her by the hair and hissing*]: Me! Me!— You bitch!

PRINCESS: Sally? I'm too overwhelmed. Can I call you back later? Sally, I'll call back later. . . . [*She drops phone in a daze of rapture.*] My picture has broken box-office records. In New York and L.A.!

CHANCE: Call her back, get her on the phone.

PRINCESS: Broken box-office records. The greatest comeback in the history of the industry, that's what she calls it. . . .

CHANCE: You didn't mention me to her.

PRINCESS [*to herself*]: I can't appear, not yet. I'll need a week in a clinic, then a week or ten days at the Morning Star Ranch at Vegas. I'd better get Ackermann down there for a series of shots before I go on to the Coast. . . .

CHANCE [*at phone*]: Come back here, call her again.

PRINCESS: I'll leave the car in New Orleans and go on by plane to, to, to—Tucson. I'd better get Strauss working on publicity for me. I'd better be sure my tracks are covered up well these last few weeks in—hell!—

CHANCE: Here. Here, get her back on this phone.

PRINCESS: Do what?

CHANCE: Talk about me and talk about Heavenly to her.

PRINCESS: Talk about a beach-boy I picked up for pleasure, distraction from panic? Now? When the nightmare is over? Involve my name, which is Alexandra Del Lago with the record of a— You've just been using me. Using me. When I needed you downstairs you shouted, "Get her a wheel chair!" Well, I didn't need a wheel chair, I came up alone, as always. I climbed back alone up the beanstalk to the ogre's country where I live, now, alone. Chance, you've gone past something you couldn't afford to go past; your time, your youth, you've passed it. It's all you had, and you've had it.

CHANCE: Who in hell's talking! Look. [*He turns her forcibly to the mirror.*] Look in that mirror. What do you see in that mirror?

PRINCESS: I see—Alexandra Del Lago, artist and star! Now it's your turn, you look and what do you see?

CHANCE: I see—Chance Wayne. . . .

PRINCESS: The face of a Franz Albertzart, a face that tomorrow's sun will touch without mercy. Of course, you were crowned with laurel in the beginning, your gold hair was wreathed with laurel, but the gold is thinning and the laurel has withered. Face it—pitiful monster. [*She touches the crown of his head.*] . . . Of course, I know I'm one too. But one with a difference. Do you know what that difference is? No, you don't know. I'll tell you. We are two monsters, but with this difference between us. Out of the passion and torment of my existence I have created a thing that I can unveil, a sculpture, almost heroic, that I can unveil, which is true. But you? You've come back to the town you were born in, to a girl that won't see you because you put such rot in her body she had to be gutted and hung on a butcher's hook, like a chicken dressed for Sunday. . . . [*He wheels about to strike at her but his raised fist changes its course and strikes down at his own belly and he bends double with a sick cry. Palm Garden wind: whisper of The Lament.*] Yes, and her brother who was one of my callers, threatens the same thing for you: castration, if you stay here.

CHANCE: That can't be done to me twice. You did that to me this morning, here on this bed, where I had the honor, where I had the great honor . . .

[*Windy sound rises: They move away from each other, he to the bed, she close to her portable dressing table.*]

PRINCESS: Age does the same thing to a woman. . . . [*Scrapes pearls and pillboxes off table top into handbag.*] Well . . .

[*All at once her power is exhausted, her fury gone. Something uncertain appears in her face and voice betraying the fact which she probably suddenly knows, that her future course is not a progression of triumphs. She still maintains a grand air as she snatches up her platinum mink stole and tosses it about her: it slides immediately off her shoulders; she doesn't seem to notice. He picks the stole up for her, puts it about her shoulders. She grunts disdainfully, her back to him; then resolution falters; she turns to face him with great, dark eyes that are fearful, lonely, and tender.*]

PRINCESS: I am going, now, on my way. [*He nods slightly, loosening the Windsor-knot of his knitted black silk tie. Her eyes stay on him.*] Well, are you leaving or staying?

CHANCE: Staying.

PRINCESS: You can't stay here. I'll take you to the next town.

CHANCE: Thanks but no thank you, Princess.

PRINCESS [*seizing his arm*]: Come on, you've got to leave with me. My name is connected with you, we checked in here together. Whatever happens to you, my name will be dragged in with it.

CHANCE: Whatever happens to me's already happened.

PRINCESS: What are you trying to prove?

CHANCE: Something's got to mean something, don't it, Princess? I mean like your life means nothing, except that you never could make it, always almost, never quite? Well, something's still got to mean something.

PRINCESS: I'll send a boy up for my luggage. You'd better come down with my luggage.

CHANCE: I'm not part of your luggage.

PRINCESS: What else can you be?

CHANCE: Nothing . . . but not part of your luggage.

[NOTE: *in this area it is very important that* CHANCE'S *attitude should be self-recognition but not self-pity—a sort of deathbed dignity and honesty apparent in it. In both* CHANCE *and the* PRINCESS, *we should return to the huddling-together of the lost, but not with sentiment, which is false, but with whatever is truthful in the moments when people share doom, face firing squads together. Because the* PRINCESS *is really equally doomed. She can't turn back the clock any more than can* CHANCE, *and the clock is equally relentless to them both. For the* PRINCESS: *a little, very temporary, return to, recapture of, the spurious glory. The report from* SALLY POWERS *may be and probably is a factually accurate report: but to indicate she is going on to further triumph would be to falsify her future. She makes this instinctive admission to herself when she sits down by* CHANCE *on the bed, facing the audience. Both are faced with castration, and in her heart she knows it. They sit side by side on the bed like two passengers on a train sharing a bench.*]

PRINCESS: Chance, we've got to go on.

CHANCE: Go on to where? I couldn't go past my youth, but I've gone past it.

[*The Lament fades in, continues through the scene to the last curtain.*]

PRINCESS: You're still young, Chance.

CHANCE: Princess, the age of some people can only be calculated by the level of—level of—rot in them. And by that measure I'm ancient.

PRINCESS: What am I?—I know, I'm dead, as old Egypt. . . . Isn't it funny? We're still sitting here together, side by side in this room, like we were occupying the same bench on a train—going on together . . . Look. That little donkey's marching around and around to draw water out of a well. . . . [*She points off at something as if outside a train window.*] Look, shepherd boy's leading a flock.—What an old country, timeless.—Look—

[*The sound of a clock ticking is heard, louder and louder.*]

CHANCE: No, listen. I didn't know there was a clock in this room.

PRINCESS: I guess there's a clock in every room people live in. . . .

CHANCE: It goes tick-tick, it's quieter than your heart-beat, but it's slow dynamite, a gradual explosion, blasting the world we lived in to burnt-out pieces. . . . Time—who could beat it, who could defeat it ever? Maybe some saints and heroes, but not Chance Wayne. I lived on something, that—time?

PRINCESS: Yes, time.

CHANCE: . . . Gnaws away, like a rat gnaws off its own foot caught in a trap, and then, with its foot gnawed off and the rat set free, couldn't run, couldn't go, bled and died. . . .

[*The clock ticking fades away.*]

TOM JUNIOR [*offstage left*]: Miss Del Lago . . .

PRINCESS: I think they're calling our—station. . . .

TOM JUNIOR [*still offstage*]: Miss Del Lago, I have got a driver for you.

[*A trooper enters and waits on gallery.*]

[*With a sort of tired grace, she rises from the bed, one hand lingering on her seat-companion's shoulder as she moves a little unsteadily to the door. When she opens it, she is confronted by* TOM JUNIOR.]

PRINCESS: Come on, Chance, we're going to change trains at this station. . . . So, come on, we've got to go on. . . . Chance, please. . . .

[CHANCE *shakes his head and the* PRINCESS *gives up. She weaves out of sight with the trooper down the corridor.*]

[TOM JUNIOR *enters from steps, pauses and then gives a low whistle to* SCOTTY, BUD, *and third man who enter and stand waiting.* TOM JUNIOR *comes down bedroom steps and stands on bottom step.*]

CHANCE [*rising and advancing to the forestage*]: I don't ask for your pity, but just for your understanding—not even that—no. Just for your recognition of me in you, and the enemy, time, in us all.

[*The curtain closes.*]

THE END

The Rose Tattoo

—◆—

O slinger! crack the nut of my eye! my heart twittered with joy under the splendour of the quicklime, the bird sings O Senectus! . . . the streams are in their beds like the cries of women and this world has more beauty than a ram's skin painted red!

St.-John Perse: *Anabasis*
T. S. ELIOT TRANSLATION

To Frank in Return for Sicily

The Timeless World of a Play

Carson McCullers concludes one of her lyric poems with the line: "Time, the endless idiot, runs screaming 'round the world." It is this continual rush of time, so violent that it appears to be screaming, that deprives our actual lives of so much dignity and meaning, and it is, perhaps more than anything else, the *arrest of time* which has taken place in a completed work of art that gives to certain plays their feeling of depth and significance. In the London notices of *Death of a Salesman* a certain notoriously skeptical critic made the remark that Willy Loman was the sort of man that almost any member of the audience would have kicked out of an office had he applied for a job or detained one for conversation about his troubles. The remark itself possibly holds some truth. But the implication that Willy Loman is consequently a chartcter with whom we have no reason to concern ourselves in drama, reveals a strikingly false conception of what plays are. Contemplation is something that exists outside of time, and so is the tragic sense. Even in the actual world of commerce, there exists in some persons a sensibility to the unfortunate situations of others, a capacity for concern and compassion, surviving from a more tender period of life outside the present whirling wire-cage of business activity. Facing Willy Loman across an office desk, meeting his nervous glance and hearing his querulous voice, we would be very likely to glance at our wrist watch and our schedule of other appointments. We would not kick him out of the office, no, but we would certainly *ease* him out with more expedition than Willy had feebly hoped for. But suppose there had been no wrist watch or office clock and suppose there had *not* been the schedule of pressing appointments, and suppose that we were not actually facing Willy across a desk—and facing a person is *not* the best way to *see* him!—suppose, in other words, that the meeting with Willy Loman had somehow occurred in a world *outside* of time. Then I think we would receive him with concern and kindness and even with respect. If the world of a play did not offer us this occasion to view its characters under that special condition of a *world without time,* then, indeed, the characters and occurrences of drama would become equally pointless, equally trivial, as corresponding meetings and happenings in life.

The classic tragedies of Greece had tremendous nobility. The actors wore great masks, movements were formal, dance-like, and the speeches had an epic quality which doubtless were as removed from the normal conversation of their contemporary society as they seem today. Yet they did not seem false to the Greek audiences: the magnitude of the events and the passions aroused by them did not seem ridiculously out of proportion to common experience. And I wonder if this was not because the Greek audiences knew, instinctively or by training, that the created world of a play is removed from that element which makes people *little* and their emotions fairly inconsequential.

Great sculpture often follows the lines of the human body: yet the repose of great sculpture suddenly transmutes those human lines to something that has an absoluteness, a purity, a beauty, which would not be possible in a living mobile form.

A play may be violent, full of motion: yet it has that special kind of repose which allows contemplation and produces the climate in which tragic importance is a possible thing, provided that certain modern conditions are met.

In actual existence the moments of love are succeeded by the moments of satiety and sleep. The sincere remark is followed by a cynical distrust. Truth is fragmentary, at best: we love and betray each other not in quite the same breath but in two breaths that occur in fairly close sequence. But the fact that passion occurred in *passing,* that it then declined into a more familiar sense of indifference, should not be regarded as proof of its inconsequence. And this is the very truth that drama wishes to bring us . . .

Whether or not we admit it to ourselves, we are all haunted by a truly awful sense of impermanence. I have always had a particularly keen sense of this at New York cocktail parties, and perhaps that is why I drink the martinis almost as fast as I can snatch them from the tray. This sense is the febrile thing that hangs in the air. Horror of insincerity, of *not meaning,* overhangs these affairs like the cloud of cigarette smoke and the hectic chatter. This horror is the only thing, almost, that is left unsaid at such functions. All social functions involving a group of people not intimately known to each other are always under this shadow. They are almost always (in an unconscious way) like that last dinner of the condemned: where steak or turkey, whatever the doomed man wants, is served in his cell as a mockingly cruel reminder of what the great-big-little-transitory world had to offer.

In a play, time is arrested in the sense of being confined. By a sort of legerdemain, events are made to remain *events,* rather than being reduced so quickly to mere *occurrences.* The audience can sit back in a comforting dusk to watch a world which is flooded with light and in which emotion and action have a dimension and dignity that they would likewise have in real existence, if only the shattering intrusion of time could be locked out.

About their lives people ought to remember that when they are finished, everything in them will be contained in a marvelous state of repose which is the same as that which they unconsciously admired in drama. The rush is temporary. The great and only possible dignity of man lies in his power deliberately to choose certain moral values by which to live as steadfastly as if he, too, like a character in a play, were immured against the corrupting rush of time. Snatching the eternal out of the desperately fleeting is the great magic trick of human existence. As far as we know, as far as there exists any kind of empiric evidence, there is no way to beat the game of *being* against *nonbeing,* in which nonbeing is the predestined victor on realistic levels.

Yet plays in the tragic tradition offer us a view of certain moral values in violent juxtaposition. Because we do not participate, except as spectators, we can view them clearly, within the limits of our emotional equipment. These people on the stage do not return our looks. We do not have to answer their questions nor make any sign of being in company with them, nor do we have to compete with their virtues nor resist their offenses. All at once, for this reason, we are able to *see* them! Our hearts are wrung by recognition and pity, so that the dusky shell of the auditorium where we are gathered anonymously together is flooded with an almost liquid warmth of unchecked human sympathies, relieved of self-consciousness, allowed to function . . .

Men pity and love each other more deeply than they per-

mit themselves to know. The moment after the phone has
been hung up, the hand reaches for a scratch pad and
scrawls a notation: "Funeral Tuesday at five, Church of the
Holy Redeemer, don't forget flowers." And the same hand
is only a little shakier than usual as it reaches, some minutes
later, for a highball glass that will pour a stupefaction over
the kindled nerves. Fear and evasion are the two little beasts
that chase each other's tails in the revolving wirecage of
our nervous world. They distract us from feeling too much
about things. Time rushes toward us with its hospital tray
of infinitely varied narcotics, even while it is preparing us
for its inevitably fatal operation . . .

So successfully have we disguised from ourselves the intensity of our own feelings, the sensibility of our own hearts,
that plays in the tragic tradition have begun to seem untrue.
For a couple of hours we may surrender ourselves to a
world of fiercely illuminated values in conflict, but when
the stage is covered and the auditorium lighted, almost immediately there is a recoil of disbelief. "Well, well!" we say
as we shuffle back up the aisle, while the play dwindles behind us with the sudden perspective of an early Chirico painting. By the time we have arrived at Sardi's, if not as soon
as we pass beneath the marquee, we have convinced ourselves
once more that life has as little resemblance to the curiously
stirring and meaningful occurrences on the stage as a jingle
has to an elegy of Rilke.

This modern condition of his theater audience is something
that an author must know in advance. The diminishing influence of life's destroyer, time, must be somehow worked
into the context of his play. Perhaps it is a certain foolery, a
certain distortion toward the grotesque, which will solve
the problem for him. Perhaps it is only restraint, putting a
mute on the strings that would like to break all bounds.
But almost surely, unless he contrives in some way to re-
late the dimensions of his tragedy to the dimensions of a
world in which time is *included*—he will be left among his
magnificent debris on a dark stage, muttering to himself:
"Those fools . . ."

And if they could hear him above the clatter of tongues,
glasses, chinaware and silver, they would give him this answer: "But you have shown us a world not ravaged by
time. We admire your innocence. But we have seen our
photographs, past and present. Yesterday evening we passed

our first wife on the street. We smiled as we spoke but we didn't really see her! It's too bad, but we know what is true and not true, and at 3 A.M. your disgrace will be in print!"

—Tennessee Williams

and from the prayers. We walked on the place where he didn't really respond, but we knew, and it was beautiful, and at a little the distance will be different."

—Tennessee Williams

Scenes

ACT ONE

SCENE 1   Evening
SCENE 2   Almost morning, the next day
SCENE 3   Noon of that day
SCENE 4   A late spring morning, three years later
SCENE 5   Immediately following
SCENE 6   Two hours later that day

ACT TWO

SCENE 1   Two hours later that day

ACT THREE

SCENE 1   Evening of the same day
SCENE 2   Just before dawn of the next day
SCENE 3   Morning

The Rose Tattoo was first produced by Cheryl Crawford at the Erlanger Theater in Chicago on December 29, 1950. It had its Broadway opening on February 3, 1951, at the Martin Beck Theatre in New York City, with Daniel Mann as director, setting by Boris Aronson and music by David Diamond. Production Associate: Bea Lawrence. Assistant to Producer: Paul Bigelow.

Cast of the New York Production

SALVATORE	SALVATORE MINEO
VIVI	JUDY RATNER
BRUNO	SALVATORE TAORMINA
ASSUNTA	LUDMILLA TORETZKA
ROSA DELLE ROSE	PHYLLIS LOVE
SERAFINA DELLE ROSE	MAUREEN STAPLETON
ESTELLE HOHENGARTEN	SONIA SOREL
THE STREGA	DAISY BELMORE
GIUSEPPINA	ROSSANA SAN MARCO
PEPPINA	AUGUSTA MERIGHI
VIOLETTA	VIVIAN NATHAN
MARIELLA	PENNY SANTON
TERESA	NANCY FRANKLIN
FATHER DE LEO	ROBERT CARRICART
A DOCTOR	ANDREW DUGGAN
MISS YORKE	DORRIT KELTON
FLORA	JANE HOFFMAN
BESSIE	FLORENCE SUNDSTROM
JACK HUNTER	DON MURRAY
THE SALESMAN	EDDIE HYANS
ALVARO MANGIACAVALLO	ELI WALLACH
A MAN	DAVID STEWART
ANOTHER MAN	MARTIN BALSAM

Author's Production Notes

The locale of the play is a village populated mostly by Sicilians somewhere along the Gulf Coast between New Orleans and Mobile. The time is the present.

As the curtain rises we hear a Sicilian folk singer with a guitar. He is singing. At each major divison of the play this song is resumed and it is completed at the final curtain.

The first lighting is extremely romantic. We see a frame cottage, in a rather poor state of repair, with a palm tree leaning dreamily over one end of it and a flimsy little entrance porch, with spindling pillars, sagging steps and broken rails, at the other end. The setting seems almost tropical, for, in addition to the palm trees, there are tall canes with feathery fronds and a fairly thick growth of pampas grass. These are growing on the slope of an embankment along which runs a highway, which is not visible, but the cars passing on it can occasionally be heard. The house has a rear door which cannot be seen. The facing wall of the cottage is either a transparency that lifts for the interior scenes, or is cut away to reveal the interior.

The romantic first lighting is that of late dusk, the sky a delicate blue with an opalescent shimmer more like water than air. Delicate points of light appear and disappear like lights reflected in a twilight harbor. The curtain rises well above the low tin roof of the cottage.

We see an interior that is as colorful as a booth at a carnival. There are many religious articles and pictures of ruby and gilt, the brass cage of a gaudy parrot, a large bowl of goldfish, cut-glass decanters and vases, rose-patterned wallpaper and a rose-colored carpet; everything is exclamatory in its brightness like the projection of a woman's heart passionately in love. There is a small shrine against the wall between the rooms, consisting of a prie-dieu and a little statue of the Madonna in a starry blue robe and gold crown. Before this burns always a vigil light in its ruby glass cup. Our purpose is to show these gaudy, childlike mysteries with

*sentiment and humor in equal measure, without ridicule and
with respect for the religious yearnings they symbolize.*

*An outdoor sign indicates that Serafina, whose home the
cottage is, does "SEWING." The interior furnishings give evidence of this vocation. The most salient feature is a collection of dressmaker's dummies. There are at least seven of
these life-size mannequins, in various shapes and attitudes.
[They will have to be made especially for the play as their
purpose is not realistic. They have pliable joints so that their
positions can be changed. Their arms terminate at the wrist.
In all their attitudes there is an air of drama, somewhat like
the poses of declamatory actresses of the old school.] Principal among them are a widow and a bride who face each
other in violent attitudes, as though having a shrill argument, in the parlor. The widow's costume is complete from
black-veiled hat to black slippers. The bride's featureless head
wears a chaplet of orange blossoms from which is depended
a flowing veil of white marquisette, and her net gown is
trimmed in white satin—lustrous, immaculate.*

*Most of the dummies and sewing equipment are confined to
the dining room which is also Serafina's work room. In that
room there is a tall cupboard on top of which are several
dusty bottles of imported Sicilian spumanti.*

Act One

It is the hour that the Italians call "prima sera," the begin-
ning of dusk. Between the house and the palm tree burns
the female star with an almost emerald luster.

The mothers of the neighborhood are beginning to call
their children home to supper, in voices near and distant,
urgent and tender, like the variable notes of wind and water.
There are three children: Bruno, Salvatore, and Vivi, ranged
in front of the house, one with a red paper kite, one with a
hoop, and the little girl with a doll dressed as a clown. They
are in attitudes of momentary respose, all looking up at some-
thing—a bird or a plane passing over—as the mothers'
voices call them.

BRUNO: The white flags are flying at the Coast Guard
station.

SALVATORE: That means fair weather.

VIVI: I love fair weather.

GIUSEPPINA: Vivi! Vieni mangiare!

PEPPINA: Salvatore! Come home!

VIOLETTA: Bruno! Come home to supper!

[The calls are repeated tenderly, musically.
[The interior of the house begins to be visible. Serafina
delle Rose is seen on the parlor sofa, waiting for her hus-
band Rosario's return. Between the curtains is a table set
lovingly for supper; there is wine in a silver ice-bucket
and a great bowl of roses.
[Serafina looks like a plump little Italian opera singer in
the role of Madame Butterfly. Her black hair is done in

143

a high pompadour that glitters like wet coal. A rose is held in place by glittering jet hairpins. Her voluptuous figure is sheathed in pale rose silk. On her feet are dainty slippers with glittering buckles and French heels. It is apparent from the way she sits, with such plump dignity, that she is wearing a tight girdle. She sits very erect, in an attitude of forced composure, her ankles daintily crossed and her plump little hands holding a yellow paper fan on which is painted a rose. Jewels gleam on her fingers, her wrists and her ears and about her throat. Expectancy shines in her eyes. For a few moments she seems to be posing for a picture.
[*Rosa delle Rose appears at the side of the house, near the palm tree. Rosa, the daughter of the house, is a young girl of twelve. She is pretty and vivacious, and has about her a particular intensity in every gesture.*]

SERAFINA: Rosa, where are you?

ROSA: Here, Mama.

SERAFINA: What are you doing, cara?

ROSA: I've caught twelve lightning bugs.

[*The cracked voice of Assunta is heard, approaching.*]

SERAFINA: I hear Assunta! Assunta!

[*Assunta appears and goes into the house, Rosa following her in. Assunta is an old woman in a gray shawl, bearing a basket of herbs, for she is fattuchiere, a woman who practices a simple sort of medicine. As she enters the children scatter.*]

ASSUNTA: Vengo, vengo. Buona sera. There is something wild in the air, no wind but everything's moving.

SERAFINA: I don't see nothing moving and neither do you.

ASSUNTA: Nothing is moving so you can see it moving, but everything is moving, and I can hear the star-noises. Hear them? Hear the star-noises?

SERAFINA: Naw, them ain't the star-noises. They're termites, eating the house up. What are you peddling, old woman, in those little white bags?

ASSUNTA: Powder, wonderful powder. You drop a pinch of it in your husband's coffee.

SERAFINA: What is it good for?

ASSUNTA: What is a husband good for! I make it out of the dry blood of a goat.

SERAFINA: Davero!

ASSUNTA: Wonderful stuff! But be sure you put it in his coffee at supper, not in his breakfast coffee.

SERAFINA: My husband don't need no powder!

ASSUNTA: Excuse me, Baronessa. Maybe he needs the opposite kind of a powder, I got that, too.

SERAFINA: Naw, naw, *no* kind of powder at all, old woman. [*She lifts her head with a proud smile.*]

[*Outside the sound of a truck is heard approaching up on the highway.*]

ROSA [*joyfully*]: Papa's truck!

[*They stand listening for a moment, but the truck goes by without stopping.*]

SERAFINA [*to Assunta*]: That wasn't him. It wasn't no 10-ton truck. It didn't rattle the shutters! Assunta, Assunta, undo a couple of hooks, the dress is tight on me!

ASSUNTA: Is it true what I told you?

SERAFINA: Yes, it is true, but nobody needed to tell me. Assunta, I'll tell you something which maybe you won't believe.

ASSUNTA: It is impossible to tell me anything that I don't believe.

SERAFINA: Va bene! Senti, Assunta!—I knew that I had conceived on the very night of conception! [*There is a phrase of music as she says this.*]

ASSUNTA: Ahhhh?

SERAFINA: Senti! That night I woke up with a burning pain on me, here, on my left breast! A pain like a needle, quick, quick, hot little stitches. I turned on the light, I uncovered my breast!—On it I saw the rose tattoo of my husband!

ASSUNTA: Rosario's tattoo?

SERAFINA: On me, on my breast, his tattoo! And when I saw it I knew that I had conceived . . .

[*Serafina throws her head back, smiling proudly, and opens her paper fan. Assunta stares at her gravely, then rises and hands her basket to Serafina.*]

ASSUNTA: Ecco! *You* sell the powders! [*She starts toward the door.*]

SERAFINA: You don't believe that I saw it?

ASSUNTA [*stopping*]: Did Rosario see it?

SERAFINA: I screamed. But when he woke up, it was gone. It only lasted a moment. But I *did* see it, and I *did* know, when I seen it, that I had conceived, that in my body another rose was growing!

ASSUNTA: Did he believe that you saw it?

SERAFINA: No. He laughed.—He laughed and I cried . . .

ASSUNTA: And he took you into his arms, and you stopped crying!

SERAFINA: Si!

ASSUNTA: Serafina, for you everything has got to be different. A sign, a miracle, a wonder of some kind. You speak to Our Lady. You say that She answers your questions. She nods or shakes Her head at you. Look, Serafina, underneath

Our Lady you have a candle. The wind through the shutters makes the candle flicker. The shadows move. Our Lady seems to be nodding!

SERAFINA: She gives me signs.

ASSUNTA: Only to you? Because you are more important? The wife of a barone? Serafina! In Sicily they called his uncle a baron, but in Sicily everybody's a baron that owns a piece of the land and a separate house for the goats!

SERAFINA: They said to his uncle "Voscenza!" and they kissed their hands to him! [*She kisses the back of her hand repeatedly, with vehemence.*]

ASSUNTA: His uncle in Sicily!—Si—But *here* what's he do? Drives a truck of bananas?

SERAFINA [*blurting out*]: No! *Not* bananas!

ASSUNTA: Not bananas?

SERAFINA: Stai zitta! [*She makes a warning gesture.*]—No —Vieni qui, Assunta! [*She beckons her mysteriously. Assunta approaches.*]

ASSUNTA: Cosa dici?

SERAFINA: On top of the truck is bananas! But underneath —something else!

ASSUNTA: Che altre cose?

SERAFINA: Whatever it is that the Brothers Romano want hauled out of the state, he hauls it for them, underneath the bananas! [*She nods her head importantly.*] And money, he gets so much it spills from his pockets! Soon I don't have to make dresses!

ASSUNTA [*turning away*]: Soon I think you will have to make a black veil!

SERAFINA: Tonight is the last time he does it! Tomorrow he quits hauling stuff for the Brothers Romano! He pays for the

10-ton truck and works for himself. We live with dignity in
America, then! Own truck! Own house! And in the house
will be everything electric! Stove—deep-freeze—*tutto!*—But
tonight, stay with me . . . I can't swallow my heart!—Not till
I hear the truck stop in front of the house and his key in the
lock of the door!—When I call him, and him shouting back,
"*Si, sono qui!*" In his hair, Assunta, he has—oil of roses. And
when I wake up at night—the air, the dark room's—full of—
roses . . . Each time is the first time with him. Time doesn't
pass . . .

[*Assunta picks up a small clock on the cupboard and holds
it to her ear.*]

ASSUNTA: Tick, tick, tick, tick.—You say the clock is a liar.

SERAFINA: No, the clock is a fool. I don't listen to it. My
clock is my heart and my heart don't say tick-tick, it says
love-love! And now I have two hearts in me, both of them
saying love-love!

[*A truck is heard approaching, then passes. Serafina drops
her fan. Assunta opens a bottle of spumanti with a loud pop.
Serafina cries out.*]

ASSUNTA: Stai tranquilla! Calmati! [*She pours her a glass of
wine.*] Drink this wine and before the glass is empty he'll be
in your arms!

SERAFINA: I can't—swallow my heart!

ASSUNTA: A woman must not have a heart that is too big to
swallow! [*She crosses to the door.*]

SERAFINA: Stay with me!

ASSUNTA: I have to visit a woman who drank rat poison because of a heart too big for her to swallow.

[*Assunta leaves. Serafina returns indolently to the sofa. She
lifts her hands to her great swelling breasts and murmurs
aloud:*]

SERAFINA: Oh, it's so wonderful, having *two* lives in the
body, not *one* but two! [*Her hands slide down to her belly,*

luxuriously.] I am heavy with life, I am big, big, big, with life!
[*She picks up a bowl of roses and goes into the back room.*]

[*Estelle Hohengarten appears in front of the house. She is
a thin blonde woman in a dress of Egyptian design, and her
blonde hair has an unnatural gloss in the clear, greenish
dusk. Rosa appears from behind the house, calling out:*]

ROSA: Twenty lightning bugs, Mama!

ESTELLE: Little girl? Little girl?

ROSA [*resentfully*]: Are you talking to me? [*There is a
pause.*]

ESTELLE: Come here. [*She looks Rosa over curiously.*]
You're a twig off the old rosebush.—Is the lady that does the
sewing in the house?

ROSA: Mama's at home.

ESTELLE: I'd like to see her.

ROSA: Mama?

SERAFINA: Dimi?

ROSA: There's a lady to see you.

SERAFINA: Oh. Tell her to wait in the parlor. [*Estelle enters
and stares curiously about. She picks up a small framed picture on the cupboard. She is looking at it as Serafina enters
with a bowl of roses. Serafina speaks sharply.*] That is my
husband's picture.

ESTELLE: Oh!—I thought it was Valentino.—With a mustache.

SERAFINA [*putting the bowl down on the table*]: You want
something?

ESTELLE: Yes. I heard you do sewing.

SERAFINA: Yes, I do sewing.

ESTELLE: How fast can you make a shirt for me?

SERAFINA: That all depends. [*She takes the picture from Estelle and puts it back on the cupboard.*]

ESTELLE: I got the piece of silk with me. I want it made into a shirt for a man I'm in love with. Tomorrow's the anniversary of the day we met . . . [*She unwraps a piece of rose-colored silk which she holds up like a banner.*]

SERAFINA [*involuntarily*]: Che bella stoffa!—Oh, that would be wonderful stuff for a lady's blouse or for a pair of pyjamas!

ESTELLE: I want a man's shirt made with it.

SERAFINA: Silk this color for a shirt for a *man?*

ESTELLE: This man is wild like a Gypsy.

SERAFINA: A woman should not encourage a man to be wild.

ESTELLE: A man that's wild is hard for a woman to hold, huh? But if he was tame—would the woman want to hold him? Huh?

SERAFINA: I am a married woman in business. I don't know nothing about wild men and wild women and I don't have much time—so . . .

ESTELLE: I'll pay you twice what you ask me.

[*Outside there is the sound of the goat bleating and the jingle of its harness; then the crash of wood splintering.*]

ROSA [*suddenly appearing at the door*]: Mama, the black goat is loose! [*She runs down the steps and stands watching the goat. Serafina crosses to the door.*]

THE STREGA [*in the distance*]: Hyeh, Billy, hyeh, hyeh, Billy!

ESTELLE: I'll pay you three times the price that you ask me for it.

SERAFINA [*shouting*]: Watch the goat! Don't let him get in our yard! [*to Estelle*]—If I ask you five dollars?

ESTELLE: I will pay you fifteen. Make it twenty; money is not the object. But it's got to be ready tomorrow.

SERAFINA: Tomorrow?

ESTELLE: Twenty-five dollars! [*Serafina nods slowly with a stunned look. Estelle smiles.*] I've got the measurements with me.

SERAFINA: Pin the measurements and your name on the silk and the shirt will be ready tomorrow.

ESTELLE: My name is Estelle Hohengarten.

[*A little boy races excitedly into the yard.*]

THE BOY: Rosa, Rosa, the black goat's in your yard!

ROSA [*calling*]: Mama, the goat's in the yard!

SERAFINA [*furiously, forgetting her visitor*]: Il becco della strega!—Scusi! [*She runs out onto the porch.*] Catch him, catch him before he gets at the vines!

[*Rosa dances gleefully. The Strega runs into the yard. She has a mop of wild grey hair and is holding her black skirts up from her bare hairy legs. The sound of the goat's bleating and the jingling of his harness is heard in the windy blue dusk.*
[*Serafina descends the porch steps. The high-heeled slippers, the tight silk skirt and the dignity of a baronessa make the descent a little gingerly. Arrived in the yard, she directs the goat-chase imperiously with her yellow paper fan, pointing this way and that, exclaiming in Italian.*
[*She fans herself rapidly and crosses back of the house. The goat evidently makes a sudden charge. Screaming, Serafina rushes back to the front of the house, all out of breath, the glittering pompadour beginning to tumble down over her forehead.*]

SERAFINA: Rosa! You go in the house! Don't look at the Strega!

[*Alone in the parlor, Estelle takes the picture of Rosario. Impetuously, she thrusts it in her purse and runs from the house, just as Serafina returns to the front yard.*]

ROSA [*refusing to move*]: Why do you call her a witch?

[*Serafina seizes her daughter's arm and propels her into the house.*]

SERAFINA: She has white eyes and every finger is crooked. [*She pulls Rosa's arm.*]

ROSA: She has a cataract, Mama, and her fingers are crooked because she has rheumatism!

SERAFINA: Malocchio—the evil eye—*that's* what she's got! And her fingers are crooked because she shook hands with the Devil. Go in the house and wash your face with salt water and throw the salt water away! *Go in! Quick!* She's coming!

[*The boy utters a cry of triumph.*
[*Serafina crosses abruptly to the porch. At the same moment the boy runs triumphantly around the house leading the captured goat by its bell harness. It is a middle-sized black goat with great yellow eyes. The Strega runs behind with the broken rope. As the grotesque little procession runs before her—the Strega, the goat and the children— Serafina cries out shrilly. She crouches over and covers her face. The Strega looks back at her with a derisive cackle.*]

SERAFINA: Malocchio! Malocchio!

[*Shielding her face with one hand, Serafina makes the sign of the horns with the other to ward off the evil eye. And the scene dims out.*]

Scene Two

It is just before dawn the next day. Father De Leo, a priest, and several black-shawled women, including Assunta, are standing outside the house. The interior of the house is very dim.

GIUSEPPINA: There is a light in the house.

PEPPINA: I hear the sewing machine!

VIOLETTA: There's Serafina! She's working. She's holding up a piece of rose-colored silk.

ASSUNTA: She hears our voices.

VIOLETTA: She's dropped the silk to the floor and she's . . .

GIUSEPPINA: Holding her throat! I think she . . .

PEPPINA: Who's going to tell her?

VIOLETTA: Father De Leo will tell her.

FATHER DE LEO: I think a woman should tell her. I think Assunta must tell her that Rosario is dead.

ASSUNTA: It will not be necessary to tell her. She will know when she sees us.

[*It grows lighter inside the house. Serafina is standing in a frozen attitude with her hand clutching her throat and her eyes staring fearfully toward the sound of voices.*]

ASSUNTA: I think she already knows what we have come to tell her!

FATHER DE LEO: Andiamo, Signore! We must go to the door.

[*They climb the porch steps. Assunta opens the door.*]

SERAFINA [*gasping*]: Don't speak!

[*She retreats from the group, stumbling blindly backward among the dressmaker's dummies. With a gasp she turns and runs out the backdoor. In a few moments we see her staggering about outside near the palm tree. She comes down in front of the house, and stares blindly off into the distance.*]

SERAFINA [*wildly*]: Don't speak!

[*The voices of the women begin keening in the house. Assunta comes out and approaches Serafina with her arms extended. Serafina slumps to her knees, whispering hoarsely: "Don't speak!" Assunta envelops her in the gray shawl of pity as the scene dims out.*]

Scene Three

It is noon of the same day. Assunta is removing a funeral wreath on the door of the house. A doctor and Father De Leo are on the porch.

THE DOCTOR: She's lost the baby. [*Assunta utters a low moan of pity and crosses herself.*] Serafina's a very strong woman and that won't kill her. But she is trying not to breathe. She's got to be watched and not allowed out of the bed. [*He removes a hypodermic and a small package from his bag and hands them to Assunta.*]—This is morphia. In the arm with the needle if she screams or struggles to get up again.

ASSUNTA: Capisco!

FATHER DE LEO: One thing I want to make plain. The body of Rosario must not be burned.

THE DOCTOR: Have you seen the "body of Rosario?"

FATHER DE LEO: Yes, I have seen his body.

THE DOCTOR: Wouldn't you say it was burned?

FATHER DE LEO: Of course the body was burned. When he was shot at the wheel of the truck, it crashed and caught fire. But deliberate cremation is not the same thing. It's an abomination in the sight of God.

THE DOCTOR: Abominations are something I don't know about.

FATHER DE LEO: The Church has set down certain laws.

155

THE DOCTOR: But the instructions of a widow have to be carried out.

FATHER DE LEO: Don't you know why she wants the body cremated? So she can keep the ashes here in the house.

THE DOCTOR: Well, why not, if that's any comfort to her?

FATHER DE LEO: Pagan idolatry is what I call it!

THE DOCTOR: Father De Leo, you love your people but you don't understand them. They find God in each other. And when they lose each other, they lose God and they're lost. And it's hard to help them.—Who is that woman?

[*Estelle Hohengarten has appeared before the house. She is black-veiled, and bearing a bouquet of roses.*]

ESTELLE: I am Estelle Hohengarten.

[*Instantly there is a great hubbub in the house. The women mourners flock out to the porch, whispering and gesticulating excitedly.*]

FATHER DE LEO: What have you come here for?

ESTELLE: To say good-bye to the body.

FATHER DE LEO: The casket is closed; the body cannot be seen. And you must never come here. The widow knows nothing about you. Nothing at all.

GIUSEPPINA: *We* know about you!

PEPPINA: Va via! Sporcacciona!

VIOLETTA: Puttana!

MARIELLA: Assassina!

TERESA: You sent him to the Romanos.

FATHER DE LEO: Shhh!

[*Suddenly the women swarm down the steps like a cloud of attacking birds, all crying out in Sicilian. Estelle crouches and bows her head defensively before their savage assault. The bouquet of roses is snatched from her black-gloved hands and she is flailed with them about the head and shoulders. The thorns catch her veil and tear it away from her head. She covers her white sobbing face with her hands.*]

FATHER DE LEO: Ferme! Ferme! Signore, fermate vi nel nome di Dio!—Have a little respect!

[*The women fall back from Estelle, who huddles weeping on the walk.*]

ESTELLE: See him, see him, just see him . . .

FATHER DE LEO: The body is crushed and burned. Nobody can see it. Now go away and don't ever come here again, Estelle Hohengarten!

THE WOMEN [*in both languages, wildly*]: Va via, va via, go way.

[*Rosa comes around the house. Estelle turns and retreats. One of the mourners spits and kicks at the tangled veil and roses. Father De Leo leaves. The others return inside, except Rosa.*
[*After a few moments the child goes over to the roses. She picks them up and carefully untangles the veil from the thorns.*
[*She sits on the sagging steps and puts the black veil over her head. Then for the first time she begins to weep, wildly, histrionically. The little boy appears and gazes at her; momentarily impressed by her performance. Then he picks up a rubber ball and begins to bounce it.*
[*Rosa is outraged. She jumps up, tears off the veil and runs to the little boy, giving him a sound smack and snatching the ball away from him.*]

ROSA: Go home! My papa is dead!

[*The scene dims out, as the music is heard again.*]

Scene Four

A June day, three years later. It is morning and the light is bright. A group of local mothers are storming Serafina's house, indignant over her delay in delivering the graduation dresses for their daughters. Most of the women are chattering continually in Sicilian, racing about the house and banging the doors and shutters. The scene moves swiftly and violently until the moment when Rosa finally comes out in her graduation dress.

GIUSEPPINA: Serafina! Serafina delle Rose!

PEPPINA: Maybe if you call her "Baronessa" she will answer the door. [*with a mocking laugh*] Call her "Baronessa" and kiss your hand to her when she opens the door.

GIUSEPPINA: [*tautingly*]: Baronessa! [*She kisses her hand toward the door.*]

. VIOLETTA: When did she promise your dress?

PEPPINA: All week she say, "Domani—domani—domani." But yestiddy I told her . . .

VIOLETTA: Yeah?

PEPPINA: Oh yeah. I says to her, "Serafina, domani's the high school graduation. I got to try the dress on my daughter *today*." "Domani," she says, "Sicuro! sicuro! sicuro!" So I start to go away. Then I hear a voice call, "Signora! Signora!" So I turn round and I see Serafina's daughter at the window.

VIOLETTA: Rosa?

PEPPINA: Yeah, Rosa. An' you know how?

VIOLETTA: How?

PEPPINA: *Naked!* Nuda, nuda! [*She crosses herself and repeats a prayer.*] In nominis padri et figlio et spiritus sancti. Aaahh!

VIOLETTA: What did she do?

PEPPINA: Do? She say, "Signora! Please, you call this numero and ask for Jack and tell Jack my clothes are lock up so I can't get out from the house." Then Serafina come and she grab-a the girl by the hair and she pull her way from the window and she slam the shutters right in my face!

GIUSEPPINA: Whatsa the matter the daughter?

VIOLETTA: Who is this boy? Where did she meet him?

PEPPINA: Boy! What boy? He's a sailor. [*At the word "sailor" the women say "Ahhh!"*] She met him at the high school dance and somebody tell Serafina. That's why she lock up the girl's clothes so she can't leave the house. She can't even go to the high school to take the examinations. Imagine!

VIOLETTA: Peppina, this time *you* go to the door, yeah?

PEPPINA: Oh yeah, I go. Now I'm getting nervous. [*The women all crowd to the door.*] Sera-feee-na!

VIOLETTA: Louder, louder!

PEPPINA: Apri la porta! Come on, come on!

THE WOMEN [*together*]: Yeah, apri la porta! . . . Come on, hurry up! . . . Open up!

GIUSEPPINA: I go get-a police.

VIOLETTA: Whatsa matta? You want more trouble?

GIUSEPPINA: Listen, I pay in advance five dollars and get

no dress. Now what she wear, my daughter, to graduate in?
A couple of towels and a rose in the hair? [*There is a noise
inside: a shout and running footsteps.*]

THE WOMEN: Something is going on in the house! I hear
someone! Don't I? Don't you?

[*A scream and running footsteps are heard. The front door
opens and Serafina staggers out onto the porch. She is
wearing a soiled pink slip and her hair is wild.*]

SERAFINA: Aiuto! Aiuto! [*She plunges back into the house.*]

[*Miss Yorke, a spinsterish high school teacher, walks
quickly up to the house. The Sicilian women, now all
chattering at once like a cloud of birds, sweep about her
as she approaches.*]

MISS YORKE: You ladies know I don't understand Italian!
So, please . . .

[*She goes directly into the house. There are more outcries
inside. The Strega comes and stands at the edge of the
yard, cackling derisively.*]

THE STREGA [*calling back to someone*]: The Wops are at
it again!—She got the daughter lock up naked in there all
week. Ho, ho, ho! She lock up all week—naked—shouting
out the window tell people to call a number and give a message to Jack. Ho, ho, ho! I guess she's in trouble already, and
only fifteen!—They ain't civilized, these Sicilians. In the old
country they live in caves in the hills and the country's run
by bandits. Ho, ho, ho! More of them coming over on the
boats all the time. [*The door is thrown open again and Serafina reappears on the porch. She is acting wildly, as if de-
mented.*]

SERAFINA [*gasping in a hoarse whisper*]: She cut her wrist,
my daughter, she cut her wrist! [*She runs out into the yard.*]
Aiiii-eeee! Aiutatemi, aiutatemi! Call the dottore! [*Assunta
rushes up to Serafina and supports her as she is about to fall
to her knees in the yard.*] Get the knife away from her! Get
the knife, please! Get the knife away from—she cut her wrist
with—Madonna! Madonna mia . . .

ASSUNTA: Smettila, smettila, Serafina.

MISS YORKE [*coming out of the back room*]: Mrs. Delle Rose, your daughter has not cut her wrist. Now come back into the house.

SERAFINA: [*panting*]: Che dice, che dice? Che cosa? Che cosa dice?

MISS YORKE: Your daughter's all right. Come back into the house. And you ladies please go away!

ASSUNTA: Vieni, Serafina. Andiamo a casa. [*She supports the heavy, sagging bulk of Serafina to the steps. As they climb the steps one of the Sicilian mothers advances from the whispering group.*]

GIUSEPPINA [*boldly*]: Serafina, we don't go away until we get our dresses.

PEPPINA: The graduation begins and the girls ain't dressed.

[*Serafina's reply to this ill-timed request is a long, animal howl of misery as she is supported into the house. Miss Yorke follows and firmly closes the door upon the women, who then go around back of the house. The interior of the house is lighted up.*]

MISS YORKE [*to Serafina*]: No, no, no, she's not bleeding. Rosa? Rosa, come here and show your mother that you are not bleeding to death.

[*Rosa appears silently and sullenly between the curtains that separate the two rooms. She has a small white handkerchief tied around one wrist. Serafina points at the wrist and cries out: "Aiieee!"*]

MISS YORKE [*severely*]: Now *stop* that, Mrs. Delle Rose!

[*Serafina rushes to Rosa, who thrusts her roughly away.*]

ROSA: Lasciami stare, Mama!—I'm so ashamed I could die. This is the way she goes around all the time. She hasn't put on clothes since my father was killed. For three years she sits at the sewing machine and never puts a dress on or goes

out of the house, and now she has locked my clothes up so
I can't go out. She wants me to be like her, a freak of the
neighborhood, the way she is! Next time, next time, I won't
cut my wrist but my throat! I don't want to live locked up
with a bottle of ashes! [*She points to the shrine.*]

ASSUNTA: Figlia, figlia, non devi parlare così!

MISS YORKE: Mrs. Delle Rose, please give me the key to
the closet so that your daughter can dress for the graduation!

SERAFINA [*surrendering the key*]: Ecco la—chiave . . .
[*Rosa snatches the key and runs back through the curtains.*]

MISS YORKE: Now why did you lock her clothes up, Mrs.
Delle Rose?

SERAFINA: The wrist is still bleeding!

MISS YORKE: No, the wrist is not bleeding. It's just a skin
cut, a scratch. But the child is exhausted from all this excitement and hasn't eaten a thing in two or three days.

ROSA [*running into the dining room*]: Four days! I only
asked her one favor. Not to let me go out but to let Jack
come to the house so she could meet him!—Then she locked
my clothes up!

MISS YORKE: Your daughter missed her final examinations
at the high school, but her grades have been so good that she
will be allowed to graduate with her class and take the examinations later.—You understand me, Mrs. Delle Rose!

[*Rosa goes into the back of the house.*]

SERAFINA [*standing at the curtains*]: See the way she looks
at me? I've got a wild thing in the house, and her wrist is still
bleeding!

MISS YORKE: Let's not have any more outbursts of emotion!

SERAFINA: Outbursts of—you make me sick! Sick! Sick at
my stomach you make me! Your school, you make all this

trouble! You give-a this dance where she gets mixed up with
a sailor.

MISS YORKE: You are talking about the Hunter girl's
brother, a sailor named Jack, who attended the dance with
his sister?

SERAFINA: "Attended with sister!"—Attended with *sister!*
—My daughter, she's nobody's sister!

[*Rosa comes out of the back room. She is radiantly beautiful in her graduation gown.*]

ROSA: Don't listen to her, don't pay any attention to her,
Miss Yorke.—I'm ready to go to the high school.

SERAFINA [*stunned by her daughter's beauty, and speaking
with a wheedling tone and gestures, as she crouches a little.*]: O tesoro, tesoro! Vieni qua, Rosa, cara!—Come here
and kiss Mama one minute!—Don't go like that, now!

ROSA: Lasciami stare!

[*She rushes out on the porch. Serafina gazes after her
with arms slowly drooping from their imploring gesture
and jaw dropping open in a look of almost comic deso-
lation.*]

SERAFINA: Ho solo te, solo te—in questo mondo!

MISS YORKE: Now, now, Mrs. Delle Rose, no more excitement, please!

SERAFINA [*suddenly plunging after them in a burst of fury*]:
Senti, senti, per favore!

ROSA: Don't you dare come out on the street like that!—
Mama!

[*She crouches and covers her face in shame, as Serafina
heedlessly plunges out into the front yard in her shocking
deshabille, making wild gestures.*]

SERAFINA: You give this dance where she gets mixed up
with a sailor. What do you think you want to do at this high
school? [*In weeping despair, Rosa runs to the porch.*] How
high is this high school? Listen, how high is this high school?
Look, look, look, I will show you! It's high as that horse's
dirt out there in the street! [*Serafina points violently out
in front of the house.*] Si! 'Sta fetentissima scuola! Scuola
maledetta!

[*Rosa cries out and rushes over to the palm tree, leaning
against it, with tears of mortification.*]

MISS YORKE: Mrs. Delle Rose, you are talking and behav-
ing extremely badly. I don't understand how a woman that
acts like you could have such a sweet and refined young girl
for a daughter!—You don't deserve it!—Really . . . [*She
crosses to the palm tree.*]

SERAFINA: Oh, you want me to talk refined to you, do you?
Then do me one thing! Stop ruining the girls at the high
school! [*As Serafina paces about, she swings her hips in the
exaggeratedly belligerent style of a parading matador.*]

ASSUNTA: Piantala, Serafina! Andiamo a casa!

SERAFINA: No, no, I ain't through talking to this here
teacher!

ASSUNTA: Serafina, look at yourself, you're not dressed!

SERAFINA: I'm dressed okay; I'm not naked! [*She glares
savagely at the teacher by the palm tree. The Sicilian mothers
return to the front yard.*]

ASSUNTA: Serafina, cara? Andiamo a casa, adesso!—Basta!
Basta!

SERAFINA: Aspetta!

ROSA: I'm so ashamed I could die, I'm so ashamed. Oh, you
don't know, Miss Yorke, the way that we live. She never puts
on a dress; she stays all the time in that dirty old pink slip!
—And talks to my father's ashes like he was living.

SERAFINA: Teacher! Teacher, senti! What do you think you

want to do at this high school? Sentite! per favore! You give this a dance! What kind of a spring dance is it? Answer this question, please, for me! What kind of a spring dance is it? She meet this boy there who don't even go to no high school. What kind of a boy? Guardate! *A sailor that wears a gold earring! That kind of a boy is the kind of boy she meets there!*—That's why I lock her clothes up so she can't go back to the high school! [*suddenly to Assunta*] She cut her wrist! It's still bleeding! [*She strikes her forehead three times with her fist.*]

ROSA: Mama, you look disgusting! [*She rushes away.*]

[*Miss Yorke rushes after her. Serafina shades her eyes with one hand to watch them departing down the street in the brilliant spring light.*]

SERAFINA: Did you hear what my daughter said to me?— "You look—disgusting."—She calls me ...

ASSUNTA: Now, Serafina, we must go in the house. [*She leads her gently to the porch of the little house.*]

SERAFINA [*proudly*]: How pretty she look, my daughter, in the white dress, like a bride! [*to all*] Excuse me! Excuse me, please! Go away! Get out of my yard!

GIUSEPPINA [*taking the bull by the horns*]: No, we ain't going to go without the dresses!

ASSUNTA: Give the ladies the dresses so the girls can get dressed for the graduation.

SERAFINA: That one there, she only paid for the goods. I charge for the work.

GIUSEPPINA: Ecco! I got the money!

THE WOMEN: We *got* the money!

SERAFINA: The names are pinned on the dresses. Go in and get them. [*She turns to Assunta.*] Did you hear what my daughter called me? She called me "disgusting!"

[*Serafina enters the house, slamming the door. After a*

moment the mothers come out, cradling the white voile dresses tenderly in their arms, murmuring "carino!" and "bellissimo!"

[*As they disappear the inside light is brought up and we see Serafina standing before a glazed mirror, looking at herself and repeating the daughter's word.*]

SERAFINA: Disgusting!

[*The music is briefly resumed to mark a division.*]

Scene Five

Immediately following. Serafina's movements gather momentum. She snatches a long-neglected girdle out of a bureau drawer and holds it experimentally about her waist. She shakes her head doubtfully, drops the girdle and suddenly snatches the $8.98 hat off the millinery dummy and plants it on her head. She turns around distractedly, not remembering where the mirror is. She gasps with astonishment when she catches sight of herself, snatches the hat off and hastily restores it to the blank head of the dummy. She makes another confused revolution or two, then gasps with fresh inspiration and snatches a girlish frock off a dummy —an Alice-blue gown with daisies crocheted on it. The dress sticks on the dummy. Serafina mutters savagely in Sicilian. She finally overcomes this difficulty but in her exasperation she knocks the dummy over. She throws off the robe and steps hopefully into the gown. But she discovers it won't fit over her hips. She seizes the girdle again; then hurls it angrily away. The parrot calls to her; she yells angrily back at the parrot: "Zitto!"

In the distance the high school band starts playing. Serafina gets panicky that she will miss the graduation ceremonies, and hammers her forehead with her fist, sobbing a little. She wriggles despairingly out of the blue dress and runs out back in her rayon slip just as Flora and Bessie appear outside the house. Flora and Bessie are two female clowns of middle years and juvenile temperament. Flora is tall and angular; Bessie is rather stubby. They are dressed for a gala. Flora runs up the steps and bangs at the cottage door.

BESSIE: I fail to understand why it's so important to pick up a polka-dot blouse when it's likely to make us miss the twelve o'clock train.

FLORA: Serafina! Serafina!

167

BESSIE: We only got fifteen minutes to get to the depot and I'll get faint on the train if I don't have m' coffee . . .

FLORA: Git a Coke on th' train, Bessie.

BESSIE: Git nothing on the train if we don't git the train!

[*Serafina runs back out of the bedroom, quite breathless, in a purple silk dress. As she passes the millinery dummy she snatches the hat off again and plants it back on her head.*]

SERAFINA: Wrist watch! Wrist watch! Where'd I put th' wrist watch? [*She hears Flora shouting and banging and rushes to the door.*]

BESSIE: Try the door if it ain't open.

FLORA [*pushing in*]: Just tell me, is it ready or not?

SERAFINA: Oh! You. Don't bother me. I'm late for the graduation of my daughter and now I can't find her graduation present.

FLORA: You got plenty of time.

SERAFINA: Don't you hear the band playing?

FLORA: They're just warming up. Now, Serafina, where is my blouse?

SERAFINA: Blouse? Not ready! I had to make fourteen graduation dresses!

FLORA: A promise is a promise and an excuse is just an excuse!

SERAFINA: I got to get to the high school!

FLORA: I got to get to the depot in that blouse!

BESSIE: We're going to the American Legion parade in New Orleans.

FLORA: There, there, there, there it is! [*She grabs the*

blouse from the machine.] Get started, woman, stitch them bandanas together! If you don't do it, I'm a-gonna report you to the Chamber of Commerce and git your license revoked!

SERAFINA [*anxiously*]: What license you talking about? I got no license!

FLORA: You hear that, Bessie? *She hasn't got no license!*

BESSIE: *She ain't even got a license?*

SERAFINA [*crossing quickly to the machine*]: I—I'll stitch them together! But if you make me late to my daughter's graduation, I'll make you sorry some way . . .

[*She works with furious rapidity. A train whistle is heard.*]

BESSIE [*wildly and striking at Flora with her purse*]: Train's pullin' out! Oh, God, you made us miss it!

FLORA: Bessie, you know there's another at 12:45!

BESSIE: It's the selfish—principle of it that makes me sick! [*She walks rapidly up and down.*]

FLORA: Set down, Bessie. Don't wear out your feet before we git to th' city . . .

BESSIE: Molly tole me the town was full of excitement. They're dropping paper sacks full of water out of hotel windows.

FLORA: Which hotel are they dropping paper sacks out of?

BESSIE: What a fool question! The Monteleone Hotel.

FLORA: That's an old-fashioned hotel.

BESSIE: It might be old-fashioned but you'd be surprised at some of the modern, up-to-date things that go on there.

FLORA: I heard, I heard that the Legionnaires caught a girl on Canal Street! They tore the clothes off her and sent her home in a taxi!

BESSIE: I double dog dare anybody to try that on me!

FLORA: You?! Huh! You never need any assistance gittin' undressed!

SERAFINA [*ominously*]: You two ladies watch how you talk in there. This here is a Catholic house. You are sitting in the same room with Our Lady and with the blessed ashes of my husband!

FLORA [*acidly*]: Well, ex-cuse *me!* [*She whispers maliciously to Bessie.*] It sure is a pleasant surprise to see you wearing a dress, Serafina, but the surprise would be twice as pleasant if it was more the right size. [*to Bessie, loudly*] She used to have a sweet figure, a little bit plump but attractive, but setting there at that sewing machine for three years in a kimona and not stepping out of the house has naturally given her hips!

SERAFINA: If I didn't have hips I would be a very uncomfortable woman when I set down.

[*The parrot squawks. Serafina imitates its squawk.*]

FLORA: Polly want a cracker?

SERAFINA: No. He don't want a cracker! What is she doing over there at that window?

BESSIE: Some Legionnaires are on the highway!

FLORA: A Legionnaire? No kidding?

[*She springs up and joins her girl friend at the window. They both laugh fatuously, bobbing their heads out the window.*]

BESSIE: He's looking this way; yell something!

FLORA [*leaning out the window*]: Mademoiselle from Armentieres, parley-voo!

BESSIE [*chiming in rapturously*]: Mademoiselle from Armentieres, parley-voo!

A VOICE OUTSIDE [*gallantly returning the salute*]: Mademoiselle from Armentieres, hadn't been kissed for forty years!

BOTH GIRLS [*together; very gaily*]: Hinky-dinky parley-voooo!

[*They laugh and applaud at the window. The Legionnaires are heard laughing. A car horn is heard as the Legionnaires drive away. Serafina springs up and rushes over to the window, jerks them away from it and slams the shutters in their faces.*]

SERAFINA [*furiously*]: I told you wimmen that you was not in a honky-tonk! Now take your blouse and git out! Get out on the streets where you kind a wimmen belong.—This is the house of Rosario delle Rose and those are his ashes in that marble urn and I won't have—unproper things going on here or dirty talk, neither!

FLORA: Who's talking dirty?

BESSIE: What a helluva nerve.

FLORA: I want you to listen!

SERAFINA: You are, you are, dirty talk, all the time men, men, men! You men-crazy things, you!

FLORA: Sour grapes—sour grapes is your trouble! You're wild with envy!

BESSIE: Isn't she green with jealousy? Huh!

SERAFINA [*suddenly and religiously*]: When I think of men I think about my husband. My husband was a Sicilian. We had love together every night of the week, we never skipped one, from the night we was married till the night he was killed in his fruit truck on that road there! [*She catches her breath in a sob.*] And maybe that is the reason I'm not man-crazy and don't like hearing the talk of women that are. But I am interested, now, in the happiness of my daughter who's graduating this morning out of high school. And now I'm going to be late, the band is playing! And I have lost her wrist watch!—her graduation present! [*She whirls about distractedly.*]

BESSIE: Flora, let's go!—The hell with that goddam blouse!

FLORA: Oh, no, just wait a minute! I don't accept insults from no one!

SERAFINA: Go on, go on to New Orleans, you two man-crazy things, you! And pick up a man on Canal Street but not in my house, at my window, in front of my dead husband's ashes! [*The high school band is playing a martial air in the distance. Serafina's chest is heaving violently; she touches her heart and momentarily seems to forget that she must go.*] I am not at all interested, I am not interested in men getting fat and bald in soldier-boy play suits, tearing the clothes off girls on Canal Street and dropping paper sacks out of hotel windows. I'm just not interested in that sort of man-crazy business. I remember my husband with a body like a young boy and hair on his head as thick and black as mine is and skin on him smooth and sweet as a yellow rose petal.

FLORA: Oh, a *rose*, was he?

SERAFINA: Yes, yes, a rose, a rose!

FLORA: Yes, a rose of a Wop!—of a gangster!—shot smuggling dope under a load of bananas!

BESSIE: Flora, Flora, let's go!

SERAFINA: My folks was peasants, contadini, but he—he come from *land*owners! *Signorile*, my husband—At night I sit here and I'm satisfied to remember, because I had the best.—Not the third best and not the second best, but the *first* best, the *only* best!—So now I stay here and am satisfied now to remember, . . .

BESSIE: Come on, come out! To the depot!

FLORA: Just wait, I wanta hear this, it's too good to miss!

SERAFINA: I count up the nights I held him all night in my arms, and I can tell you how many. Each night for twelve years. Four thousand—three hundred—and eighty. The number of nights I held him all night in my arms. Sometimes I didn't sleep, just held him all night in my arms. And I am satisfied with it. I grieve for him. Yes, my pillow at night's never dry—but I'm satisfied to remember. And I would feel cheap and degraded and not fit to live with my daughter or under the roof with the urn of his blessed ashes, those— ashes of a rose—if after that memory, after knowing that man, I went to some other, some middle-aged man, not young, not full of young passion, but getting a pot belly on him and losing his hair and smelling of sweat and liquor— and trying to fool myself that *that* was love-making! I *know* what love-making was. And I'm satisfied just to remember . . . [*She is panting as though she had run upstairs.*] Go on, you do it, you go on the streets and let them drop their sacks of dirty water on you!—I'm satisfied to remember the love of a man that was mine—*only mine!* Never touched by the hand of *nobody! Nobody* but *me!*—Just me! [*She gasps and runs out to the porch. The sun floods her figure. It seems to astonish her. She finds herself sobbing. She digs in her purse for her handkerchief.*]

FLORA [*crossing to the open door*]: Never touched by no-body?

SERAFINA [*with fierce pride*]: Never nobody but me!

FLORA: *I* know somebody that could a tale unfold! And not so far from here neither. Not no further than the Square Roof is, that place on Esplanade!

BESSIE: Estelle Hohengarten!

FLORA: Estelle Hohengarten!—the blackjack dealer from Texas!

BESSIE: Get into your blouse and let's go!

FLORA: Everybody's known it but Serafina. I'm just telling the facts that come out at the inquest while she was in bed with her eyes shut tight and the sheet pulled over her head like a female ostrich! Tie this damn thing on me! It was a ro- mance, not just a fly-by-night thing, but a steady affair that went on for more than a year.

[*Serafina has been standing on the porch with the door open behind her. She is in the full glare of the sun. She appears to have been struck senseless by the words shouted inside. She turns slowly about. We see that her dress is un-*

*fastened down the back, the pink slip showing. She reaches
out gropingly with one hand and finds the porch column
which she clings to while the terrible words strike con-
stantly deeper. The high school band continues as a merci-
less counterpoint.*]

BESSIE: Leave her in ignorance. Ignorance is bliss.

FLORA: He had a rose tattoo on his chest, the stuck-up
thing, and Estelle was so gone on him she went down to
Bourbon Street and had one put on her. [*Serafina comes onto
the porch and Flora turns to her, viciously.*] Yeah, a rose
tattoo on her chest same as the Wop's!

SERAFINA [*very softly*]: Liar . . . [*She comes inside; the
word seems to give her strength.*]

BESSIE [*nervously*]: Flora, let's go, let's go!

SERAFINA [*in a terrible voice*]: Liar!—*Lie*-arrrrr!

[*She slams the wooden door shut with a violence that
shakes the walls.*]

BESSIE [*shocked into terror*]: Let's get outa here, Flora!

FLORA: Let her howl her head off. I don't care.

[*Serafina has snatched up a broom.*]

BESSIE: What's she up to?

FLORA: I don't care what she's up to!

BESSIE: I'm a-scared of these Wops.

FLORA: I'm not afraid of nobody!

BESSIE: She's gonna hit you.

FLORA: She'd better not hit me!

[*But both of the clowns are in retreat to the door. Sera-
fina suddenly rushes at them with the broom. She flails
Flora about the hips and shoulders. Bessie gets out. But
Flora is trapped in a corner. A table is turned over. Bessie,*

outside, screams for the police and cries: "Murder! Murder!" *The high school band is playing "The Stars and Stripes Forever." Flora breaks wildly past the flailing broom and escapes out of the house. She also takes up the cry for help. Serafina follows them out. She is flailing the brilliant noon air with the broom. The two women run off, screaming.*]

FLORA [*calling back*]: I'm going to have her arrested! Police, police! I'm going to have you arrested!

SERAFINA: *Have* me arrested, *have* me, you dirt, you devil, you *liar!* Li-i-arrrr!

[*She comes back inside the house and leans on the work table for a moment, panting heavily. Then she rushes back to the door, slams it and bolts it. Then she rushes to the windows, slams the shutters and fastens them. The house is now dark except for the vigil light in the ruby glass cup before the Madonna, and the delicate beams admitted through the shutter slats.*]

SERAFINA [*in a crazed manner*]: Have me—have me—arrested—dirty slut—bitch—liar! [*She moves about helplessly, not knowing what to do with her big, stricken body. Panting for breath, she repeats the word "liar" monotonously and helplessly as she thrashes about. It is necessary for her, vitally necessary for her, to believe that the woman's story is a malicious invention. But the words of it stick in her mind and she mumbles them aloud as she thrashes crazily around the small confines of the parlor.*] Woman—Estelle—[*The sound of band music is heard.*] Band, band, already—started. —Going to miss—graduation. Oh! [*She retreats toward the Madonna.*] Estelle, Estelle Hohengarten?—"A shirt for a man I'm in love with! This man—is—wild like a Gypsy."—Oh, oh, Lady—The—rose-colored—silk. [*She starts toward the dining room, then draws back in terror.*] No, no, no, no, no! I don't remember! It wasn't that name, I don't remember the name! [*The band music grows louder.*] High school—graduation—late! I'll be—late for it.—Oh, Lady, give me a —sign! [*She cocks her head toward the statue in a fearful listening attitude.*] Che? Che dice, Signora? Oh, Lady! Give me a sign!

[*The scene dims out.*]

Scene Six

It is two hours later. The interior of the house is in complete darkness except for the vigil light. With the shutters closed, the interior is so dark that we do not know Serafina is present. All that we see clearly is the starry blue robe of Our Lady above the flickering candle of the ruby glass cup. After a few moments we hear Serafina's voice, very softly, in the weak, breathless tone of a person near death.

SERAFINA [*very softly*]: Oh, Lady, give me a sign . . .

[*Gay, laughing voices are heard outside the house. Rosa and Jack appear, bearing roses and gifts. They are shouting back to others in a car.*]

JACK: Where do we go for the picnic?

A GIRL'S VOICE [*from the highway*]: We're going in three sailboats to Diamond Key.

A MAN'S VOICE: Be at Municipal Pier in half an hour.

ROSA: Pick us up here! [*She races up the steps.*] Oh, the door's locked! Mama's gone *out!* There's a key in that birdbath.

[*Jack opens the door. The parlor lights up faintly as they enter.*]

JACK: It's dark in here.

ROSA: Yes, Mama's gone out!

JACK: How do you know she's out?

176

ROSA: The door was locked and all the shutters are closed! Put down those roses.

JACK: Where shall I . . .

ROSA: Somewhere, anywhere!—Come here! [*He approaches her rather diffidently.*] I want to teach you a little Dago word. The word is "bacio."

JACK: What does this word mean?

ROSA: This and this and this! [*She rains kisses upon him till he forcibly removes her face from his.*] Just think. A week ago Friday—I didn't know boys existed!—Did you know girls existed before the dance?

JACK: Yes, I knew they existed . . .

ROSA [*holding him*]: Do you remember what you said to me on the dance floor? "Honey, you're dancing too close?"

JACK: Well, it was hot in the Gym and the—floor was crowded.

ROSA: When my girl friend was teaching me how to dance, I asked her, "How do you know which way the boy's going to move?" And she said, "You've got to feel he's going to move with your body!" I said, "How do you feel with your body?" And she said, "By pressing up close!"—That's why I pressed up close! I didn't realize that I was—Ha, ha! Now you're blushing! Don't go *away!*—And a few minutes later you said to me, "Gee, you're beautiful!" I said, "Excuse me," and ran to the ladies' room. Do you know why? To look at myself in the mirror! And I saw that I was! For the first time in my life I was beautiful! You'd made me beautiful when you *said* that I was!

JACK [*humbly*]: You *are* beautiful, Rosa! So much, I . . .

ROSA: *You've* changed, *too.* You've stopped laughing and joking. Why have you gotten so old and serious, Jack?

JACK: Well, honey, you're sort of . . .

ROSA: What am I "sort of?"

JACK [*finding the exact word*]: *Wild!* [*She laughs. He seizes the bandaged wrist.*] I didn't know nothing like this was going to happen.

ROSA: Oh, that, that's nothing! I'll take the handkerchief off and you can forget it.

JACK: How could you do a thing like that over me? I'm— nothing!

ROSA: Everybody is nothing until you love them!

JACK: Give me that handkerchief. I want to show it to my shipmates. I'll say, "This is the blood of a beautiful girl who cut her wrist with a knife because she loved me!"

ROSA: Don't be so pleased with yourself. It's mostly Mer-curochrome!

SERAFINA [*violently, from the dark room adjoining*]: *Stai zitta!—Cretina!*

[*Rosa and Jack draw abruptly apart.*]

JACK [*fearfully*]: I knew somebody was here!

ROSA [*sweetly and delicately*]: Mama? Are you in there, Mama?

SERAFINA: No, no, no, I'm not, I'm dead and buried!

ROSA: Yes, Mama's in there!

JACK: Well, I—better go and—wait outside for a— while . . .

ROSA: You stay right here!—Mama?—Jack is with me.— Are you dressed up nicely? [*There is no response.*] Why's it so dark in here?—Jack, open the shutters!—I want to intro-duce you to my mother . . .

JACK: Hadn't I better go and . . .

ROSA: No. Open the shutters!

[*The shutters are opened and Rosa draws apart the curtains between the two rooms. Sunlight floods the scene. Serafina is revealed slumped in a chair at her work table in the dining room near the Singer sewing machine. She is grotesquely surrounded by the dummies, as though she had been holding a silent conference with them. Her appearance, in slovenly deshabille, is both comic and shocking.*]

ROSA [*terribly embarrassed*]: Mama, Mama, you said you were dressed up pretty! Jack, stay out for a minute! What's happened, Mama?

[*Jack remains in the parlor. Rosa pulls the curtains, snatches a robe and flings it over Serafina. She brushes Serafina's hair back from her sweat-gleaming face, rubs her face with a handkerchief and dusts it with powder. Serafina submits to this cosmetic enterprise with a dazed look.*]

ROSA [*gesturing vertically*]: Su, su, su, su, su, su, su, su, su! [*Serafina sits up slightly in her chair, but she is still looking stupefied. Rosa returns to the parlor and opens the curtains again.*]

ROSA: Come in, Jack! Mama is ready to meet you!

[*Rosa trembles with eagerness as Jack advances nervously from the parlor. But before he enters Serafina collapses again into her slumped position, with a low moan.*]

ROSA [*violently*]: Mama, Mama, su, Mama! [*Serafina sits half erect.*] She didn't sleep good last night.—Mama, this is Jack Hunter!

JACK: Hello, Mrs. Delle Rose. It sure is a pleasure to meet you.

[*There is a pause. Serafina stares indifferently at the boy.*]

ROSA: Mama, Mama, say something!

JACK: Maybe your Mama wants me to . . . [*He makes an awkward gesture toward the door.*]

ROSA: No, no, Mama's just tired. Mama makes dresses; she made a whole lot of dresses for the graduation! How many, Mama, how many graduation dresses did you have to make?

SERAFINA [*dully*]: Fa niente . . .

JACK: I was hoping to see you at the graduation, Mrs. Delle Rose.

ROSA: I guess that Mama was too worn out to go.

SERAFINA: Rosa, shut the front door, shut it and lock it. There was a—policeman . . . [*There is a pause.*] What?—What?

JACK: My sister was graduating. My mother was there and my aunt was there—a whole bunch of cousins—I was hoping that you could—all—get together . . .

ROSA: Jack brought you some flowers.

JACK: I hope you are partial to roses as much as I am. [*He hands her the bouquet. She takes them absently.*]

ROSA: Mama, say something, say something simple like "Thanks."

SERAFINA: Thanks.

ROSA: Jack, tell Mama about the graduation; describe it to her.

JACK: My mother said it was just like fairyland.

ROSA: Tell her what the boys wore!

JACK: What did—what did they wear?

ROSA: Oh, you know what they wore. They wore blue coats and white pants and each one had a carnation! And there were three couples that did an old-fashioned dance, a minuet, Mother, to Mendelssohn's *Spring Song!* Wasn't it lovely, Jack? But one girl slipped; she wasn't used to long dresses! She slipped and fell on her—ho, ho! Wasn't it funny, Jack, wasn't it, wasn't it, Jack?

JACK [*worriedly*]: I think that your Mama . . .

ROSA: Oh, my prize, my prize, I have forgotten my prize!

JACK: Where is it?

ROSA: You set them down by the sewing sign when you looked for the key.

JACK: Aw, excuse me, I'll get them. [*He goes out through the parlor. Rosa runs to her mother and kneels by her chair.*]

ROSA [*in a terrified whisper*]: Mama, something has happened! What has happened, Mama? Can't you tell me, Mama? Is it because of this morning? Look. I took the bandage off, it was only a scratch! So, Mama, forget it! Think it was just a bad dream that never happened! Oh, Mama! [*She gives her several quick kisses on the forehead. Jack returns with two big books tied in white satin ribbon.*]

JACK: Here they are.

ROSA: Look what I got, Mama.

SERAFINA [*dully*]: What?

ROSA: The *Digest of Knowledge!*

JACK: Everything's in them, from Abracadabra to Zoo! My sister was jealous. She just got a diploma!

SERAFINA [*rousing a bit*]: Diploma, where is it? Didn't you get no diploma?

ROSA: Si, si, Mama! Eccolo! Guarda, guarda! [*She holds up the diploma tied in ribbon.*]

SERAFINA: Va bene.—Put it in the drawer with your father's clothes.

JACK: Mrs. Delle Rose, you should be very, very proud of your daughter. She stood in front of the crowd and recited a poem.

ROSA: Yes, I did. Oh, I was so excited!

JACK: And Mrs. Delle Rose, your daughter, Rosa, was so pretty when she walked on the stage—that people went "Ooooooooooo!"—like that! Y'know what I mean? They all went—"Ooooooooooo!" Like a—like a—*wind* had—blown over! Because your daughter, Rosa, was so—*lovely* looking! [*He has crouched over to Serafina to deliver this description close to her face. Now he straightens up and smiles proudly at Rosa.*] How does it feel to be the mother of the prettiest girl in the world?

ROSA [*suddenly bursting into pure delight*]: Ha, ha, ha, ha, ha, ha! [*She throws her head back in rapture.*]

SERAFINA [*rousing*]: Hush!

ROSA: Ha, ha, ha, ha, ha, ha, ha, ha, ha, ha! [*She cannot control her ecstatic laughter. She presses her hand to her mouth but the laughter still bubbles out.*]

SERAFINA [*suddenly rising in anger*]: Pazza, pazza, pazza! Finiscila! Basta, via! [*Rosa whirls around to hide her convulsions of joy. To Jack:*] Put the prize books in the parlor, and shut the front door; there was a policeman come here because of—some trouble . . . [*Jack takes the books.*]

ROSA: Mama, I've never seen you like this! What will Jack think, Mama?

SERAFINA: Why do I care what Jack thinks?—You wild, wild crazy thing, you—with the eyes of your—father . . .

JACK [*returning*]: Yes, ma'am, Mrs. Delle Rose, you certainly got a right to be very proud of your daughter.

SERAFINA [*after a pause*]: I am proud of the—memory of her—father.—He was a baron . . . [*Rosa takes Jack's arm.*] And who are *you?* What are you?—per piacere!

ROSA: Mama, I just introduced him; his name is Jack Hunter.

SERAFINA: Hunt-er?

JACK: Yes, ma'am, Hunter. Jack Hunter.

SERAFINA: What are you hunting?—Jack?

ROSA: Mama!

SERAFINA: What all of 'em are hunting? To have a good time, and the Devil care who pays for it? I'm sick of men, I'm almost as sick of men as I am of wimmen.—Rosa, get out while I talk to this boy!

ROSA: I didn't bring Jack here to be insulted!

JACK: Go on, honey, and let your Mama talk to me. I think your Mama has just got a slight wrong—impression . . .

SERAFINA [*ominously*]: Yes, I got an impression!

ROSA: I'll get dressed! Oh, Mama, don't spoil it for me!— the happiest day of my life! [*She goes into the back of the house.*]

JACK [*after an awkward pause*]: Mrs. Delle Rose . . .

SERAFINA [*correcting his pronunciation*]: Delle Rose!

JACK: Mrs. Delle Rose, I'm sorry about all this. Believe me, Mrs. Delle Rose, the last thing I had in mind was getting mixed up in a family situation. I come home after three months to sea, I docked at New Orleans, and come here to see my folks. My sister was going to a high school dance. She took me with her, and there I met your daughter.

SERAFINA: What did you do?

JACK: At the high school dance? We danced! My sister had told me that Rose had a very strict mother and wasn't allowed to go on dates with boys so when it was over, I said, "I'm sorry you're not allowed to go out." And she said, "Oh! What gave you the idea I *wasn't!*" So then I thought my sister had made a mistake and I made a date with her for the next night.

SERAFINA: What did you do the next night?

JACK: The next night we went to the movies.

SERAFINA: And what did you do—that night?

JACK: At the movies? We ate a bag of popcorn and watched the movie!

SERAFINA: She come home at midnight and said she had been with a girl friend studying "civics."

JACK: Whatever story she told you, it ain't my fault!

SERAFINA: And the night after that?

JACK: Last Tuesday? We went roller skating!

SERAFINA: And afterward?

JACK: After the skating? We went to a drugstore and had an ice cream soda!

SERAFINA: Alone?

JACK: At the drugstore? No. It was crowded. And the skating rink was full of people skating!

SERAFINA: You mean that you haven't been alone with my Rosa?

JACK: Alone or not alone, what's the point of that question? I still don't see the point of it.

SERAFINA: We are Sicilians. We don't leave the girls with the boys they're not engaged to!

JACK: Mrs. Delle Rose, this is the United States.

SERAFINA: But we are Sicilians, and we are not cold-blooded.—My girl is a *virgin!* She *is*—or she *was*—I would like to know—*which!*

JACK: Mrs. Delle Rose! I got to tell you something. You might not believe it. It is a hard thing to say. But I am—*also* a—*virgin* . . .

SERAFINA: *What? No.* I do not believe it.

JACK: Well, it's true, though. This is the first time—I . . .

SERAFINA: First time you *what?*

JACK: The first time I really wanted to . . .

SERAFINA: Wanted to what?

JACK: Make—love . . .

SERAFINA: You? A sailor?

JACK [*sighing deeply*]: Yes, ma'am. I had opportunities to!—But I—always thought of my mother . . . I always asked myself, would she or would she not—think—this or that person was—decent!

SERAFINA: But with my daughter, my Rosa, your mother tells you *okay?*—go ahead, son!

JACK: Mrs. Delle Rose! [*with embarrassment*]—Mrs. Delle Rose, I . . .

SERAFINA: Two weeks ago I was slapping her hands for scratching mosquito bites. She rode a bicycle to school. Now all at once—I've got a wild thing in the house. She says she's in love. And you? Do you say *you're* in love?

JACK [*solemnly*]: Yes, ma'am, I do, I'm in love!—very much . . .

SERAFINA: Bambini, tutti due, bambini!

[*Rosa comes out, dressed for the picnic.*]

ROSA: I'm ready for Diamond Key!

SERAFINA: Go out on the porch. Diamond Key!

ROSA [*with a sarcastic curtsy*]: Yes, Mama!

SERAFINA: What are you? Catholic?

JACK: Me? Yes, ma'am, Catholic.

SERAFINA: You don't look Catholic to me!

ROSA [*shouting, from the door*]: Oh, God, Mama, how do Catholics look? How do they look different from anyone else?

SERAFINA: Stay out till I call you! [*Rosa crosses to the bird-bath and prays. Serafina turns to Jack.*] Turn around, will you?

JACK: Do what, ma'am?

SERAFINA: I said, *turn around!* [*Jack awkwardly turns around.*] Why do they make them Navy pants so tight?

ROSA [*listening in the yard*]: Oh, my God . . .

JACK [*flushing*]: That's a question you'll have to ask the Navy, Mrs. Delle Rose.

SERAFINA: And that gold earring, what's the gold earring for?

ROSA [*yelling from the door*]: For crossing the equator, Mama; he crossed it three times. He was initiated into the court of Neptune and gets to wear a gold earring! He's a shellback!

[*Serafina springs up and crosses to slam the porch door. Rosa runs despairingly around the side of the house and leans, exhausted with closed eyes, against the trunk of a palm tree. The Strega creeps into the yard, listening.*]

SERAFINA: You see what I got. A wild thing in the house!

JACK: Mrs. Delle Rose, I guess that Sicilians are very emotional people . . .

SERAFINA: I want nobody to take advantage of that!

JACK: You got the wrong idea about me, Mrs. Delle Rose.

SERAFINA: I know what men want—not to eat popcorn with girls or to slide on ice! And boys are the same, only younger.—Come here. Come here!

[*Rosa hears her mother's passionate voice. She rushes from the palm tree to the backdoor and pounds on it with her fists.*]

ROSA: Mama! Mama! Let me in the door, Jack!

JACK: Mrs. Delle Rose, your daughter is calling you.

SERAFINA: Let her call!—Come here. [*She crosses to the shrine of Our Lady.*] *Come here!*

[*Despairing of the backdoor, Rosa rushes around to the front. A few moments later she pushes open the shutters of the window in the wall and climbs half in. Jack crosses apprehensively to Serafina before the Madonna.*]

SERAFINA: You said you're Catholic, ain't you?

JACK: Yes, ma'am.

SERAFINA: Then kneel down in front of Our Lady!

JACK: Do—do what, did you say?

SERAFINA: I said to get down on your knees in front of Our Lady!

[*Rosa groans despairingly in the window. Jack kneels awkwardly upon the hassock.*]

ROSA: Mama, Mama, *now* what?!

[*Serafina rushes to the window, pushes Rosa out and slams the shutters.*]

SERAFINA [*returning to Jack*]: Now say after me what I say!

JACK: Yes, ma'am.

[*Rosa pushes the shutters open again.*]

SERAFINA: I promise the Holy Mother that I will respect the innocence of the daughter of . . .

ROSA [*in anguish*]: Ma-*maaa!*

SERAFINA: Get back out of that window!—Well? Are you gonna say it?

JACK: Yes, ma'am. What was it, again?

SERAFINA: I promise the Holy Mother . . .

JACK: I promise the Holy Mother . . .

SERAFINA: As I hope to be saved by the Blessed Blood of Jesus . . .

JACK: As I hope to be saved by the . . .

SERAFINA: Blessed Blood of . . .

JACK: Jesus . . .

SERAFINA: That I will respect the innocence of the daughter, Rosa, of Rosario delle Rose.

JACK: That I will respect the innocence—of—Rosa . . .

SERAFINA: Cross yourself! [*He crosses himself.*] Now get up, get up, get up! I am satisfied now . . .

[*Rosa jumps through the window and rushes to Serafina with arms outflung and wild cries of joy.*]

SERAFINA: Let me go, let me breathe! [*Outside the Strega cackles derisively.*]

ROSA: Oh, wonderful Mama, don't breathe! Oh, Jack! *Kiss* Mama! *Kiss Mama!* Mama, please kiss Jack!

SERAFINA: Kiss? Me? No, no, no, no!—Kiss my *hand* . . .

[*She offers her hand, shyly, and Jack kisses it with a loud smack. Rosa seizes the wine bottle.*]

ROSA: Mama, get some wine glasses!

[*Serafina goes for the glasses, and Rosa suddenly turns to*

*Jack. Out of her mother's sight, she passionately grabs
hold of his hand and presses it, first to her throat, then to
her lips and finally to her breast. Jack snatches her hand
away as Serafina returns with the glasses. Voices are heard
calling from the highway.*]

VOICES OUTSIDE: Ro-osa!—Ro-osa!—Ro-osa!

[*A car horn is heard blowing.*]

SERAFINA: Oh, I forgot the graduation present.

[*She crouches down before the bureau and removes a
fancily wrapped package from its bottom drawer. The car
horn is honking, and the voices are calling.*]

ROSA: They're calling for us! *Coming!* Jack! [*She flies out
the door, calling back to her mother.*] G'bye, Mama!

JACK [*following Rosa*]: Good-bye, Mrs. Delle Rose!

SERAFINA [*vaguely*]: It's a Bulova wrist watch with seventeen jewels in it . . . [*She realizes that she is alone.*] Rosa!
[*She goes to the door, still holding out the present. Outside
the car motor roars, and the voices shout as the car goes off.
Serafina stumbles outside, shielding her eyes with one hand,
extending the gift with the other.*] Rosa, Rosa, your present!
Regalo, regalo—tesoro!

[*But the car has started off, with a medley of voices shouting farewells, which fade quickly out of hearing. Serafina
turns about vaguely in the confusing sunlight and gropes
for the door. There is a derisive cackle from the witch
next door. Serafina absently opens the package and removes the little gold watch. She winds it and then holds it
against her ear. She shakes it and holds it again to her
ear. Then she holds it away from her and glares at it
fiercely.*]

SERAFINA [*pounding her chest three times*]: Tick—tick—
tick! [*She goes to the Madonna and faces it.*] Speak to me,
Lady! Oh, Lady, give me a sign!

[*The scene dims out.*]

Act Two

It is two hours later the same day.

Serafina comes out onto the porch, barefooted, wearing a rayon slip. Great shadows have appeared beneath her eyes; her face and throat gleam with sweat. There are dark stains of wine on the rayon slip. It is difficult for her to stand, yet she cannot sit still. She makes a sick moaning sound in her throat almost continually.

A hot wind rattles the canebrake. Vivi, the little girl, comes up to the porch to stare at Serafina as at a strange beast in a cage. Vivi is chewing a licorice stick which stains her mouth and her fingers. She stands chewing and staring. Serafina evades her stare. She wearily drags a broken gray wicker chair down off the porch, all the way out in front of the house, and sags heavily into it. It sits awry on a broken leg.

Vivi sneaks toward her. Serafina lurches about to face her angrily. The child giggles and scampers back to the porch.

SERAFINA [*sinking back into the chair*]: Oh, Lady, Lady, Lady, give me a—sign . . . [*She looks up at the white glare of the sky.*]

[*Father De Leo approaches the house. Serafina crouches low in the chair to escape his attention. He knocks at the door. Receiving no answer, he looks out into the yard, sees her, and approaches her chair. He comes close to address her with a gentle severity.*]

FATHER DE LEO: Buon giorno, Serafina.

SERAFINA [*faintly, with a sort of disgust*]: Giorno . . .

FATHER DE LEO: I'm surprised to see you sitting outdoors like this. What is that thing you're wearing?—I think it's an

193

undergarment!—It's hanging off one shoulder, and your head, Serafina, looks as if you had stuck it in a bucket of oil. Oh, I see now why the other ladies of the neighborhood aren't taking their afternoon naps! They find it more entertaining to sit on the porches and watch the spectacle you are putting on for them!—Are you listening to me?—I must tell you that the change in your appearance and behavior since Rosario's death is shocking—shocking! A woman can be dignified in her grief but when it's carried too far it becomes a sort of self-indulgence. Oh, I knew this was going to happen when you broke the Church law and had your husband cremated! [*Serafina lurches up from the chair and shuffles back to the porch. Father De Leo follows her.*]—Set up a little idolatrous shrine in your house and give worship to a bottle of ashes. [*She sinks down upon the steps.*]—Are you listening to me?

[*Two women have appeared on the embankment and descend toward the house. Serafina lurches heavily up to meet them, like a weary bull turning to face another attack.*]

SERAFINA: You ladies, what you want? I don't do sewing! Look, I quit doing sewing. [*She pulls down the "SEWING" sign and hurls it away.*] Now you got places to go, you ladies, go places! Don't hang around front of my house!

FATHER DE LEO: The ladies want to be friendly.

SERAFINA: Naw, they don't come to be friendly. They think they know something that Serafina don't know; they think I got *these* on my head! [*She holds her fingers like horns at either side of her forehead.*] Well, I ain't got them! [*She goes padding back out in front of the house. Father De Leo follows.*]

FATHER DE LEO: You called me this morning in distress over something.

SERAFINA: I called you this morning but now it is afternoon.

FATHER DE LEO: I had to christen the grandson of the Mayor.

SERAFINA: The Mayor's important people, not Serafina!

FATHER DE LEO: You don't come to confession.

SERAFINA [*starting back toward the porch*]: No, I don't come, I don't go, I—Ohhh! [*She pulls up one foot and hops on the other.*]

FATHER DE LEO: You stepped on something?

SERAFINA [*dropping down on the steps*]: No, no, no, no, no, I don't step on—noth'n . . .

FATHER DE LEO: Come in the house. We'll wash it with antiseptic. [*She lurches up and limps back toward the house.*] Walking barefooted you will get it infected.

SERAFINA: Fa niente . . .

[*At the top of the embankment a little boy runs out with a red kite and flourishes it in the air with rigid gestures, as though he were giving a distant signal. Serafina shades her eyes with a palm to watch the kite, and then, as though its motions conveyed a shocking message, she utters a startled soft cry and staggers back to the porch. She leans against a pillar, running her hand rapidly and repeatedly through her hair. Father De Leo approaches her again, somewhat timidly.*]

FATHER DE LEO: Serafina?

SERAFINA: Che, che, che cosa vuole?

FATHER DE LEO: I am thirsty. Will you go in the house and get me some water?

SERAFINA: Go in. Get you some water. The faucet is working.—I can't go in the house.

FATHER DE LEO: Why can't you go in the house?

SERAFINA: The house has a tin roof on it. I got to breathe.

FATHER DE LEO: You can breathe in the house.

SERAFINA: No, I can't breathe in the house. The house has a tin roof on it and I . . .

[*The Strega has been creeping through the canebrake pretending to search for a chicken.*]

THE STREGA: Chick, chick, chick, chick chick? [*She crouches to peer under the house.*]

SERAFINA: What's that? Is that the . . . ? Yes, the Strega! [*She picks up a flower pot containing a dead plant and crosses the yard.*] Strega! Strega! [*The Strega looks up, retreating a little.*] Yes, you, I mean you! You ain't look for no chick! Getta hell out of my yard! [*The Strega retreats, viciously muttering, back into the canebrake. Serafina makes the protective sign of the horns with her fingers. The goat bleats.*]

FATHER DE LEO: You have no friends, Serafina.

SERAFINA: I don't want friends.

FATHER DE LEO: You are still a young woman. Eligible for—loving and—bearing again! I remember you dressed in pale blue silk at Mass one Easter morning, yes, like a lady wearing a—piece of the—weather! Oh, how proudly you walked, *too* proudly!—But now you crouch and shuffle about barefooted; you live like a convict, dressed in the rags of a convict. You have no companions; women you don't mix with. You . . .

SERAFINA: No, I don't mix with them women. [*glaring at the women on the embankment*] The dummies I got in my house, I mix with them better because they don't make up no lies!—What kind of women are them? [*mimicking fiercely*] "Eee, Papa, eeee, baby, eee, me, me, me!" At thirty years old they got no more use for the letto matrimoniale, no. The big bed goes to the basement! They get little beds from Sears Roebuck and sleep on their bellies!

FATHER DE LEO: Attenzione!

SERAFINA: They make the life without glory. Instead of the heart they got the deep-freeze in the house. The men, they don't feel no glory, not in the house with them women; they go to the bars, fight in them, get drunk, get fat, put horns on the women because the women don't give them the love which is glory.—I did, I give him the glory. To me the big bed was beautiful like a religion. Now I lie on it with dreams, with memories only! But it is still beautiful to me and I don't believe that the man in my heart gave me horns! [*The women whisper.*] What, what are they saying? Does ev'rybody know something that I don't know?—No, all I want is a sign, a sign from Our Lady, to tell me the lie is a lie! And then I . . . [*The women laugh on the embankment. Serafina starts fiercely toward them. They scatter.*] Squeak, squeak, squawk, squawk! Hens—like water thrown on them! [*There is the sound of mocking laughter.*]

FATHER DE LEO: People are laughing at you on all the porches.

SERAFINA: I'm laughing, too. Listen to me, I'm laughing! [*She breaks into loud, false laughter, first from the porch, then from the foot of the embankment, then crossing in front of the house.*] Ha, ha, ha, ha, ha, ha, ha! Now ev'rybody is laughing. Ha, ha, ha, ha, ha, ha!

FATHER DE LEO: Zitta ora!—Think of your daughter.

SERAFINA [*understanding the word "daughter"*]: You, *you* think of my daughter! Today you give out the diplomas, today you at the high school you give out the prizes, diplomas! You give to my daughter a set of books call the *Digest of Knowledge!* What does she know? How to be cheap already?—Oh, yes, that is what to learn, how to be cheap and to cheat!—You know what they do at this high school? They ruin the girls there! They give the spring dance because the girls are man-crazy. And there at that dance my daughter goes with a sailor that has in his ear a gold ring! And pants so tight that a woman ought not to look at him! This morning, this morning she cuts with a knife her wrist if I don't let her go!—Now all of them gone to some island, they call it a picnic, all of them, gone in a—boat!

FATHER DE LEO: There *was* a school picnic, chaperoned by the teachers.

SERAFINA: Oh, lo so, lo so! The man-crazy old-maid teachers!—They all run wild on the island!

FATHER DE LEO: Serafina delle Rose! [*He picks up the chair by the back and hauls it to the porch when she starts to resume her seat.*]—I *command* you to go in the house.

SERAFINA: Go in the house? I will. I will go in the house if you will answer one question.—Will you answer one question?

FATHER DE LEO: I will if I know the answer.

SERAFINA: Aw, you know the answer!—You used to hear the confessions of my husband. [*She turns to face the priest.*]

FATHER DE LEO: Yes, I heard his confessions . . .

SERAFINA [*with difficulty*]: Did he ever speak to you of a woman?

[*A child cries out and races across in front of the house. Father De Leo picks up his panama hat. Serafina paces slowly toward him. He starts away from the house.*]

SERAFINA [*rushing after him*]: Aspettate! Aspettate un momento!

FATHER DE LEO [*fearfully, not looking at her*]: Che volete?

SERAFINA: Rispondetemi! [*She strikes her breast.*] Did he speak of a woman to you?

FATHER DE LEO: You know better than to ask me such a question. I don't break the Church laws. The secrets of the confessional are sacred to me. [*He walks away.*]

SERAFINA [*pursuing and clutching his arm*]: I got to know. You could tell me.

FATHER DE LEO: Let go of me, Serafina!

SERAFINA: Not till you tell me, Father. Father, you tell me, please tell me! Or I will go mad! [*in a fierce whisper*] I will go back in the house and smash the urn with the ashes—if you don't tell me! I will go mad with the doubt in my heart and I will smash the urn and scatter the ashes—of my husband's body!

FATHER DE LEO: What could I tell you? If you would not believe the known facts about him . . .

SERAFINA: Known facts, who knows the known facts?

[*The neighbor women have heard the argument and begin to crowd around, muttering in shocked whispers at Serafina's lack of respect.*]

FATHER DE LEO [*frightened*]: Lasciatemi, lasciatemi stare!—Oh, Serafina, I am too old for this—please!—Everybody is . . .

SERAFINA [*in a fierce, hissing whisper*]: Nobody knew my rose of the world but me and now they can lie because the rose ain't living. They want the marble urn broken; they want me to smash it. They want the rose ashes scattered because I had too much glory. They don't want glory like *that* in nobody's heart. They want—mouse-squeaking!—known facts.—Who knows the known facts? You—padres—wear black because of the fact that the facts are known by nobody!

FATHER DE LEO: Oh, Serafina! There are people watching!

SERAFINA: Let them watch something. That will be a change for them.—It's been a long time I wanted to break out like this and now I . . .

FATHER DE LEO: I am too old a man; I am not strong enough. I am sixty-seven years old! Must I call for help, now?

SERAFINA: Yes, call! Call for help, but I won't let you go till you tell me!

FATHER DE LEO: You're not a respectable woman.

SERAFINA: No, I'm not a respectable; I'm a woman.

FATHER DE LEO: No, you are not a woman. You are an animal!

SERAFINA: Si, si, animale! Sono animale! Animale. Tell them all, shout it all to them, up and down the whole block! The Widow Delle Rose is not respectable, she is not even a woman, she is an animal! She is attacking the priest! She will

tear the black suit off him unless he tells her the whores in
this town are lying to her!

[*The neighbor women have been drawing closer as the
argument progresses, and now they come to Father De
Leo's rescue and assist him to get away from Serafina,
who is on the point of attacking him bodily. He cries out,
"Officer! Officer!" but the women drag Serafina from him
and lead him away with comforting murmurs.*]

SERAFINA [*striking her wrists together*]: Yes, it's me, it's
me! ! Lock me up, lock me, lock me up! Or I will—*smash!*—
the marble . . . [*She throws her head far back and presses her
fists to her eyes. Then she rushes crazily to the steps and falls
across them.*]

ASSUNTA: Serafina! Figlia! Figlia! Andiamo a casa!

SERAFINA: Leave me alone, old woman.

[*She returns slowly to the porch steps and sinks down
on them, sitting like a tired man, her knees spread apart
and her head cupped in her hands. The children steal back
around the house. A little boy shoots a beanshooter at
her. She starts up with a cry. The children scatter, shriek-
ing. She sinks back down on the steps, then leans back,
staring up at the sky, her body rocking.*]

SERAFINA: Oh, Lady, Lady, Lady, give me a sign!

[*As if in mocking answer, a novelty salesman appears
and approaches the porch. He is a fat man in a seersucker
suit and a straw hat with a yellow, red and purple band.
His face is beet-red and great moons of sweat have soaked
through the armpits of his jacket. His shirt is lavender,
and his tie, pale blue with great yellow polka dots, is a
butterfly bow. His entrance is accompanied by a brief,
satiric strain of music.*]

THE SALESMAN: Good afternoon, lady. [*She looks up
slowly. The salesman talks sweetly, as if reciting a prayer.*] I
got a little novelty here which I am offering to just a few
lucky people at what we call an introductory price. Know
what I mean? Not a regular price but a price which is less
than what it costs to manufacture the article, a price we are

making for the sake of introducing the product in the Gulf
Coast territory. Lady, this thing here that I'm droppin' right
in youah lap is bigger than television; it's going to revolu-
tionize the domestic life of America.—Now I don't do house
to house canvassing. I sell directly to merchants but when I
stopped over there to have my car serviced, I seen you taking
the air on the steps and I thought I would just drop over
and . . .

[*There is the sound of a big truck stopping on the highway, and a man's voice, Alvaro's, is heard, shouting.*]

ALVARO: Hey! Hey, you road hog!

THE SALESMAN [*taking a sample out of his bag*]: Now,
lady, this little article has a deceptive appearance. First of
all, I want you to notice how *compact* it is. It takes up no
more space than . . .

[*Alvaro comes down from the embankment. He is about
twenty-five years old, dark and very good-looking. He is
one of those Mediterranean types that resemble glossy
young bulls. He is short in stature, has a massively sculp-
tured torso and bluish-black curls. His face and manner
are clownish; he has a charming awkwardness. There is
a startling, improvised air about him; he frequently seems
surprised at his own speeches and actions, as though he
had not at all anticipated them. At the moment when we
first hear his voice the sound of timpani begins, at first
very pianissimo, but building up as he approaches, till it
reaches a vibrant climax with his appearance to Serafina
beside the house.*]

ALVARO: Hey.

THE SALESMAN [*without glancing at him*]: Hay is for
horses!—Now, madam, you see what happens when I press
this button?

[*The article explodes in Serafina's face. She slaps it away
with an angry cry. At the same time Alvaro advances,
trembling with rage, to the porch steps. He is sweating
and stammering with pent-up fury at a world of frustra-
tions which are temporarily localized in the gross figure
of this salesman.*]

ALVARO: Hey, you! Come here! What the hell's the idea, back there at that curve? You make me drive off the highway!

THE SALESMAN [to Serafina]: Excuse me for just one minute. [He wheels menacingly about to face Alvaro.] Is something giving you gas pains, Maccaroni?

ALVARO: My name is not Maccaroni.

THE SALESMAN: All right. Spaghetti.

ALVARO [almost sobbing with passion]: I am not maccaroni. I am not spaghetti. I am a human being that drives a truck of bananas. I drive a truck of bananas for the Southern Fruit Company for a living, not to play cowboys and Indians on no highway with no rotten road hog. You got a 4-lane highway between Pass Christian and here. I give you the sign to pass me. You tail me and give me the horn. You yell "Wop" at me and "Dago." "Move over, Wop, move over, Dago." Then at the goddam curve, you go pass me and make me drive off the highway and yell back "Son of a bitch of a Dago!" I don't like that, no, no! And I am glad you stop here. Take the cigar from your mouth, take out the cigar!

THE SALESMAN: Take it out for me, greaseball.

ALVARO: If I take it out I will push it down your throat. I got three dependents! If I fight, I get fired, but I will fight and get fired. Take out the cigar!

[Spectators begin to gather at the edge of the scene. Serafina stares at the truck driver, her eyes like a somnambule's. All at once she utters a low cry and seems about to fall.]

ALVARO: Take out the cigar, take out, take out the cigar!

[He snatches the cigar from the salesman's mouth and the salesman brings his knee up violently into Alvaro's groin. Bending double and retching with pain, Alvaro staggers over to the porch.]

THE SALESMAN [shouting, as he goes off]: I got your license number, Maccaroni! I know your boss!

ALVARO [*howling*]: Drop dead! [*He suddenly staggers up
the steps.*] Lady, lady, I got to go in the house!

[*As soon as he enters, he bursts into rending sobs, leaning against a wall and shaking convulsively. The spectators outside laugh as they scatter. Serafina slowly enters
the house. The screen door rasps loudly on its rusty springs
as she lets it swing gradually shut behind her, her eyes
remaining fixed with a look of stupefied wonder upon the
sobbing figure of the truck driver. We must understand
her profound unconscious response to this sudden contact with distress as acute as her own. There is a long
pause as the screen door makes its whining, catlike noise
swinging shut by degrees.*]

SERAFINA: Somebody's—in my house? [*finally, in a hoarse,
tremulous whisper*] What are you—doing in here? Why have
you—come in my house?

ALVARO: Oh, lady—leave me alone!—Please—now!

SERAFINA: You—got no business—in here . . .

ALVARO: I got to cry after a fight. I'm sorry, lady. I . . .
[*The sobs still shake him. He leans on a dummy.*]

SERAFINA: Don't lean on my dummy. Sit down if you can't
stand up.—What is the matter with you?

ALVARO: I always cry after a fight. But I don't want people
to see me. It's not like a man. [*There is a long pause; Serafina's attitude seems to warm toward the man.*]

SERAFINA: A man is not no different from no one else . . .
[*All at once her face puckers up, and for the first time in the
play Serafina begins to weep, at first soundlessly, then audibly.
Soon she is sobbing as loudly as Alvaro. She speaks between
sobs.*]—I always cry—when somebody else is crying . . .

ALVARO: No, no, lady, *don't* cry! Why should *you* cry? I
will stop. I will stop in a minute. This is not like a man. I am
ashamed of myself. I will stop now; please, lady . . .

[*Still crouching a little with pain, a hand clasped to his abdomen, Alvaro turns away from the wall. He blows his nose between two fingers. Serafina picks up a scrap of white voile and gives it to him to wipe his fingers.]*

SERAFINA: Your jacket is torn.

ALVARO [*sobbing*]: My company jacket is torn?

SERAFINA: Yes . . .

ALVARO: Where is it torn?

SERAFINA [*sobbing*]: Down the—back.

ALVARO: Oh, Dio!

SERAFINA: Take it off. I will sew it up for you. I do— sewing.

ALVARO: Oh, Dio! [*sobbing*] I got three dependents! [*He holds up three fingers and shakes them violently at Serafina.*]

SERAFINA: Give me—give me your jacket.

ALVARO: He took down my license number!

SERAFINA: People are always taking down license numbers and telephone numbers and numbers that don't mean nothing—all them numbers . . .

ALVARO: Three, three dependents! Not citizens, even! No relief checks, no nothing! [*Serafina sobs.*] He is going to complain to the boss.

SERAFINA: I wanted to cry all day.

ALVARO: He said he would fire me if I don't stop fighting!

SERAFINA: Stop crying so I can stop crying.

ALVARO: I am a sissy. Excuse me. I am ashame.

SERAFINA: Don't be ashame of nothing, the world is too crazy for people to be ashame in it. I'm not ashame and I had two fights on the street and my daughter called me "disgusting." I got to sew this by hand; the machine is broke in a fight with two women.

ALVARO: That's what—they call a cat fight . . . [*He blows his nose.*]

SERAFINA: Open the shutters, please, for me. I can't see to work. [*She has crossed to her work table. He goes over to the window. As he opens the shutters, the light falls across his fine torso, the undershirt clinging wetly to his dark olive skin. Serafina is struck and murmurs: "Ohhh . . ." There is the sound of music.*]

ALVARO: What, lady?

SERAFINA [*in a strange voice*]: The light on the body was like a man that lived here . . .

ALVARO: Che dice?

SERAFINA: Niente.—Ma com'è strano!—Lei è Napoletano? [*She is threading a needle.*]

ALVARO: Io sono Siciliano! [*Serafina sticks her finger with her needle and cries out.*] Che fa?

SERAFINA: I—stuck myself with the—needle!—You had—better wash up . . .

ALVARO: Dov'è il gabinetto?

SERAFINA [*almost inaudibly*]: Dietro. [*She points vaguely back.*]

ALVARO: Con permesso! [*He moves past her. As he does so, she picks up a pair of broken spectacles on the work table. Holding them up by the single remaining side piece, like a lorgnette, she inspects his passing figure with an air of stupefaction. As he goes out, he says:*] A kick like that can have serious consequences! [*He goes into the back of the house.*]

SERAFINA [*after a pause*]: Madonna Santa!—*My husband's body*, with the head of a *clown!* [*She crosses to the Madonna.*] O Lady, O Lady! [*She makes an imploring gesture.*] Speak to me!—What are you saying?—Please, Lady, I can't hear you!

Is it a sign? Is is a sign of something? What does it mean?
Oh, *speak to me*, Lady!—Everything is too strange!

[*She gives up the useless entreaty to the impassive statue.
Then she rushes to the cupboard, clambers up on a chair
and seizes a bottle of wine from the top shelf. But she
finds it impossible to descend from the chair. Clasping
the dusty bottle to her breast, she crouches there, helplessly whimpering like a child, as Alvaro comes back in.*]

ALVARO: Ciao!

SERAFINA: I can't get up.

ALVARO: You mean you can't get down?

SERAFINA: I mean I—can't get down . . .

ALVARO: Con permesso, Signora! [*He lifts her down from
the chair.*]

SERAFINA: Grazie.

ALVARO: I am ashame of what happen. Crying is not like a
man. Did anyone see me?

SERAFINA: Nobody saw you but me. To me it don't matter.

ALVARO: You are simpatica, molto!—It was not just the
fight that makes me break down. I was like this all today!
[*He shakes his clenched fists in the air.*]

SERAFINA: You and—me, too!—What was the trouble today?

ALVARO: My name is Mangiacavallo which means "Eat-a-
horse." It's a comical name, I know. Maybe two thousand
and seventy years ago one of my grandfathers got so hungry
that he ate up a horse! That ain't my fault. Well, today at the
Southern Fruit Company I find on the pay envelope not
"Mangiacavallo" but "EAT A HORSE" in big print! Ha, ha,
ha, very funny!—I open the pay envelope! In it I find a
notice.—The wages have been *garnishee!* You know what
garnishee is? [*Serafina nods gravely.*] Garnishee!—Eat a
horse!—Road hog!—All in one day is too much! I go crazy,

I boil, I cry, and I am ashame but I am not able to help it!—Even a Wop truck driver's a human being! And human beings must cry . . .

SERAFINA: Yes, they must cry. I couldn't cry all day but now I have cried and I am feeling much better.—I will sew up the jacket . . .

ALVARO [*licking his lips*]: What is that in your hand? A bottle of vino?

SERAFINA: This is spumanti. It comes from the house of the family of my husband. The Delle Rose! A very great family. I was a peasant, but I married a baron!—No, I still don't believe it! I married a baron when I didn't have shoes!

ALVARO: Excuse me for asking—but where is the Baron, now? [*Serafina points gravely to the marble urn*.]. Where did you say?

SERAFINA: Them're his ashes in that marble urn.

ALVARO: Ma! Scusatemi! Scusatemi! [*crossing himself*]—I hope he is resting in peace.

SERAFINA: It's him you reminded me of—when you opened the shutters. Not the face but the body.—Please get me some ice from the icebox in the kitchen. I had a—very bad day . . .

ALVARO: Oh, ice! Yes—ice—I'll get some . . . [*As he goes out, she looks again through the broken spectacles at him.*]

SERAFINA: *Non posso crederlo!*—A clown of a face like that with my husband's body!

[*There is the sound of ice being chopped in the kitchen. She inserts a corkscrew in the bottle but her efforts to open it are clumsily unsuccessful. Alvaro returns with a little bowl of ice. He sets it down so hard on the table that a piece flies out. He scrambles after it, retrieves it and wipes it off on his sweaty undershirt.*]

SERAFINA: I think the floor would be cleaner!

ALVARO: Scusatemi!—I wash it again?

SERAFINA: Fa niente!

ALVARO: I am a—clean!—I . . .

SERAFINA: Fa niente, niente!—The bottle should be in the ice but the next best thing is to pour the wine over the bottle.

ALVARO: You mean over the ice?

SERAFINA: I mean over the . . .

ALVARO: Let me open the bottle. Your hands are not used to rough work. [*She surrenders the bottle to him and regards him through the broken spectacles again.*]

SERAFINA: These little bits of white voile on the floor are not from a snowstorm. I been making voile dresses for high school graduation.—One for my daughter and for thirteen other girls.—All of the work I'm not sure didn't kill me!

ALVARO: The wine will make you feel better.

[*There is a youthful cry from outside.*]

SERAFINA: There is a wild bunch of boys and girls in this town. In Sicily the boys would dance with the boys because a girl and a boy could not dance together unless they was going to be married. But here they run wild on islands!—boys, girls, man-crazy teachers . . .

ALVARO: Ecco! [*The cork comes off with a loud pop. Serafina cries out and staggers against the table. He laughs. She laughs with him, helplessly, unable to stop, unable to catch her breath.*]—I like a woman that laughs with all her heart.

SERAFINA: And a woman that cries with her heart?

ALVARO: I like everything that a woman does with her heart.

[*Both are suddenly embarrassed and their laughter dies out. Serafina smooths down her rayon slip. He hands her a glass of the sparkling wine with ice in it. She murmurs "Grazie."*

[*Unconsciously the injured finger is lifted again to her*

lip and she wanders away from the table with the glass held shakily.]

ALVARO [*continuing nervously*]: I see you had a bad day.

SERAFINA: Sono così—stanca . . .

ALVARO [*suddenly springing to the window and shouting*]: Hey, you kids, git down off that truck! Keep your hands off them bananas! [*At the words "truck" and "bananas" Serafina gasps again and spills some wine on her slip.*] Little buggers! —Scusatemi . . .

SERAFINA: You haul—you haul bananas?

ALVARO: Si, Signora.

SERAFINA: Is it a 10-ton truck?

ALVARO: An 8-ton truck.

SERAFINA: My husband hauled bananas in a 10-ton truck.

ALVARO: Well, he was a baron.

SERAFINA: Do you haul just bananas?

ALVARO: Just bananas. What else would I haul?

SERAFINA: My husband hauled bananas, but underneath the bananas was something else. He was—wild like a— Gypsy.—"Wild—like a—Gypsy?" Who said that?—I hate to start to remember, and then not remember . . .

[*The dialogue between them is full of odd hesitations, broken sentences and tentative gestures. Both are nervously exhausted after their respective ordeals. Their fumbling communication has a curious intimacy and sweetness, like the meeting of two lonely children for the first time. It is oddly luxurious to them both, luxurious as the first cool wind of evening after a scorching day. Serafina idly picks up a little Sicilian souvenir cart from a table.*]

SERAFINA: The priest was against it.

ALVARO: What was the priest against?

SERAFINA: My keeping the ashes. It was against the Church law. But I had to have something and that was all I could have. [*She sets down the cart.*]

ALVARO: I don't see nothing wrong with it.

SERAFINA: You don't?

ALVARO: No! Niente!—The body would've decayed, but ashes always stay clean.

SERAFINA [*eagerly*]: Si, si, bodies decay, but ashes always stay clean! Come here. I show you this picture—my wedding. [*She removes a picture tenderly from the wall.*] Here's me a bride of fourteen, and this—this—this! [*drumming the picture with her finger and turning her face to Alvaro with great lustrous eyes*] My husband! [*There is a pause. He takes the picture from her hand and holds it first close to his eyes, then far back, then again close with suspirations of appropriate awe.*] Annnh?—Annnnh?—Che dice!

ALVARO [*slowly, with great emphasis*]: Che bell' uomo! Che bell' uomo!

SERAFINA [*replacing the picture*]: A rose of a man. On his chest he had the tattoo of a rose. [*then, quite suddenly*]—Do you believe strange things, or do you doubt them?

ALVARO: If strange things didn't happen, I wouldn't be here. You wouldn't be here. We wouldn't be talking together.

SERAFINA: Davvero! I'll tell you something about the tattoo of my husband. My husband, he had this rose tattoo on his chest. One night I woke up with a burning pain on me here. I turn on the light. I look at my naked breast and on it I see the rose tattoo of my husband, on me, on *my* breast, *his* tattoo.

ALVARO: Strano!

SERAFINA: And that was the night that—I got to speak frankly to tell you . . .

ALVARO: Speak frankly! We're grown-up people.

SERAFINA: That was the night I conceived my son—the little boy that was lost when I lost my husband . . .

ALVARO: Che cosa—strana!—Would you be willing to show me the rose tattoo?

SERAFINA: Oh, it's gone now, it only lasted a moment. But I did see it. I saw it clearly.—Do you believe me?

ALVARO: Lo credo!

SERAFINA: I don't know why I told you. But I like what you said. That bodies decay but ashes always stay clean—immacolate!—But, you know, there are some people that want to make everything dirty. Two of them kind of people come in the house today and told me a terrible lie in front of the ashes.—So awful a lie that if I thought it was true—I would smash the urn—and throw the ashes away! [*She hurls her glass suddenly to the floor.*] Smash it, *smash it like that!*

ALVARO: Ma!—Baronessa!

[*Serafina seizes a broom and sweeps the fragments of glass away.*]

SERAFINA: And take this broom and sweep them out the backdoor like so much trash!

ALVARO [*impressed by her violence and a little awed*]: What lie did they tell you?

SERAFINA: No, no, no! I don't want to talk about it! [*She throws down the broom.*] I just want to forget it; it wasn't true, it was false, false, false!—as the hearts of the bitches that told it . . .

ALVARO: Yes. I would forget anything that makes you unhappy.

SERAFINA: The memory of a love don't make you unhappy unless you believe a lie that makes it dirty. I don't believe in the lie. The ashes are clean. The memory of the rose in my heart is perfect!—Your glass is weeping . . .

ALVARO: *Your* glass is weeping too.

[*While she fills his glass, he moves about the room, looking here and there. She follows him. Each time he picks up an article for inspection she gently takes it from him and examines it herself with fresh interest.*]

ALVARO: Cozy little homelike place you got here.

SERAFINA: Oh, it's—molto modesto.—You got a nice place too?

ALVARO: I got a place with three dependents in it.

SERAFINA: What—dependents?

ALVARO [*counting them on his fingers*]: One old maid sister, one feeble-minded grandmother, one lush of a pop that's not worth the powder it takes to blow him to hell.—They got the parchesi habit. They play the game of parchesi, morning, night, noon. Passing a bucket of beer around the table . . .

SERAFINA: They got the beer habit, too?

ALVARO: Oh, yes. And the numbers habit. This spring the old maid sister gets female trouble—mostly mental, I think—she turns the housekeeping over to the feeble-minded grandmother, a very sweet old lady who don't think it is necessary to pay the grocery bill so long as there's money to play the numbers. She plays the numbers. She has a perfect system except it don't ever work. And the grocery bill goes up, up, up, up, up!—so high you can't even see it!—Today the Ideal Grocery Company garnishees my wages . . . There, now! I've told you my life . . . [*The parrot squawks. He goes over to the cage.*] Hello, Polly, how's tricks?

SERAFINA: The name ain't Polly. It ain't a she; it's a he.

ALVARO: How can you tell with all them tail feathers? [*He sticks his finger in the cage, pokes at the parrot and gets bitten.*] Owww!

SERAFINA [*vicariously*]: Ouuu . . . [*Alvaro sticks his injured finger in his mouth. Serafina puts her corresponding finger in her mouth. He crosses to the telephone.*] I told you watch out.—What are you calling, a doctor?

ALVARO: I am calling my boss in Biloxi to explain why I'm late.

SERAFINA: The call to Biloxi is a ten-cent call.

ALVARO: Don't worry about it.

SERAFINA: I'm not worried about it. You will pay it.

ALVARO: You got a sensible attitude toward life . . . Give me the Southern Fruit Company in Biloxi—seven-eight-seven!

SERAFINA: You are a bachelor. With three dependents? [*She glances below his belt.*]

ALVARO: I'll tell you my hopes and dreams!

SERAFINA: Who? Me?

ALVARO: I am hoping to meet some sensible older lady. Maybe a lady a little bit older than me.—I don't care if she's a little too plump or not such a stylish dresser! [*Serafina self-consciously pulls up a dangling strap.*] The important thing in a lady is understanding. Good sense. And I want her to have a well-furnished house and a profitable little business of some kind . . . [*He looks about him significantly.*]

SERAFINA: And such a lady, with a well-furnished house and business, what does she want with a man with three dependents with the parchesi and the beer habit, playing the numbers!

ALVARO: Love and affection!—in a world that is lonely—and cold!

SERAFINA: It might be lonely but I would not say "cold" on this particular day!

ALVARO: Love and affection is what I got to offer on hot or cold days in this lonely old world and is what I am look-

ing for. I got nothing else. Mangiacavallo has nothing. In
fact, he is the grandson of the village idiot of Ribera!

SERAFINA [*uneasily*]: I see you like to make—jokes!

ALVARO: No, no joke!—Davvero!—He chased my grandmother in a flooded rice field. She slip on a wet rock.—
Ecco! Here I am.

SERAFINA: You ought to be more respectful.

ALVARO: What have I got to respect? The rock my grandmother slips on?

SERAFINA: Yourself at least! Don't you work for a living?

ALVARO: If I *don't* work for a living I would respect myself
more. Baronessa, I am a healthy young man, existing without
no love life. I look at the magazine pictures. Them girls in
the advertisement—you know what I mean? A little bitty
thing here? A little bitty thing there?

[*He touches two portions of his anatomy. The latter por-
tion embarrasses Serafina, who quietly announces:*]

SERAFINA: The call is ten cents for three minutes. Is the
line busy?

ALVARO: Not the line, but the boss.

SERAFINA: And the charge for the call goes higher. That
ain't the phone of a millionaire you're using!

ALVARO: I think you talk a poor mouth. [*He picks up the
piggy bank and shakes it.*] This pig sounds well fed to me.

SERAFINA: Dimes and quarters.

ALVARO: Dimes and quarters're better than nickels and
dimes. [*Serafina rises severely and removes the piggy bank
from his grasp.*] Ha, ha, ha! You think I'm a bank robber?

SERAFINA: I think you are maleducato! Just get your boss
on the phone or hang the phone up.

ALVARO: What, what! Mr. Siccardi? How tricks at the Southern Fruit Comp'ny this hot afternoon? Ha, ha, ha!—Mangiacavallo!—What? You got the complaint already? Sentite, per favore! This road hog was—Mr. Siccardi? [*He jiggles the hook; then slowly hangs up.*] A man with three dependents!—out of a job . . . [*There is a pause.*]

SERAFINA: Well, you better ask the operator the charges.

ALVARO: Oofla! A man with three dependents—out of a job!

SERAFINA: I can't see to work no more. I got a suggestion to make. Open the bottom drawer of that there bureau and you will find a shirt in white tissue paper and you can wear that one while I am fixing this. And call for it later. [*He crosses to the bureau.*]—It was made for somebody that never called for it. [*He removes the package.*] Is there a name pinned to it?

ALVARO: Yes, it's . . .

SERAFINA [*fiercely, but with no physical movement*]: Don't tell me the name! Throw it away, out the window!

ALVARO: Perchè?

SERAFINA: Throw it, throw it away!

ALVARO [*crumpling the paper and throwing it through the window*]: Ecco fatto! [*There is a distant cry of children as he unwraps the package and holds up the rose silk shirt, exclaiming in Latin delight at the luxury of it.*] Colore di rose! Seta! Seta pura!—Oh, this shirt is too good for Mangiacavallo! Everything here is too good for Mangiacavallo!

SERAFINA: Nothing's too good for a man if the man is good.

ALVARO: The grandson of a village idiot is not that good.

SERAFINA: No matter whose grandson you are, put it on; you are welcome to wear it.

ALVARO [*slipping voluptuously into the shirt*]: Sssssssss!

SERAFINA: How does it feel, the silk, on you?

ALVARO: It feels like a girl's hands on me! [*There is a pause, while he shows her the whiteness of his teeth.*]

SERAFINA [*holding up her broken spectacles*]: It will make you less trouble.

ALVARO: There is nothing more beautiful than a gift between people!—Now you are smiling!—You like me a little bit better?

SERAFINA [*slowly and tenderly*]: You know what they should of done when you was a baby? They should of put tape on your ears to hold them back so when you grow up they wouldn't stick out like the wings of a little kewpie! [*She touches his ear, a very slight touch, betraying too much of her heart. Both laugh a little and she turns away, embarrassed.*]

[*Outside the goat bleats and there is the sound of splintering timber. One of the children races into the front yard, crying out.*]

SALVATORE: Mizz' Dell' Rose! The black goat's in your yard!

SERAFINA: Il becco della strega!

[*Serafina dashes to the window, throws the shutters violently open and leans way out. This time, she almost feels relief in this distraction. The interlude of the goat chase has a quality of crazed exaltation. Outside is heard the wild bleating of the goat and the jingling of his harness.*]

SERAFINA: Miei pomodori! Guarda i miei pomodori!

THE STREGA [*entering the front yard with a broken length of rope, calling out*]: Heyeh, Billy! Heyeh. Heyeh, Billy!

SERAFINA [*making the sign of horns with her fingers*]: There is the Strega! She lets the goat in my yard to eat my tomatoes! [*backing from the window*] She has the eye; she has the malocchio, and so does the goat! The goat has the evil eye, too. He got in my yard the night that I lost

Rosario and my boy! Madonna, Madonna mia! Get that goat out of my yard! [*She retreats to the Madonna, making the sign of the horns with her fingers, while the goat chase continues outside.*]

ALVARO: Now take it easy! I will catch the black goat and give him a kick that he will never forget!

[*Alvaro runs out the front door and joins in the chase. The little boy is clapping together a pair of tin pan lids which sound like cymbals. The effect is weird and beautiful with the wild cries of the children and the goat's bleating. Serafina remains anxiously halfway between the shutters and the protecting Madonna. She gives a furious imitation of the bleating goat, contorting her face with loathing. It is the fury of woman at the desire she suffers. At last the goat is captured.*]

BRUNO: Got him, got him, got him!

ALVARO: Vieni presto, Diavolo!

[*Alvaro appears around the side of the house with a tight hold on the broken rope around the goat's neck. The boy follows behind, gleefully clapping the tin lids together, and further back follows the Strega, holding her broken length of rope, her gray hair hanging into her face and her black skirts caught up in one hand, revealing bare feet and hairy legs. Serafina comes out on the porch as the grotesque little procession passes before it, and she raises her hand with the fingers making horns as the goat and the Strega pass her. Alvaro turns the goat over to the Strega and comes panting back to the house.*]

ALVARO: Niente paura!—I got to go now.—You have been troppo gentile, Mrs. . . .

SERAFINA: I am the widow of the Baron Delle Rose.— Excuse the way I'm—not dressed . . . [*He keeps hold of her hand as he stands on the porch steps. She continues very shyly, panting a little.*] I am not always like this.—Sometimes I fix myself up!—When my husband was living, when my husband comes home, when he was living—I had a clean dress on! And sometimes even, I—put a rose in my hair . . .

ALVARO: A rose in your hair would be pretty!

SERAFINA: But for a widow—it ain't the time of roses . . .

[*The sound of music is heard, of a mandolin playing.*]

ALVARO: Naw, you make a mistake! It's always for everybody the time of roses! The rose is the heart of the world like the heart is the—heart of the—body! But you, Baronessa— you know what I think you have done?

SERAFINA: What—what have I—done?

ALVARO: You have put your heart in the marble urn with the ashes. [*Now singing is heard along with the music, which continues to the end of the scene.*] And if in a storm sometime, or sometime when a 10-ton truck goes down the highway—the marble urn was to *break!* [*He suddenly points up at the sky.*] Look! Look, Baronessa!

SERAFINA [*startled*]: Look? Look? I don't see!

ALVARO: I was pointing at your heart, broken out of the urn and away from the ashes!—*Rondinella felice!* [*He makes an airy gesture toward the fading sky.*]

SERAFINA: Oh! [*He whistles like a bird and makes graceful winglike motions with his hands.*] Buffone, buffone— piantatela! I take you serious—then you make it a joke . . . [*She smiles involuntarily at his antics.*]

ALVARO: When can I bring the shirt back?

SERAFINA: When do you pass by again?

ALVARO: I will pass by tonight for supper. Volete?

SERAFINA: Then look at the window tonight. If the shutters are open and there is a light in the window, you can stop by for your—jacket—but if the shutters are closed, you better not stop because my Rosa will be home. Rosa's my daughter. She has gone to a picnic—maybe—home early—but you know how picnics are. They—wait for the moon to—start singing.—Not that there's nothing wrong in two grown-up people having a quiet conversation!—but Rosa's fifteen—I got to be careful to set her a perfect example.

ALVARO: I will look at the window.—I will look at the win-dooow! [*He imitates a bird flying off with gay whistles.*]

SERAFINA: Buffone!

ALVARO [*shouting from outside*]: Hey, you little buggers, climb down off that truck! Lay offa them bananas!

[*His truck is heard starting and pulling away. Serafina stands motionless on the porch, searching the sky with her eyes.*]

SERAFINA: Rosario, forgive me! Forgive me for thinking the awful lie could be true!

[*The light in the house dims out. A little boy races into the yard holding triumphantly aloft a great golden bunch of bananas. A little girl pursues him with shrill cries. He eludes her. They dash around the house. The light fades and the curtain falls.*]

Act Three

*It is the evening of the same day. The neighborhood chil-
dren are playing games around the house. One of them is
counting by fives to a hundred, calling out the numbers, as
he leans against the palm tree.*

*Serafina is in the parlor, sitting on the sofa. She is seated
stiffly and formally, wearing a gown that she has not worn
since the death of her husband, and with a rose in her hair.
It becomes obvious from her movements that she is wearing
a girdle that constricts her unendurably.*

[*There is the sound of a truck approaching up on the
highway. Serafina rises to an odd, crouching position. But
the truck passes by without stopping. The girdle is becoming quite intolerable to Serafina and she decides to take
it off, going behind the sofa to do so. With much grunting,
she has gotten it down as far as her knees, when there is
the sound outside of another truck approaching. This time
the truck stops up on the highway, with a sound of screech-
ing brakes. She realizes that Alvaro is coming, and her
efforts to get out of the girdle, which is now pinioning her
legs, become frantic. She hobbles from behind the sofa as
Alvaro appears in front of the house.*]

ALVARO [*gaily*]: Rondinella felice! I will look at win-
dooooo! Signora Delle Rose!

[*Serafina's response to this salutation is a groan of anguish.
She hobbles and totters desperately to the curtains between
the rooms and reaches them just in time to hide herself as
Alvaro comes into the parlor from the porch through the
screen door. He is carrying a package and a candy box.*]

ALVARO: C'è nessuno?

223

SERAFINA [*at first inaudibly*]: Si, si, sono qui. [*then loudly and hoarsely, as she finally gets the girdle off her legs*] Si, si, sono qui! [*To cover her embarrassment, she busies herself with fixing wineglasses on a tray.*]

ALVARO: I hear the rattle of glasses! Let me help you! [*He goes eagerly through the curtain but stops short, astonished.*]

SERAFINA: Is—something the—matter?

ALVARO: I didn't expect to see you looking so pretty! You are a *young* little widow!

SERAFINA: You are—fix yourself up ...

ALVARO: I been to The Ideal Barber's! I got the whole works!

SERAFINA [*faintly, retreating from him a little*]: You got—rose oil—in your hair ...

ALVARO: Olio di rose! You like the smell of it? [*Outside there is a wild, distant cry of children, and inside a pause. Serafina shakes her head slowly with the infinite wound of a recollection.*]—You—*don't*—like—the smell of it? Oh, then I wash the smell *out*, I go and ... [*He starts toward the back. She raises her hand to stop him.*]

SERAFINA: No, no, no, fa—niente.—I—*like* the smell of it ...

[*A little boy races into the yard, ducks some invisible missile, sticks out his tongue and yells: "Yahhhhh!" Then he dashes behind the house.*]

SERAFINA: Shall we—set down in the parlor?

ALVARO: I guess that's better than standing up in the dining room. [*He enters formally.*]—Shall we set down on the sofa?

SERAFINA: You take the sofa. I will set down on this chair.

ALVARO [*disappointed*]: You don't like to set on a sofa?

SERAFINA: I lean back too far on that sofa. I like a straight back behind me . . .

ALVARO: That chair looks not comfortable to me.

SERAFINA: This chair is a comfortable chair.

ALVARO: But it's more easy to talk with two on a sofa!

SERAFINA: I talk just as good on a chair as I talk on a sofa . . . [*There is a pause. Alvaro nervously hitches his shoulder.*] Why do you hitch your shoulders like that?

ALVARO: Oh, that!—That's a—nervous—habit . . .

SERAFINA: I thought maybe the suit don't fit you good . . .

ALVARO: I bought this suit to get married in four years ago.

SERAFINA: But didn't get married?

ALVARO: I give her, the girl, a zircon instead of a diamond. She had it examined. The door was slammed in my face.

SERAFINA: I think that maybe I'd do the same thing myself.

ALVARO: Buy the zircon?

SERAFINA: No, slam the door.

ALVARO: Her eyes were not sincere-looking. You've got sincere-looking eyes. Give me your hand so I can tell your fortune! [*She pushes her chair back from him.*] I see two men in your life. One very handsome. One not handsome. His ears are too big but not as big as his heart! He has three dependents.—In fact he has four dependents! Ha, ha, ha!

SERAFINA: What is the fourth dependent?

ALVARO: The one that every man's got, his biggest expense, worst troublemaker and chief liability! Ha, ha, ha!

SERAFINA: I hope you are not talking vulgar. [*She rises and turns her back to him. Then she discovers the candy box.*] What's that fancy red box?

ALVARO: A present I bought for a nervous but nice little lady!

SERAFINA: Chocolates? Grazie! Grazie! But I'm too fat.

ALVARO: You are not fat, you are just pleasing and plump. [*He reaches way over to pinch the creamy flesh of her upper arm.*]

SERAFINA: No, please. Don't make me nervous. If I get nervous again I will start to cry . . .

ALVARO: Let's talk about something to take your mind off your troubles. You say you got a young daughter?

SERAFINA [*in a choked voice*]: Yes. I got a young daughter. Her name is Rosa.

ALVARO: Rosa, Rosa! She's pretty?

SERAFINA: She has the eyes of her father, and his wild, stubborn blood! Today was the day of her graduation from high school. She looked so pretty in a white voile dress with a great big bunch of—roses . . .

ALVARO: Not no prettier than her Mama, I bet—with that rose in your hair!

SERAFINA: She's only fifteen.

ALVARO: Fifteen?

SERAFINA [*smoothing her blue silk lap with a hesitant hand*]: Yes, only fifteen . . .

ALVARO: But has a boy friend, does she?

SERAFINA: She met a sailor.

ALVARO: Oh, Dio! No wonder you seem to be nervous.

SERAFINA: I didn't want to let her go out with this sailor. He had a gold ring in his ear.

ALVARO: Madonna Santa!

SERAFINA: This morning she cut her wrist—not much but enough to bleed—with a kitchen knife!

ALVARO: Tch, tch! A very wild girl!

SERAFINA: I had to give in and let her bring him to see me. He said he was Catholic. I made him kneel down in front of Our Lady there and give Her his promise that he would respect the innocence of my Rosa!—But how do I know that he was a Catholic, *really*?

ALVARO [*taking her hand*]: Poor little worried lady! But you got to face facts. Sooner or later the innocence of your daughter cannot be respected.—Did he—have a—tattoo?

SERAFINA [*startled*]: Did who have—what?

ALVARO: The sailor friend of your daughter, did he have a tattoo?

SERAFINA: Why do you ask me that?

ALVARO: Just because most sailors have a tattoo.

SERAFINA: How do I know if he had a tattoo or not!

ALVARO: *I* got a tattoo!

SERAFINA: *You* got a tattoo?

ALVARO: Si, si, veramente!

SERAFINA: What kind of tattoo you got?

ALVARO: What kind you think?

SERAFINA: Oh, I think—you have got—a South Sea girl without clothes on . . .

ALVARO: No South Sea girl.

SERAFINA: Well, maybe a big red heart with MAMA written across it.

ALVARO: Wrong again, Baronessa.

[*He takes off his tie and slowly unbuttons his shirt, gazing at her with an intensely warm smile. He divides the unbuttoned shirt, turning toward her his bare chest. She utters a gasp and rises.*]

SERAFINA: No, no, no!—*Not ā rose!* [*She says it as if she were evading her feelings.*]

ALVARO: Si, si, una rosa!

SERAFINA: I—don't feel good! The air is . . .

ALVARO: Che fate, che fate, che dite?

SERAFINA: The house has a tin roof on it!—The air is—I got to go outside the house to breathe! Scu—scusatemi! [*She goes out onto the porch and clings to one of the spindling porch columns for support, breathing hoarsely with a hand to her throat. He comes out slowly.*]

ALVARO [*gently*]: I didn't mean to surprise you!—Mi dispiace molto!

SERAFINA [*with enforced calm*]: Don't—talk about it! Anybody could have a rose tattoo.—It don't mean nothing.—You know how a tin roof is. It catches the heat all day and it don't cool off until—midnight . . .

ALVARO: No, no, not until midnight. [*She makes a faint laughing sound, is quite breathless and leans her forehead against the porch column. He places his fingers delicately against the small of her back.*] It makes it hot in the bedroom —so that you got to sleep without nothing on you . . .

SERAFINA: No, you—can't stand the covers . . .

ALVARO: You can't even stand a—*nightgown!* [*His fingers press her back.*]

SERAFINA: Please. There is a strega next door; she's always watching!

ALVARO: It's been so long since I felt the soft touch of a woman! [*She gasps loudly and turns to the door.*] Where are you going?

SERAFINA: I'm going back in the house! [*She enters the parlor again, still with forced calm.*]

ALVARO [*following her inside*]: Now, now, what is the matter?

SERAFINA: I got a feeling like I have—forgotten something.

ALVARO: What?

SERAFINA: I can't remember.

ALVARO: It couldn't be nothing important if you can't remember. Let's open the chocolate box and have some candy.

SERAFINA [*eager for any distraction*]: Yes! Yes, open the box!

[*Alvaro places a chocolate in her hand. She stares at it blankly.*]

ALVARO: Eat it, eat the chocolate. If you don't eat it, it will melt in your hand and make your fingers all gooey!

SERAFINA: Please, I . . .

ALVARO: Eat it!

SERAFINA [*weakly and gagging*]: I can't, I can't, I would choke! Here, you eat it.

ALVARO: Put it in my mouth! [*She puts the chocolate in his mouth.*] Now, look. Your fingers are gooey!

SERAFINA: Oh!—I better go wash them! [*She rises unsteadily. He seizes her hands and licks her fingers.*]

ALVARO: Mmmm! Mmmmm! Good, very good!

SERAFINA: Stop that, stop that, stop that! That—ain't—nice . . .

ALVARO: I'll lick off the chocolate for you.

SERAFINA: No, no, no!—I am the mother of a fifteen-year-old girl!

ALVARO: You're as old as your arteries, Baronessa. Now set back down. The fingers are now white as snow!

SERAFINA: You don't—understand—how I feel . . .

ALVARO: You don't understand how *I* feel.

SERAFINA [*doubtfully*]: How do you—feel? [*In answer, he stretches the palms of his hands out toward her as if she were a fireplace in a freezing-cold room.*]—What does—*that*—mean?

ALVARO: The night is warm but I feel like my hands are—freezing!

SERAFINA: Bad—circulation . . .

ALVARO: No, too *much* circulation! [*Alvaro becomes tremulously pleading, shuffling forward a little, slightly crouched like a beggar.*] Across the room I feel the sweet warmth of a lady!

SERAFINA [*retreating, doubtfully*]: Oh, you talk a sweet mouth. I think you talk a sweet mouth to fool a woman.

ALVARO: No, no, I know—I know that's what warms the world, that is what makes it the summer! [*He seizes the hand she holds defensively before her and presses it to his own breast in a crushing grip.*] Without it, the rose—the rose would not grow on the bush; the fruit would not grow on the tree!

SERAFINA: I know, and the truck—the truck would not haul the bananas! But, Mr. Mangiacavallo, that is my hand, not a sponge. I got bones in it. Bones break!

ALVARO: Scusatemi, Baronessa! [*He returns her hand to*

her with a bow.] For me it is winter, because I don't have in my life the sweet warmth of a lady. I live with my hands in my pockets! [*He stuffs his hands violently into his pants' pockets, then jerks them out again. A small cellophane-wrapped disk falls on the floor, escaping his notice, but not Serafina's.*]—You don't like the poetry!—How can a man talk to you?

SERAFINA [*ominously*]: I like the poetry good. Is that a piece of the poetry that you dropped out of your pocket? [*He looks down.*]—No, no, right by your foot!

ALVARO [*aghast as he realizes what it is that she has seen*]: Oh, that's—that's nothing! [*He kicks it under the sofa.*]

SERAFINA [*fiercely*]: You talk a sweet mouth about women. Then drop such a thing from your pocket?—Va via, vigliacco! [*She marches grandly out of the room, pulling the curtains together behind her. He bangs his head despairingly between his hands. Then he approaches the curtains timidly.*]

ALVARO [*in a small voice*]: Baronessa?

SERAFINA: Pick up what you dropped on the floor and go to the Square Roof with it. Buona notte!

ALVARO: Baronessa! [*He parts the curtains and peeks through them.*]

SERAFINA: I told you good night. Here is no casa privata. Io, non sono puttana!

ALVARO: Understanding is—very—necessary!

SERAFINA: I understand plenty. You think you got a good thing, a thing that is cheap!

ALVARO: You make a mistake, Baronessa! [*He comes in and drops to his knees beside her, pressing his cheek to her flank. He speaks rhapsodically.*] So soft is a lady! So, so, so, so, so soft—is a lady!

SERAFINA: Andate via, sporcaccione, andate a casa! Lasciatemi! Lasciatemi stare!

[*She springs up and runs into the parlor. He pursues. The chase is grotesquely violent and comic. A floor lamp is overturned. She seizes the chocolate box and threatens to slam it into his face if he continues toward her. He drops to his knees, crouched way over, and pounds the floor with his fists, sobbing.*]

ALVARO: Everything in my life turns out like this!

SERAFINA: Git up, git up, git up!—you village idiot's grandson! There is people watching you through that window, the —Strega next door . . . [*He rises slowly.*] And where is the shirt that I loaned you? [*He shuffles abjectly across the room, then hands her a neatly wrapped package.*]

ALVARO: My sister wrapped it up for you.—My sister was very happy I met this *nice* lady!

SERAFINA: Maybe she thinks I will pay the grocery bill while she plays the numbers!

ALVARO: She don't think nothing like that. She is an old maid, my sister. She wants—nephews—nieces . . .

SERAFINA: You tell her for me I don't give nephews and nieces!

[*Alvaro hitches his shoulders violently in his embarrassment and shuffles over to where he had left his hat. He blows the dust off it and rubs the crown on his sleeve. Serafina presses a knuckle to her lips as she watches his awkward gestures. She is a little abashed by his humility. She speaks next with the great dignity of a widow whose respectability has stood the test.*]

SERAFINA: Now, Mr. Mangiacavallo, please tell me the truth about something. *When* did you get the tattoo put on your chest?

ALVARO [*shyly and sadly, looking down at his hat*]: I got it tonight—after supper . . .

SERAFINA: That's what I thought. You had it put on because I told you about my husband's tattoo.

ALVARO: I wanted to be—close to you . . . to make you—
happy . . .

SERAFINA: Tell it to the marines! [*He puts on his hat with
an apologetic gesture.*] You got the tattoo and the chocolate
box after supper, and then you come here to fool me!

ALVARO: I got the chocolate box a long time ago.

SERAFINA: How long ago? If that is not too much a personal question!

ALVARO: I got it the night the door was slammed in my
face by the girl that I give—the zircon . . .

SERAFINA: Let that be a lesson. Don't try to fool women.
You are not smart enough!—Now take the shirt back. You
can keep it.

ALVARO: Huh?

SERAFINA: Keep it. I don't want it back.

ALVARO: You just now said that you did.

SERAFINA: It's a man's shirt, ain't it?

ALVARO: You just now accused me of trying to steal it off
you.

SERAFINA: Well, you been making me nervous!

ALVARO: Is it my fault you been a widow too long?

SERAFINA: You make a mistake!

ALVARO: *You* make a mistake!

SERAFINA: Both of us make a mistake!

[*There is a pause. They both sigh profoundly.*]

ALVARO: We should of have been friends, but I think we
meet the wrong day.—Suppose I go out and come in the
door again and we start all over?

SERAFINA: No, I think it's no use. The day was wrong to begin with, because of two women. Two women, they told me today that my husband had put on my head the nanny-goat's horns!

ALVARO: How is it possible to put horns on a widow?

SERAFINA: That was before, before! They told me my husband was having a steady affair with a woman at the Square Roof. What was the name on the shirt, on the slip of paper? Do you remember the name?

ALVARO: You told me to . . .

SERAFINA: Tell me! Do you remember?

ALVARO: I remember the name because I know the woman. The name was Estelle Hohengarten.

SERAFINA: Take me there! Take me to the Square Roof!— Wait, wait!

[*She plunges into the dining room, snatches a knife out of the sideboard drawer and thrusts it in her purse. Then she rushes back, with the blade of the knife protruding from the purse.*]

ALVARO [*noticing the knife*]: They—got a cover charge there . . .

SERAFINA: I will charge them a cover! Take me there now, this minute!

ALVARO: The fun don't start till midnight.

SERAFINA: I will start the fun sooner.

ALVARO: The floor show commences at midnight.

SERAFINA: I will commence it! [*She rushes to the phone.*] Yellow Cab, please, Yellow Cab. I want to go to the Square Roof out of my house! Yes, you come to my house and take me to the Square Roof right this minute! My number is—what is my number? Oh my God, what is my number?—64 is my number on Front Street! Subito, subito—quick!

[*The goat bleats outside.*]

ALVARO: Baronessa, the knife's sticking out of your purse. [*He grabs the purse.*] What do you want with this weapon?

SERAFINA: To cut the lying tongue out of a woman's mouth! Saying she has on her breast the tattoo of my husband because he had put on me the horns of a goat! I cut the heart out of that woman, she cut the heart out of me!

ALVARO: Nobody's going to cut the heart out of nobody!

[*A car is heard outside, and Serafina rushes to the porch.*]

SERAFINA [*shouting*]: Hey, Yellow Cab, Yellow Cab, Yellow—Cab . . . [*The car passes by without stopping. With a sick moan she wanders into the yard. He follows her with a glass of wine.*]—Something hurts—in my heart . . .

ALVARO [*leading her gently back to the house*]: Baronessa, drink this wine on the porch and keep your eyes on that star. [*He leads her to a porch pillar and places the glass in her trembling hand. She is now submissive.*] You know the name of that star? That star is Venus. She is the only female star in the sky. Who put her up there? Mr. Siccardi, the transportation manager of the Southern Fruit Company? No. She was put there by God. [*He enters the house and removes the knife from her purse.*] And yet there's some people that don't believe in nothing. [*He picks up the telephone.*] Esplanade 9-7-0.

SERAFINA: What are you doing?

ALVARO: Drink that wine and I'll settle this whole problem for you. [*on the telephone*] I want to speak to the blackjack dealer, please, Miss Estelle Hohengarten . . .

SERAFINA: Don't talk to that woman, she'll lie!

ALVARO: Not Estelle Hohengarten. She deals a straight game of cards.—Estelle? This is Mangiacavallo. I got a question to ask you which is a personal question. It has to do with a very good-looking truck driver, not living now but once on a time thought to have been a very well-known character at the Square Roof. His name was . . . [*He*

turns questioningly to the door where Serafina is standing.]
What was his name, Baronessa?

SERAFINA [*hardly breathing*]: Rosario delle Rose!

ALVARO: Rosario delle Rose was the name. [*There is a pause.*]—È vero?—Mah! Che peccato . . .

[*Serafina drops her glass and springs into the parlor with a savage outcry. She snatches the phone from Alvaro and screams into it.*]

SERAFINA [*wildly*]: This is the wife that's speaking! What do you know of my husband, what is the lie?

[*A strident voice sounds over the wire.*]

THE VOICE [*loud and clear*]: Don't you remember? I brought you the rose-colored silk to make him a shirt. You said, "For a man?" and I said, "Yes, for a man that's wild like a Gypsy!" But if you think I'm a liar, come here and let me show you his rose tattooed on my chest!

[*Serafina holds the phone away from her as though it had burst into flame. Then, with a terrible cry, she hurls it to the floor. She staggers dizzily toward the Madonna. Alvaro seizes her arm and pushes her gently onto the sofa.*]

ALVARO: Piano, piano, Baronessa! This will be gone, this will pass in a moment. [*He puts a pillow behind her, then replaces the telephone.*]

SERAFINA [*staggering up from the sofa*]: The room's— going round . . .

ALVARO: You ought to stay lying down a little while longer. I know, I know what you need! A towel with some ice in it to put on your forehead—Baronessa.—You stay right there while I fix it! [*He goes into the kitchen, and calls back.*] Torno subito, Baronessa!

[*The little boy runs into the yard. He leans against the bending trunk of the palm, counting loudly.*]

THE LITTLE BOY: Five, ten, fifteen, twenty, twenty-five, thirty . . .

[*There is the sound of ice being chopped in the kitchen.*]

SERAFINA: Dove siete, dove siete?

ALVARO: In cucina!—Ghiaccio . . .

SERAFINA: Venite qui!

ALVARO: Subito, subito . . .

SERAFINA [*turning to the shrine, with fists knotted*]: Non voglio, non voglio farlo!

[*But she crosses slowly, compulsively toward the shrine, with a trembling arm stretched out.*]

THE LITTLE BOY: Seventy-five, eighty, eighty-five, ninety, ninety-five, one hundred! [*then, wildly*] Ready or not you shall be caught!

[*At this cry, Serafina seizes the marble urn and hurls it violently into the furthest corner of the room. Then, instantly, she covers her face. Outside the mothers are heard calling their children home. Their voices are tender as music, fading in and out. The children appear slowly at the side of the house, exhausted from their wild play.*]

GIUSEPPINA: Vivi! Vi-vi!

PEPINA: Salvatore!

VIOLETTA: Bruno! Come home, come home!

[*The children scatter. Alvaro comes in with the ice pick.*]

ALVARO: I broke the point of the ice pick.

SERAFINA: [*removing her hands from her face*]: I don't want ice . . . [*She looks about her, seeming to gather a fierce strength in her body. Her voice is hoarse, her body trembling with violence, eyes narrow and flashing, her fists clenched.*] Now I show you how wild and strong like a man a woman

can be! [*She crosses to the screen door, opens it and shouts.*]
Buona notte, Mr. Mangiacavallo!

ALVARO: You—you make me go *home*, now?

SERAFINA: No, no; senti, cretino! [*in a strident whisper*]
You make out like you are going. You drive the truck out of
sight where the witch can't see it. Then you come back and I
leave the backdoor open for you to come in. Now, tell me
good-bye so all the neighbors can hear you! [*She shouts.*]
Arrivederci!

ALVARO: Ha, ha! Capish! [*He shouts too.*] Arrivederci! [*He
runs to the foot of the embankment steps.*]

SERAFINA [*still more loudly*]: Buona notte!

ALVARO: Buona notte, Baronessa!

SERAFINA [*in a choked voice*]: Give them my love; give
everybody—my love . . . Arrivederci!

ALVARO: Ciao!

[*Alvaro scrambles on down the steps and goes off. Serafina comes down into the yard. The goat bleats. She mut-
ters savagely to herself.*]

SERAFINA: Sono una bestia, una bestia feroce!

[*She crosses quickly around to the back of the house. As
she disappears, the truck is heard driving off; the lights
sweep across the house. Serafina comes in through the
backdoor. She is moving with great violence, gasping and
panting. She rushes up to the Madonna and addresses her
passionately with explosive gestures, leaning over so that
her face is level with the statue's.*]

SERAFINA: Ora, ascolta, Signora! You hold in the cup of
your hand this little house and you smash it! You break this
little house like the shell of a bird in your hand, because you
have hate Serafina?—Serafina that *loved* you! No, no, no,
you don't speak! I don't believe in you, Lady! You're just a
poor little doll with the paint peeling off, and now I blow out

the light and I forget you the way you forget Serafina! [*She blows out the vigil light.*] *Ecco—fatto!*

[*But now she is suddenly frightened; the vehemence and boldness have run out. She gasps a little and backs away from the shrine, her eyes rolling apprehensively this way and that. The parrot squawks at her. The goat bleats. The night is full of sinister noises, harsh bird cries, the sudden flapping of wings in the canebrake, a distant shriek of Negro laughter. Serafina retreats to the window and opens the shutters wider to admit the moonlight. She stands panting by the window with a fist pressed to her mouth. In the back of the house a door slams open. Serafina catches her breath and moves as though for protection behind the dummy of the bride. Alvaro enters through the backdoor, calling out softly and hoarsely, with great excitement.*]

ALVARO: Dove? Dove sei, cara?

SERAFINA [*faintly*]: Sono qui . . .

ALVARO: You have turn out the light!

SERAFINA: The moon is enough . . . [*He advances toward her. His white teeth glitter as he grins. Serafina retreats a few steps from him. She speaks tremulously, making an awkward gesture toward the sofa.*] Now we can go on with our— conversation . . . [*She catches her breath sharply.*]

[*The curtain comes down.*]

Scene Two

It is just before daybreak of the next day. Rosa and Jack appear at the top of the embankment steps.

ROSA: I thought they would never leave. [*She comes down the steps and out in front of the house, then calls back to him.*] Let's go down there.

[*He obeys hesitatingly. Both are very grave. The scene is played as close as possible to the audience. She sits very straight. He stands behind her with his hands on her shoulders.*]

ROSA [*leaning her head back against him*]: This was the happiest day of my life, and this is the saddest night . . . [*He crouches in front of her.*]

SERAFINA [*from inside the house*]: Aaaaaahhhhhhh!

JACK [*springing up, startled*]: What's that?

ROSA [*resentfully*]: Oh! That's Mama dreaming about my father.

JACK: I—feel like a—*heel!* I feel like a rotten heel!

ROSA: Why?

JACK: That promise I made your mother.

ROSA: I hate her for it.

JACK: Honey—Rosa, she—wanted to protect you.

[*There is a long-drawn cry from the back of the house:* "Ohhhh—Rosario!"]

ROSA: She wanted me not to have what she's dreaming about . . .

JACK: Naw, naw, honey, she—wanted to—protect you . . .

[*The cry from within is repeated softly.*]

ROSA: Listen to her making love in her sleep! Is that what she wants *me* to do, just—*dream* about it?

JACK [*humbly*]: She knows that her Rosa *is* a rose. And she wants her rose to have someone—better than *me* . . .

ROSA: *Better* than—*you!* [*She speaks as if the possibility were too preposterous to think of.*]

JACK: You see me through—rose-colored—glasses . . .

ROSA: I see you with love!

JACK: Yes, but your Mama sees me with—common sense . . . [*Serafina cries out again.*] I got to be going! [*She keeps a tight hold on him. A rooster crows.*] Honey, it's so late the roosters are crowing!

ROSA: They're fools, they're fools, it's early!

JACK: Honey, on that island I almost forgot my promise. Almost, but not quite. Do you understand, honey?

ROSA: Forget the promise!

JACK: I made it on my knees in front of Our Lady. I've got to leave now, honey.

ROSA [*clasping him fiercely*]: You'd have to break my arms to!

JACK: Rosa, Rosa! You want to drive me crazy?

ROSA: I want you not to remember.

JACK: You're a very young girl! Fifteen—fifteen is too young!

ROSA: Caro, caro, carissimo!

JACK: You got to save some of those feelings for when you're grown up!

ROSA: Carissimo!

JACK: Hold some of it back until you're grown!

ROSA: I have been grown for two years!

JACK: No, no, that ain't what I . . .

ROSA: Grown enough to be married, and have a—baby!

JACK [*springing up*]: Oh, good—Lord! [*He circles around her, pounding his palm repeatedly with his fist and champing his teeth together with a grimace. Suddenly he speaks.*] I got to be going!

ROSA: You want me to scream? [*He groans and turns away from her to resume his desperate circle. Rosa is blocking the way with her body.*]—I know, I know! You don't want me! [*Jack groans through his gritting teeth.*] No, no, you don't want me . . .

JACK: Now you listen to me! You almost got into trouble today on that island! You almost did, but not quite!—But it didn't quite happen and no harm is done and you can just—forget it . . .

ROSA: It is the only thing in my life that I want to remember!—When are you going back to New Orleans?

JACK: Tomorrow.

ROSA: When does your—ship sail?

JACK: Tomorrow.

ROSA: Where to?

JACK: Guatemala.

SERAFINA [*from the house*]: Aahh!

ROSA: Is that a long trip?

JACK: After Guatemala, Buenos Aires. After Buenos Aires, Rio. Then around the Straits of Magellan and back up the west coast of South America, putting in at three ports before we dock at San Francisco.

ROSA: I don't think I will—ever see you again . . .

JACK: The ship won't sink!

ROSA [*faintly and forlornly*]: No, but—I think it could just happen once, and if it don't happen that time, it never can—later . . . [*A rooster crows. They face each other sadly and quietly.*] You don't need to be very old to understand how it works out. One time, one time, only once, it could be—God! —to remember.—Other times? Yes—they'd be something.— But only once, God—to remember . . . [*With a little sigh she crosses to pick up his white cap and hand it gravely to him.*] —I'm sorry to you it didn't—mean—that much . . .

JACK [*taking the cap and hurling it to the ground*]: Look! Look at my knuckles! You see them scabs on my knuckles? You know how them scabs got there? They got there because I banged my knuckles that hard on the deck of the sailboat!

ROSA: Because it—didn't quite happen? [*Jack jerks his head up and down in grotesquely violent assent to her question. Rosa picks up his cap and returns it to him again.*]—Because of the promise to Mama! I'll never forgive her . . . [*There is a pause.*] What time in the afternoon must you be on the boat?

JACK: Why?

ROSA: Just tell me what time.

JACK: Five!—Why?

ROSA: What will you be doing till five?

JACK: Well, I could be a goddam liar and tell you I was going to—pick me a hatful of daisies in—Audubon Park.—Is that what you want me to tell you?

ROSA: No, tell me the truth.

JACK: All right, I'll tell you the truth. I'm going to check in at some flea-bag hotel on North Rampart Street. Then I'm going to get loaded! And then I'm going to get . . . [*He doesn't complete the sentence but she understands him. She places the hat more becomingly on his blond head.*]

ROSA: Do me a little favor. [*Her hand slides down to his cheek and then to his mouth.*] Before you get loaded and before you—before you—

JACK: Huh?

ROSA: Look in the waiting room at the Greyhound bus station, please. At twelve o'clock, noon!

JACK: Why?

ROSA: You might find me there, waiting for you . . .

JACK: What—what good would that do?

ROSA: I never been to a hotel but I know they have numbers on doors and sometimes—numbers are—lucky.—Aren't they?—Sometimes?—Lucky?

JACK: You want to buy me a ten-year stretch in the brig?

ROSA: I want you to give me that little gold ring on your ear to put on my finger.—I want to give you my heart to keep forever! And ever! And ever! [*Slowly and with a barely audible sigh she leans her face against him.*] Look for me! I will be there!

JACK [*breathlessly*]: In all of my life, I never felt nothing so sweet as the feel of your little warm body in my arms . . .

[*He breaks away and runs toward the road. From the foot of the steps he glares fiercely back at her like a tiger*

*through the bars of a cage. She clings to the two porch
pillars, her body leaning way out.*]

ROSA: Look for me! I will be there!

[*Jack runs away from the house. Rosa returns inside.
Listlessly she removes her dress and falls on the couch in
her slip, kicking off her shoes. Then she begins to cry, as
one cries only once in a lifetime, and the scene dims out.*]

Scene Three

The time is three hours later.

We see first the exterior view of the small frame building against a night sky which is like the starry blue robe of Our Lady. It is growing slightly paler.

[The faint light discloses Rosa asleep on the couch. The covers are thrown back for it has been a warm night, and on the concave surface of the white cloth, which is like the dimly lustrous hollow of a shell, is the body of the sleeping girl which is clad only in a sheer white slip.

[A cock crows. A gentle wind stirs the white curtains inward and the tendrils of vine at the windows, and the sky lightens enough to distinguish the purple trumpets of the morning glory against the very dim blue of the sky in the planet Venus remains still undimmed.

[In the back of the cottage someone is heard coughing hoarsely and groaning in the way a man does who has drunk very heavily the night before. Bedsprings creak as a heavy figure rises. Light spills dimly through the curtains, now closed, between the two front rooms.

[There are heavy, padding footsteps and Alvaro comes stumbling rapidly into the dining room with the last bottle of spumanti in the crook of an arm, his eyes barely open, legs rubbery, saying, "Wuh-wuh-wuh-wuh-wuh-wuh . . ." like the breathing of an old dog. The scene should be played with the pantomimic lightness, almost fantasy, of an early Chaplin comedy. He is wearing only his trousers and his chest is bare. As he enters he collides with the widow dummy, staggers back, pats her inflated bosom in a timid, apologetic way, remarking:]

ALVARO: Scusami, Signora, I am the grandson of the village idiot of Ribera!

[Alvaro backs into the table and is propelled by the impact all the way to the curtained entrance to the parlor. He draws the curtains apart and hangs onto them, peering into the room. Seeing the sleeping girl, he blinks several times, suddenly makes a snoring sound in his nostrils and waves one hand violently in front of his eyes as if to dispel a vision. Outside the goat utters a long "Baaaaaaaaaaaa!" As if in response, Alvaro whispers, in the same basso key, "Che bella!" The first vowel of "bella" is enormously prolonged like the "baaa" of the goat. On his rubbery legs he shuffles forward a few steps and leans over to peer more intently at the vision. The goat bleats again. Alvaro whispers more loudly: "Che bel-la!" He drains the spumanti, then staggers to his knees, the empty bottle rolling over the floor. He crawls on his knees to the foot of the bed, then leans against it like a child peering into a candy shop window, repeating: "Che bel-la, che bel-la!" with antiphonal responses from the goat outside. Slowly, with tremendous effort, as if it were the sheer side of a precipice, he clambers upon the couch and crouches over the sleeping girl in a leapfrog position, saying "Che bel-la!" quite loudly, this time, in a tone of innocently joyous surprise. All at once Rosa wakens. She screams, even before she is quite awake, and springs from the couch so violently that Alvaro topples over to the floor.

[Serafina cries out almost instantly after Rosa. She lunges through the dining room in her torn and disordered nightgown. At the sight of the man crouched by the couch a momentary stupefaction turns into a burst of savage fury. She flies at him like a great bird, tearing and clawing at his stupefied figure. With one arm Alvaro wards off her blows, plunging to the floor and crawling into the dining room. She seizes a broom with which she flails him about the head, buttocks and shoulders while he scrambles awkwardly away. The assault is nearly wordless. Each time she strikes at him she hisses: "Sporcaccione!" He continually groans: "Dough, dough, dough!" At last he catches hold of the widow dummy which he holds as a shield before him while he entreats the two women.]

ALVARO: Senti, Baronessa! Signorina! I didn't know what I was doin', I was dreamin', I was just dreamin'! I got turn around in the house; I got all twisted! I thought that you was your Mama!—Sono ubriaco! Per favore!

ROSA [*seizing the broom*]: That's enough, Mama!

SERAFINA [*rushing to the phone*]: Police!

ROSA [*seizing the phone*]: No, no, no, no, no, no!—You want everybody to know?

SERAFINA [*weakly*]: Know?—Know *what*, cara?

ROSA: Just give him his clothes, now, Mama, and let him get out! [*She is clutching a bedsheet about herself.*]

ALVARO: Signorina—young lady! I swear I was *dreaming!*

SERAFINA: Don't speak to my daughter! [*then, turning to Rosa*]—Who is this man? How did this man get here?

ROSA [*coldly*]: Mama, don't say any more. Just give him his clothes in the bedroom so he can get out!

ALVARO [*still crouching*]: I am so sorry, so sorry! I don't remember a thing but that I was dreaming!

SERAFINA [*shoving him toward the back of the room with her broom*]: Go on, go get your clothes on, you—idiot's grandson, you!—Svelto, svelto, più svelto! [*Alvaro continues his apologetic mumbling in the back room.*] Don't talk to me, don't say nothing! Or I will kill you!

[*A few moments later Alvaro rushes around the side of the house, his clothes half buttoned and his shirttails out.*]

ALVARO: But, Baronessa, I *love* you! [*A teakettle sails over his head from behind the house. The Strega bursts into laughter. Despairingly, Alvaro retreats, tucking his shirttails in and shaking his head.*] Baronessa, Baronessa, I love you!

[*As Alvaro runs off, the Strega is heard cackling:*]

THE STREGA'S VOICE: The Wops are at it again. Had a truck driver in the house all night!

[*Rosa is feverishly dressing. From the bureau she has snatched a shimmering white satin slip, disappearing for a moment behind a screen to put it on as Serafina comes*] *padding sheepishly back into the room, her nightgown now covered by a black rayon kimona sprinkled with poppies, her voice tremulous with fear, shame and apology.*]

ROSA [*behind the screen*]: Has the man gone?

SERAFINA: That—man?

ROSA: Yes, "that man!"

SERAFINA [*inventing desperately*]: I don't know how he got in. Maybe the backdoor was open.

ROSA: Oh, yes, maybe it was!

SERAFINA: Maybe he—climbed in a window . . .

ROSA: Or fell down the chimney, maybe! [*She comes from behind the screen, wearing the white bridal slip.*]

SERAFINA: Why you put on the white things I save for your wedding?

ROSA: Because I want to. That's a good enough reason. [*She combs her hair savagely.*]

SERAFINA: I want you to understand about that man. That was a man that—that was—that was a man that . . .

ROSA: You can't think of a lie?

SERAFINA: He was a—truck driver, cara. He got in a fight, he was chase by—policemen!

ROSA: They chased him into your bedroom?

SERAFINA: I took pity on him, I give him first aid, I let him sleep on the floor. He give me his promise—he . . .

ROSA: Did he kneel in front of Our Lady? Did he promise that he would respect your innocence?

SERAFINA: Oh, cara, cara! [*abandoning all pretense*] He was Sicilian; he had rose oil in his hair and the rose tattoo of your father. In the dark room I couldn't see his clown face. I closed my eyes and dreamed that he was your father! I closed my eyes! I dreamed that he was your father . . .

ROSA: Basta, basta, non voglio sentire più niente! The only thing worse than a liar is a liar that's also a hypocrite!

SERAFINA: Senti, per favore! [*Rosa wheels about from the mirror and fixes her mother with a long and withering stare. Serafina cringes before it.*] Don't look at me like that with the eyes of your father! [*She shields her face as from a terrible glare.*]

ROSA: Yes, I am looking at you with the eyes of my father. I see you the way *he* saw you. [*She runs to the table and seizes the piggy bank.*] Like this, this pig! [*Serafina utters a long, shuddering cry like a cry of childbirth.*] I need five dollars. I'll take it out of this! [*Rosa smashes the piggy bank to the floor. There is the sound of a train whistle. Rosa is now fully dressed, but she hesitates, a little ashamed of her cruelty —but only a little. Serafina cannot meet her daughter's eyes. At last the girl speaks.*]

SERAFINA: How beautiful—is my daughter! Go to the boy!

ROSA [*as if she might be about to apologize*]: Mama? He didn't touch me—he just said—"Che bella!"

[*Serafina turns slowly, shamefully, to face her. She is like a peasant in the presence of a young princess. Rosa stares at her a moment longer, then suddenly catches her breath and runs out of the house. As the girl leaves, Serafina calls:*]

SERAFINA: Rosa, Rosa, the—wrist watch! [*Serafina snatches up the little gift box and runs out onto the porch with it. She starts to call her daughter again, holding the gift out toward her, but her breath fails her.*] Rosa, Rosa, the—wrist watch . . . [*Her arms fall to her side. She turns, the gift still ungiven. Senselessly, absently, she holds the watch to her ear again. She shakes it a little, then utters a faint, startled laugh.*]

[*Assunta appears beside the house and walks directly in, as though Serafina had called her.*]

SERAFINA: Assunta, the urn is broken. The ashes are spilt on the floor and I can't touch them.

[*Assunta stoops to pick up the pieces of the shattered urn. Serafina has crossed to the shrine and relights the candle before the Madonna.*]

ASSUNTA: There are no ashes.

SERAFINA: Where—where are they? Where have the ashes gone?

ASSUNTA [*crossing to the shrine*]: The wind has blown them away.

[*Assunta places what remains of the broken urn in Serafina's hands. Serafina turns it tenderly in her hands and then replaces it on the top of the prie-dieu before the Madonna.*]

SERAFINA: A man, when he burns, leaves only a handful of ashes. No woman can hold him. The wind must blow him away.

[*Alvaro's voice is heard, calling from the top of the highway embankment.*]

ALVARO'S VOICE: Rondinella felice!

[*The neighborhood women hear Alvaro calling, and there is a burst of mocking laughter from some of them. Then they all converge on the house from different directions and gather before the porch.*]

PEPPINA: Serafina delle Rose!

GIUSEPPINA: Baronessa! Baronessa delle Rose!

PEPPINA: There is a man on the road without the shirt!

GIUSEPPINA [*with delight*]: Si, si! Senza camicia!

PEPPINA: All he got on his chest is a rose tattoo! [*to the women*] She lock up his shirt so he can't go to the high school?

[*The women shriek with laughter. In the house Serafina snatches up the package containing the silk shirt, while Assunta closes the shutters of the parlor windows.*]

SERAFINA: Un momento! [*She tears the paper off the shirt and rushes out onto the porch, holding the shirt above her head defiantly.*] Ecco la camicia!

[*With a soft cry, Serafina drops the shirt, which is immediately snatched up by Peppina. At this point the music begins again, with a crash of percussion, and continues to the end of the play. Peppina flourishes the shirt in the air like a banner and tosses it to Giuseppina, who is now on the embankment. Giuseppina tosses it on to Mariella, and she in her turn to Violetta, who is above her, so that the brilliantly colored shirt moves in a zigzag course through the pampas grass to the very top of the embankment, like a streak of flame shooting up a dry hill. The women call out as they pass the shirt along:*]

PEPPINA: Guardate questa camicia! Coloro di rose!

MARIELLA [*shouting up to Alvaro*]: Corragio, signor!

GIUSEPPINA: Avanti, avanti, signor!

VIOLETTA [*at the top of the embankment, giving the shirt a final flourish above her*]: Corragio, corragio! The Baronessa is waiting!

[*Bursts of laughter are mingled with the cries of the women. Then they sweep away like a flock of screaming birds, and Serafina is left upon the porch, her eyes closed, a hand clasped to her breast. In the meanwhile, inside the house, Assunta has poured out a glass of wine. Now she comes to the porch, offering the wine to Serafina and murmuring:*]

ASSUNTA: Stai tranquilla.

SERAFINA [*breathlessly*]: Assunta, I'll tell you something that maybe you won't believe.

ASSUNTA [*with tender humor*]: It is impossible to tell me anything that I don't believe.

SERAFINA: Just now I felt on my breast the burning again of the rose. I know what it means. It means that I have conceived! [*She lifts the glass to her lips for a moment and then returns it to Assunta.*] Two lives again in the body! Two, two lives again, two!

ALVARO'S VOICE [*nearer now, and sweetly urgent*]: Rondinella felice!

[*Alvaro is not visible on the embankment but Serafina begins to move slowly toward his voice.*]

ASSUNTA: Dove vai, Serafina?

SERAFINA [*shouting now, to Alvaro*]: Vengo, vengo, amore! [*She starts up the embankment toward Alvaro and the curtain falls as the music rises with her in great glissandi of sound.*]

The Night of the Iguana

And so, as kinsmen met a night,
We talked between the rooms,
Until the moss had reached our lips,
And covered up our names.

EMILY DICKINSON

The play takes place in the summer of 1940 in a rather rustic and very Bohemian hotel, the Costa Verde, which, as its name implies, sits on a jungle-covered hilltop overlooking the "caleta," or "morning beach" of Puerto Barrio in Mexico. But this is decidedly not the Puerto Barrio of today. At that time—twenty years ago—the west coast of Mexico had not yet become the Las Vegas and Miami Beach of Mexico. The villages were still predominantly primitive Indian villages, and the still-water morning beach of Puerto Barrio and the rain forests above it were among the world's wildest and loveliest populated places.

The setting for the play is the wide verandah of the hotel. This roofed verandah, enclosed by a railing, runs around all four sides of the somewhat dilapidated, tropical-style frame structure, but on the stage we see only the front and one side. Below the verandah, which is slightly raised above the stage level, are shrubs with vivid trumpet-shaped flowers and a few cactus plants, while at the sides we see the foliage of the encroaching jungle. A tall coconut palm slants upward at one side, its trunk notched for a climber to chop down coconuts for rum-cocos. In the back wall of the verandah are the doors of a line of small cubicle bedrooms which are screened with mosquito-net curtains. For the night scenes they are lighted from within, so that each cubicle appears as a little interior stage, the curtains giving a misty effect to their dim inside lighting. A path which goes down through the rain forest to the highway and the beach, its opening masked by foliage, leads off from one side of the verandah. A canvas hammock is strung from posts on the verandah and there are a few old wicker rockers and rattan lounging chairs at one side.

The Night of the Iguana was presented at the Royale Theatre in New York on December 28, 1961 by Charles Bowden, in association with Violla Rubber. It was directed by Frank Corsaro; the stage setting was designed by Oliver Smith; lighting by Jean Rosenthal; costumes by Noel Taylor; audio effects by Edward Beyer. The cast, in order of appearance, was as follows:

MAXINE FAULK	BETTE DAVIS
PEDRO	JAMES FARENTINO
PANCHO	CHRISTOPHER JONES
REVEREND SHANNON	PATRICK O'NEAL
HANK	THESEUS GEORGE
HERR FAHRENKOPF	HEINZ HOHENWALD
FRAU FAHRENKOPF	LUCY LANDAU
WOLFGANG	BRUCE GLOVER
HILDA	LARYSSA LAURET
JUDITH FELLOWES	PATRICIA ROE
HANNAH JELKES	MARGARET LEIGHTON
CHARLOTTE GOODALL	LANE BRADBURY
JONATHAN COFFIN (NONNO)	ALAN WEBB
JAKE LATTA	LOUIS GUSS

Production owned and presented by "The Night of the Iguana" Joint Venture (the joint venture consisting of Charles Bowden and Two Rivers Enterprises, Inc.).

Act One

*As the curtain rises, there are
sounds of a party of excited female tourists arriving by bus on
the road down the hill below the Costa Verde Hotel.* MRS.
MAXINE FAULK, *the proprietor of the hotel, comes around the
turn of the verandah. She is a stout, swarthy woman in her
middle forties—affable and rapaciously lusty. She is wearing
a pair of levis and a blouse that is half unbuttoned. She is
followed by* PEDRO, *a Mexican of about twenty—slim and
attractive. He is an employee in the hotel and also her casual
lover.* PEDRO *is stuffing his shirt under the belt of his pants and
sweating as if he had been working hard in the sun.* MRS.
FAULK *looks down the hill and is pleased by the sight of someone coming up from the tourist bus below.*

MAXINE [*calling out*]: Shannon! [*A man's voice from below
answers:* "Hi!"] Hah! [MAXINE *always laughs with a single
harsh, loud bark, opening her mouth like a seal expecting a
fish to be thrown to it.*] My spies told me that you were back
under the border! [*to* PEDRO] Anda, hombre, anda!

[MAXINE'S *delight expands and vibrates in her as* SHANNON
*labors up the hill to the hotel. He does not appear on the
jungle path for a minute or two after the shouting between
them starts.*]

MAXINE: Hah! My spies told me you went through Saltillo
last week with a busload of women—a whole busload of females, all females, hah! How many you laid so far? Hah!

SHANNON [*from below, panting*]: Great Caesar's ghost . . .
stop . . . shouting!

MAXINE: No wonder your ass is draggin', hah!

9

SHANNON: Tell the kid to help me up with this bag.

MAXINE [*shouting directions*]: Pedro! Anda—la maleta. Pancho, no seas flojo! Va y trae el equipaje del señor.

[PANCHO, *another young Mexican, comes around the verandah and trots down the jungle path.* PEDRO *has climbed up a coconut tree with a machete and is chopping down nuts for rum-cocos.*]

SHANNON [*shouting, below*]: Fred? Hey, Fred!

MAXINE [*with a momentary gravity*]: Fred can't hear you, Shannon. [*She goes over and picks up a coconut, shaking it against her ear to see if it has milk in it.*]

SHANNON [*still below*]: Where is Fred—gone fishing?

[MAXINE *lops the end off a coconut with the machete, as* PANCHO *trots up to the verandah with* SHANNON'S *bag—a beat-up Gladstone covered with travel stickers from all over the world. Then* SHANNON *appears, in a crumpled white linen suit. He is panting, sweating and wild-eyed. About thirty-five,* SHANNON *is "black Irish." His nervous state is terribly apparent; he is a young man who has cracked up before and is going to crack up again—perhaps repeatedly.*]

MAXINE: Well! Lemme look at you!

SHANNON: Don't look at me, get dressed!

MAXINE: Gee, you look like you had it!

SHANNON: You look like you been having it, too. Get dressed!

MAXINE: Hell, I'm dressed. I never dress in September. Don't you know I never dress in September?

SHANNON: Well, just, just—button your shirt up.

MAXINE: How long you been off it, Shannon?

SHANNON: Off what?

MAXINE: The wagon . . .

SHANNON: Hell, I'm dizzy with fever. Hundred and three this morning in Cuernavaca.

MAXINE: Watcha got wrong with you?

SHANNON: Fever . . . fever . . . Where's Fred?

MAXINE: Dead.

SHANNON: Did you say *dead*?

MAXINE: That's what I said. Fred is dead.

SHANNON: How?

MAXINE: Less'n two weeks ago, Fred cut his hand on a fish-hook, it got infected, infection got in his blood stream, and he was dead inside of forty-eight hours. [*to* PANCHO] Vete!

SHANNON: Holy smoke. . . .

MAXINE: I can't quite realize it yet. . . .

SHANNON: You don't seem—inconsolable about it.

MAXINE: Fred was an old man, baby. Ten years older'n me. We hadn't had sex together in. . . .

SHANNON: What's that got to do with it?

MAXINE: Lie down and have a rum-coco.

SHANNON: No, no. I want a cold beer. If I start drinking rum-cocos now I won't stop drinking rum-cocos. So Fred is dead? I looked forward to lying in this hammock and talking to Fred.

MAXINE: Well Fred's not talking now, Shannon. A diabetic

gets a blood infection, he goes like that without a decent hospital in less'n a week. [*A bus horn is heard blowing from below*.] Why don't your busload of women come on up here? They're blowing the bus horn down there.

SHANNON: Let 'em blow it, blow it. . . . [*He sways a little*.] I got a fever. [*He goes to the top of the path, divides the flowering bushes and shouts down the hill to the bus*.] Hank! Hank! Get them out of the bus and bring 'em up here! Tell 'em the rates are OK. Tell 'em the. . . . [*His voice gives out, and he stumbles back to the verandah, where he sinks down onto the low steps, panting*.] Absolutely the worst party I've ever been out with in ten years of conducting tours. For God's sake, help me with 'em because I can't go on. I got to rest here a while. [*She gives him a cold beer*.] Thanks. Look and see if they're getting out of the bus. [*She crosses to the masking foliage and separates it to look down the hill*.] Are they getting out of the bus or are they staying in it, the stingy—daughters of—bitches. . . . Schoolteachers at a Baptist Female College in Blowing Rock, Texas. Eleven, eleven of them.

MAXINE: A football squad of old maids.

SHANNON: Yeah, and I'm the football. Are they out of the bus?

MAXINE: One's gotten out—she's going into the bushes.

SHANNON: Well, I've got the ignition key to the bus in my pocket—this pocket—so they can't continue without me unless they walk.

MAXINE: They're still blowin' that horn.

SHANNON: Fantastic. I can't lose this party. Blake Tours has put me on probation because I had a bad party last month that tried to get me sacked and I am now on probation with Blake Tours. If I lose this party I'll be sacked for sure . . . Ah, my God, are they still all in the bus? [*He heaves himself off the steps and staggers back to the path, dividing the foliage to look down it, then shouts*.] Hank! Get them out of the busssss! Bring them up heeee-re!

HANK'S VOICE [*from below*]: They wanta go back in tooooooowwww-n.

SHANNON: They *can't* go back in toooowwwwn!—Whew— Five years ago this summer I was conducting round-the-world tours for Cook's. Exclusive groups of retired Wall Street financiers. We traveled in fleets of Pierce Arrows and Hispano Suizas.—Are they getting out of the bus?

MAXINE: You're going to pieces, are you?

SHANNON: No! Gone! Gone! [*He rises and shouts down the hill again.*] Hank! come up here! Come on up here a minute! I wanta talk to you about this situation!—Incredible, fantastic . . . [*He drops back on the steps, his head falling into his hands.*]

MAXINE: They're not getting out of the bus.—Shannon . . . you're not in a nervous condition to cope with this party, Shannon, so let them go and you stay.

SHANNON: You know my situation: I lose this job, what's next? There's nothing lower than Blake Tours, Maxine honey. —Are they getting out of the bus? Are they getting out of it now?

MAXINE: Man's comin' up the hill.

SHANNON: Aw. Hank. You gotta help me with him.

MAXINE: I'll give him a rum-coco.

[HANK *comes grinning onto the verandah.*]

HANK: Shannon, them ladies are not gonna come up here, so you better come on back to the bus.

SHANNON: Fantastic.—I'm not going down to the bus and I've got the ignition key to the bus in my pocket. It's going to stay in my pocket for the next three days.

HANK: You can't get away with that, Shannon. Hell, they'll
walk back to town if you don't give up the bus key.

SHANNON: They'd drop like flies from sunstrokes on that
road. . . . Fantastic, absolutely fantastic . . . [*Panting and
sweating, he drops a hand on* HANK's *shoulder.*] Hank, I want
your co-operation. Can I have it? Because when you're out
with a difficult party like this, the tour conductor—me—and
the guide—you—have got to stick together to control the
situations as they come up against us. It's a test of strength
between two men, in this case, and a busload of old wet *hens!*
You know that, don't you?

HANK: Well. . . . [*He chuckles.*] There's this kid that's crying on the back seat all the time, and that's what's rucked up
the deal. Hell, I don't know if you did or you didn't, but they
all think that you did 'cause the kid keeps crying.

SHANNON: *Hank? Look!* I don't care what they think. A tour
conducted by T. Lawrence Shannon is in his charge, completely—where to go, when to go, every detail of it. Otherwise I resign. So go on back down there and get them out of
that bus before they suffocate in it. Haul them out by force if
necessary and herd them up here. Hear me? Don't give me
any argument about it. Mrs. Faulk, honey? Give him a menu,
give him one of your sample menus to show the ladies. She's
got a Chinaman cook here, you won't believe the menu. The
cook's from Shanghai, handled the kitchen at an exclusive club
there. I got him here for her, and he's a bug, a fanatic about—
whew!—continental cuisine . . . can even make beef Stroga-
noff and thermidor dishes. Mrs. Faulk, honey? Hand him one
of those—whew!—one of those fantastic sample menus.
[MAXINE *chuckles, as if perpetrating a practical joke, as she
hands him a sheet of paper.*] Thanks. Now, here. Go on back
down there and show them this fantastic menu. Describe the
view from the hill, and . . . [HANK *accepts the menu with a
chuckling shake of the head.*] And have a cold Carta Blanca
and. . . .

HANK: You better go down with me.

SHANNON: I can't leave this verandah for at least forty-eight hours. *What in blazes is this?* A little animated cartoon by Hieronymus Bosch?

[*The German family which is staying at the hotel, the* FAHRENKOPFS, *their daughter and son-in-law, suddenly make a startling, dreamlike entrance upon the scene. They troop around the verandah, then turn down into the jungle path. They are all dressed in the minimal concession to decency and all are pink and gold like baroque cupids in various sizes —Rubenesque, splendidly physical. The bride,* HILDA, *walks astride a big inflated rubber horse which has an ecstatic smile and great winking eyes. She shouts "Horsey, horsey, giddap!" as she waddles astride it, followed by her Wagnerian-tenor bridegroom,* WOLFGANG, *and her father,* HERR FAHRENKOPF, *a tank manufacturer from Frankfurt. He is carrying a portable shortwave radio, which is tuned in to the crackle and guttural voices of a German broadcast reporting the Battle of Britain.* FRAU FAHRENKOPF, *bursting with rich, healthy fat and carrying a basket of food for a picnic at the beach, brings up the rear. They begin to sing a Nazi marching song.*]

SHANNON: Aw—Nazis. How come there's so many of them down here lately?

MAXINE: Mexico's the front door to South America—and the back door to the States, that's why.

SHANNON: Aw, and you're setting yourself up here as a receptionist at both doors, now that Fred's dead? [MAXINE *comes over and sits down on him in the hammock.*] Get off my pelvis before you crack it. If you want to crack something, crack some ice for my forehead. [*She removes a chunk of ice from her glass and massages his forehead with it.*]—Ah, God. . . .

MAXINE [*chuckling*]: Ha, so you took the young chick and the old hens are squawking about it, Shannon?

SHANNON: The kid asked for it, no kidding, but she's seventeen—less, a month less'n seventeen. So it's serious, it's very serious, because the kid is not just emotionally precocious, she's a musical prodigy, too.

MAXINE: What's that got to do with it?

SHANNON: Here's what it's got to do with it, she's traveling under the wing, the military escort, of this, this—butch vocal teacher who organizes little community sings in the bus. Ah, God! I'm surprised they're not singing now, they must've already suffocated. Or they'd be singing some morale-boosting number like "She's a Jolly Good Fellow" or "Pop Goes the Weasel."—Oh, God. . . . [MAXINE *chuckles up and down the scale.*] And each night after supper, after the complaints about the supper and the check-up on the checks by the math instructor, and the vomiting of the supper by several ladies, who have inspected the kitchen—then the kid, the canary, will give a vocal recital. She opens her mouth and out flies Carrie Jacobs Bond or Ethelbert Nevin. I mean after a day of one indescribable torment after another, such as three blowouts, and a leaking radiator in Tierra Caliente. . . . [*He sits up slowly in the hammock as these recollections gather force.*] And an evening climb up sierras, through torrents of rain, around hairpin turns over gorges and chasms measureless to man, and with a Thermos-jug under the driver's seat which the Baptist College ladies think is filled with icewater but which I know is filled with iced tequila—I mean after such a day has finally come to a close, the musical prodigy, Miss Charlotte Goodall, right after supper, before there's a chance to escape, will give a heartbreaking and earsplitting rendition of Carrie Jacobs Bond's "End of a Perfect Day"—with absolutely no humor. . . .

MAXINE: Hah!

SHANNON: Yeah, "Hah!" Last night—no, night before last, the bus burned out its brake linings in Chilpancingo. This town has a hotel . . . this hotel has a piano, which hasn't been tuned since they shot Maximilian. This Texas songbird opens her mouth and out flies "I Love You Truly," and it flies straight at *me*, with *gestures,* all right at *me,* till her chaperone, this Diesel-driven vocal instructor of hers, slams the piano lid down and hauls her out of the mess hall. But as she's hauled out Miss Bird-Girl opens her mouth and out flies, "Larry, Larry, I love you, I love you truly!" That night, when I went to my room, I found that I had a roommate.

MAXINE: The musical prodigy had moved in with you?

SHANNON: The *spook* had moved in with me. In that hot room with one bed, the width of an ironing board and about as hard, the spook was up there on it, sweating, stinking, grinning up at me.

MAXINE: Aw, the spook. [*She chuckles.*] So you've got the spook with you again.

SHANNON: That's right, he's the only passenger that got off the bus with me, honey.

MAXINE: Is he here now?

SHANNON: Not far.

MAXINE: On the verandah?

SHANNON: He might be on the other side of the verandah. Oh, he's around somewhere, but he's like the Sioux Indians in the Wild West fiction, he doesn't attack before sundown, he's an after-sundown shadow. . . .

[SHANNON *wriggles out of the hammock as the bus horn gives one last, long protesting blast.*]

MAXINE:
> I have a little shadow
> That goes in and out with me,
> And what can be the use of him
> Is more than I can see.
>
> He's very, very like me,
> From his heels up to his head,
> And he always hops before me
> When I hop into my bed.

SHANNON: That's the truth. He sure hops in the bed with me.

MAXINE: When you're sleeping alone, or . . . ?

SHANNON: I haven't slept in three nights.

MAXINE: Aw, you will tonight, baby.

[*The bus horn sounds again.* SHANNON *rises and squints down the hill at the bus.*]

SHANNON: How long's it take to sweat the faculty of a Baptist Female College out of a bus that's parked in the sun when it's a hundred degrees in the shade?

MAXINE: They're staggering out of it now.

SHANNON: Yeah, I've won *this* round, I reckon. What're they doing down there, can you see?

MAXINE: They're crowding around your pal Hank.

SHANNON: Tearing him to pieces?

MAXINE: One of them's slapped him, he's ducked back into the bus, and she is starting up here.

SHANNON: Oh, Great Caesar's ghost, it's the butch vocal teacher.

MISS FELLOWES [*in a strident voice, from below*]: Shannon! Shannon!

SHANNON: For God's sake, help me with her.

MAXINE: You know I'll help you, baby, but why don't you lay off the young ones and cultivate an interest in normal grown-up women?

MISS FELLOWES [*her voice coming nearer*]: Shannon!

SHANNON [*shouting down the hill*]: Come on up, Miss Fellowes, everything's fixed. [*to* MAXINE] Oh, God, here she comes chargin' up the hill like a bull elephant on a rampage!

[MISS FELLOWES *thrashes through the foliage at the top of the jungle path*.]

SHANNON: Miss Fellowes, never do that! Not at high noon in a tropical country in summer. Never charge up a hill like you were leading a troop of cavalry attacking an almost impregnable. . . .

MISS FELLOWES [*panting and furious*]: I don't want advice or instructions, I want the *bus key!*

SHANNON: Mrs. Faulk, this is Miss Judith Fellowes.

MISS FELLOWES: Is this man making a deal with you?

MAXINE: I don't know what you—

MISS FELLOWES: Is this man getting a *kickback* out of you?

MAXINE: Nobody gets any kickback out of me. I turn away more people than—

MISS FELLOWES [*cutting in*]: This isn't the Ambos Mundos. It says in the brochure that in Puerto Barrio we stay at the Ambos Mundos in the heart of the city.

SHANNON: Yes, on the plaza—tell her about the plaza.

MAXINE: What about the plaza?

SHANNON: It's hot, noisy, stinking, swarming with flies. Pariah dogs dying in the—

MISS FELLOWES: How is this place better?

SHANNON: The view from this verandah is equal and I think better than the view from Victoria Peak in Hong Kong, the view from the roof-terrace of the Sultan's palace in—

MISS FELLOWES [*cutting in*]: I want the view of a clean bed, a bathroom with plumbing that works, and food that is eatable and digestible and not contaminated by filthy—

SHANNON: *Miss Fellowes!*

MISS FELLOWES: Take your hand off my arm.

SHANNON: Look at this sample menu. The cook is a Chinese imported from Shanghai by *me!* Sent here by *me,* year before last, in nineteen thirty-eight. He was the chef at the Royal Colonial Club in—

MISS FELLOWES [*cutting in*]: You got a telephone here?

MAXINE: Sure, in the office.

MISS FELLOWES: I want to use it— I'll call collect. Where's the office?

MAXINE [*to* PANCHO]: Llévala al teléfono!

[*With* PANCHO *showing her the way,* MISS FELLOWES *stalks off around the verandah to the office.* SHANNON *falls back, sighing desperately, against the verandah wall.*]

MAXINE: Hah!

SHANNON: Why did you have to . . . ?

MAXINE: Huh?

SHANNON: Come out looking like this! For you it's funny but for me it's. . . .

MAXINE: This is how I *look*. What's wrong with how I *look?*

SHANNON: I told you to button your shirt. Are you so proud of your boobs that you won't button your shirt up?—Go in the office and see if she's calling Blake Tours to get me fired.

MAXINE: She better not unless she pays for the call.

[*She goes around the turn of the verandah.*]

[MISS HANNAH JELKES *appears below the verandah steps and*

stops short as SHANNON *turns to the wall, pounding his fist against it with a sobbing sound in his throat.*]

HANNAH: Excuse me.

[SHANNON *looks down at her, dazed.* HANNAH *is remarkable-looking—ethereal, almost ghostly. She suggests a Gothic cathedral image of a medieval saint, but animated. She could be thirty, she could be forty: she is totally feminine and yet androgynous-looking—almost timeless. She is wearing a cotton print dress and has a bag slung on a strap over her shoulder.*]

HANNAH: Is this the Costa Verde Hotel?

SHANNON [*suddenly pacified by her appearance*]: Yes. Yes, it is.

HANNAH: Are you . . . you're not, the hotel manager, are you?

SHANNON: No. She'll be right back.

HANNAH: Thank you. Do you have any idea if they have two vacancies here? One for myself and one for my grandfather who's waiting in a taxi down there on the road. I didn't want to bring him up the hill—till I'd made sure they have rooms for us first.

SHANNON: Well, there's plenty of room here out-of-season— like now.

HANNAH: Good! Wonderful! I'll get him out of the taxi.

SHANNON: Need any help?

HANNAH: No, thank you. We'll make it all right.

[*She gives him a pleasant nod and goes back off down the path through the rain forest. A coconut plops to the ground; a parrot screams at a distance.* SHANNON *drops into the hammock and stretches out. Then* MAXINE *reappears.*]

SHANNON: How about the call? Did she make a phone call?

MAXINE: She called a judge in Texas—Blowing Rock, Texas. Collect.

SHANNON: She's trying to get me fired and she is also trying to pin on me a rape charge, a charge of statutory rape.

MAXINE: What's "statutory rape"? I've never known what that was.

SHANNON: That's when a man is seduced by a girl under twenty. [*She chuckles.*] It's not funny, Maxine honey.

MAXINE: Why do you want the young ones—or think that you do?

SHANNON: I don't want any, any—regardless of age.

MAXINE: Then why do you take them, Shannon? [*He swallows but does not answer.*]—Huh, Shannon.

SHANNON: People need human contact, Maxine honey.

MAXINE: What size shoe do you wear?

SHANNON: I don't get the point of that question.

MAXINE: These shoes are shot and if I remember correctly, you travel with only one pair. Fred's estate included one good pair of shoes and your feet look about his size.

SHANNON: I loved ole Fred but I don't want to fill his shoes, honey.

[*She has removed* SHANNON'S *beat-up, English-made oxfords.*]

MAXINE: Your socks are shot. Fred's socks would fit you, too, Shannon. [*She opens his collar.*] Aw-aw, I see you got on your gold cross. That's a bad sign, it means you're thinking again about goin' back to the Church.

SHANNON: This is my last tour, Maxine. I wrote my old Bishop this morning a complete confession and a complete capitulation.

[*She takes a letter from his damp shirt pocket.*]

MAXINE: If this is the letter, baby, you've sweated through it, so the old bugger couldn't read it even if you mailed it to him this time.

[*She has started around the verandah, and goes off as* HANK *reappears up the hill-path, mopping his face.* SHANNON'S *relaxed position in the hammock aggravates* HANK *sorely.*]

HANK: Will you get your ass out of that hammock?

SHANNON: No, I will not.

HANK: Shannon, git out of that hammock! [*He kicks at* SHANNON'S *hips in the hammock.*]

SHANNON: Hank, if you can't function under rough circumstances, you are in the wrong racket, man. I gave you instructions, the instructions were simple. I said get them out of the bus and. . . .

[MAXINE *comes back with a kettle of water, a towel and other shaving equipment.*]

HANK: Out of the hammock, Shannon! [*He kicks* SHANNON *again, harder.*]

SHANNON [*warningly*]: That's enough, Hank. A little familiarity goes a long way, but not as far as you're going. [MAXINE *starts lathering his face.*] What's this, what are you . . . ?

MAXINE: Haven't you ever had a shave-and-haircut by a lady barber?

HANK: The kid has gone into hysterics.

MAXINE: Hold still, Shannon.

SHANNON: Hank, hysteria is a natural phenomenon, the common denominator of the female nature. It's the big female weapon, and ~~the test of a man is his ability to cope~~ with it, and I can't believe you can't. If I believed that you couldn't, I would not be able—

MAXINE: Hold still!

SHANNON: I'm holding still. [*to* HANK] No, I wouldn't be able to take you out with me again. So go on back down there and—

HANK: You want me to go back down there and tell them you're getting a shave up here in a hammock?

MAXINE: Tell them that Reverend Larry is going back to the Church so they can go back to the Female College in Texas.

HANK: I want another beer.

MAXINE: Help yourself, piggly-wiggly, the cooler's in my office right around there. [*She points around the corner of the verandah.*]

SHANNON [*as* HANK *goes off*]: It's horrible how you got to bluff and keep bluffing even when hollering "Help!" is all you're up to, Maxine. *You cut me!*

MAXINE: You didn't hold still.

SHANNON: Just trim the beard a little.

MAXINE: I know. Baby, tonight we'll go night-swimming, whether it storms or not.

SHANNON: Ah, God. . . .

MAXINE: The Mexican kids are wonderful night-swimmers. . . . Hah, when I found 'em they were taking the two-hundred-foot dives off the Quebrada, but the Quebrada Hotel kicked 'em out for being over-attentive to the lady guests there. That's how I got hold of them.

SHANNON: Maxine, you're bigger than life and twice as unnatural, honey.

MAXINE: No one's bigger than life-size, Shannon, or even ever that big, except maybe Fred. [*She shouts "Fred?" and gets a faint answering echo from an adjoining hill.*] Little Sir Echo is all that answers for him now, Shannon, but. . . . [*She pats some bay rum on his face.*] Dear old Fred was always a mystery to me. He was so patient and tolerant with me that it was insulting to me. A man and a woman have got to challenge each other, y'know what I mean. I mean I hired those diving-boys from the Quebrada six months before Fred died, and did he care? Did he give a damn when I started night-swimming with them? No. He'd go night-*fishing*, all night, and when I got up the next day, he'd be preparing to go out fishing again, but he just caught the fish and threw them back in the sea.

[HANK *returns and sits drinking his beer on the steps.*]

SHANNON: The mystery of old Fred was simple. He was just cool and decent, that's all the mystery of him. . . . Get your pair of night-swimmers to grab my ladies' luggage out of the bus before the vocal-teacher gets off the phone and stops them.

MAXINE [*shouting*]: Pedro! Pancho! Muchachos! Trae las maletas al anejo! Pronto! [*The Mexican boys start down the path.* MAXINE *sits in the hammock beside* SHANNON.] You I'll put in Fred's old room, next to me.

SHANNON: You want me in his socks and his shoes and in his room next to *you*? [*He stares at her with a shocked surmise of her intentions toward him, then flops back down in the hammock with an incredulous laugh.*] Oh no, honey. I've just been hanging on till I could get in this hammock on this verandah over the rain forest and the still-water beach, that's all that can pull me through this last tour in a condition to go back to my . . . original . . . vocation.

MAXINE: Hah, you still have some rational moments when you face the fact that churchgoers don't go to church to hear atheistical sermons.

SHANNON: Goddamit, I never preached an atheistical sermon in a church in my life, and. . . .

[MISS FELLOWES *has charged out of the office and rounds the verandah to bear down on* SHANNON *and* MAXINE, *who jumps up out of the hammock.*]

MISS FELLOWES: I've completed my call, which I made collect to Texas.

[MAXINE *shrugs, going by her around the verandah.* MISS FELLOWES *runs across the verandah.*]

SHANNON [*sitting up in the hammock*]: Excuse me, Miss Fellowes, for not getting out of this hammock, but I . . . Miss Fellowes? Please sit down a minute, I want to confess something to you.

MISS FELLOWES: That ought to be int'restin'! *What?*

SHANNON: Just that—well, like everyone else, at some point or other in life, my life has cracked up on me.

MISS FELLOWES: How does that compensate *us?*

SHANNON: I don't think I know what you mean by *compensate*, Miss Fellowes. [*He props himself up and gazes at her with the gentlest bewilderment, calculated to melt a heart of stone.*] I mean I've just confessed to you that I'm at the end of my rope, and you say, "How does that compensate *us?*" Please, Miss Fellowes. Don't make me feel that any adult human being puts personal compensation before the dreadful, bare fact of a man at the end of his rope who still has to try to go on, to continue, as if he'd never been better or stronger in his whole existence. No, don't do that, it would. . . .

MISS FELLOWES: It would *what?*

SHANNON: Shake if not shatter everything left of my faith in essential . . . human . . . *goodness!*

MAXINE [*returning, with a pair of socks*]: Hah!

MISS FELLOWES: Can you sit there, I mean lie there—yeah, I mean *lie* there . . . ! and talk to me about—

MAXINE: Hah!

MISS FELLOWES: "Essential human goodness"? Why, just plain human decency is beyond your imagination, Shannon, so lie there, lie there and *lie* there, we're *going!*

SHANNON [*rising from the hammock*]: Miss Fellowes, I thought that I was conducting this party, not you.

MISS FELLOWES: You? You just now *admitted* you're incompetent, as well as. . . .

MAXINE: Hah.

SHANNON: Maxine, will you—

MISS FELLOWES [*cutting in with cold, righteous fury*]: *Shannon,* we girls have worked and slaved all year at Baptist Female College for this Mexican tour, and the tour is a cheat!

SHANNON [*to himself*]: Fantastic!

MISS FELLOWES: Yes, *cheat!* You haven't stuck to the schedule and you haven't stuck to the itinerary advertised in the brochure which Blake Tours put out. Now either Blake Tours is cheating us or you are cheating Blake Tours, and I'm putting wheels in motion—I don't care *what* it costs me —I'm. . . .

SHANNON: Oh, Miss Fellowes, isn't it just as plain to you as it is to me that your hysterical insults, which are not at all easy for any born and bred gentleman to accept, are not . . . *motivated, provoked* by . . . anything as *trivial* as the, the . . . the motivations that you're, you're . . . *ascribing* them to? Now can't we talk about the *real, true* cause of. . . .

MISS FELLOWES: Cause of *what?*

[CHARLOTTE GOODALL *appears at the top of the hill.*]

SHANNON: —Cause of your *rage* Miss Fellowes, your—

MISS FELLOWES: *Charlotte!* Stay down the hill in the *bus!*

CHARLOTTE: Judy, they're—

MISS FELLOWES: *Obey me! Down!*

[CHARLOTTE *retreats from view like a well-trained dog.* MISS FELLOWES *charges back to* SHANNON *who has gotten out of the hammock. He places a conciliatory hand on her arm.*]

MISS FELLOWES: *Take your hand off my arm!*

MAXINE: Hah!

SHANNON: *Fantastic.* Miss Fellowes, please! No more shouting? Please? Now I really must ask you to let this party of ladies come up here and judge the accommodations for themselves and compare them with what they saw passing through town. Miss Fellowes, there is such a thing as charm and beauty in some places, as much as there's nothing but dull, ugly imitation of highway motels in Texas and—

[MISS FELLOWES *charges over to the path to see if* CHARLOTTE *has obeyed her.* SHANNON *follows, still propitiatory.* MAXINE *says* "Hah," *but she gives him an affectionate little pat as he goes by her. He pushes her hand away as he continues his appeal to* MISS FELLOWES.]

MISS FELLOWES: I've taken a look at those rooms and they'd make a room at the "Y" look like a suite at the Ritz.

SHANNON: Miss Fellowes, I am employed by Blake Tours and so I'm not in a position to tell you quite frankly what mistakes they've made in their advertising brochure. They just don't know Mexico. I do. I know it as well as I know five out of all six continents on the—

MISS FELLOWES: *Continent! Mexico?* You never even studied geography if you—

SHANNON: My degree from Sewanee is *Doctor* of *Divinity*, but for the past ten years geography's been my *specialty*, Miss Fellowes, honey! Name any tourist agency I haven't worked for! You couldn't! I'm only, now, with Blake Tours because I—

MISS FELLOWES: Because you *what?* Couldn't keep your hands off innocent, under-age girls in your—

SHANNON: Now, Miss Fellowes. . . . [*He touches her arm again.*]

MISS FELLOWES: Take your hand off my arm!

SHANNON: For days I've known you were furious and unhappy, but—

MISS FELLOWES: *Oh!* You think it's just *me* that's unhappy! Hauled in that stifling bus over the byways, off the highways, shook up and bumped up so you could get your rake-off, is that what you—

SHANNON: What I know is, all I know is, that you are the *leader* of the *insurrection!*

MISS FELLOWES: All of the girls in this party have dysentery!

SHANNON: That you can't hold me to blame for.

MISS FELLOWES: I *do* hold you to blame for it.

SHANNON: Before we entered Mexico, at New Laredo, Texas, I called you ladies together in the depot on the Texas side of the border and I passed out mimeographed sheets of instructions on what to eat and what *not* to eat, what to drink, what *not* to drink in the—

MISS FELLOWES: It's not *what* we ate but *where* we ate that gave us dysentery!

SHANNON [*shaking his head like a metronome*]: It is not dysentery.

MISS FELLOWES: The result of eating in places that would
be condemned by the Board of Health in—

SHANNON: Now wait a minute—

MISS FELLOWES: For disregarding all rules of sanitation.

SHANNON: It is not dysentery, it is not amoebic, it's nothing
at all but—

MAXINE: Montezuma's Revenge! That's what we call it.

SHANNON: I even passed out pills. I passed out bottles of
Enteroviaform because I knew that some of you ladies would
rather be victims of Montezuma's Revenge than spend cinco
centavos on bottled water in stations.

MISS FELLOWES: You sold those pills at a profit of fifty
cents per bottle.

MAXINE: Hah-hah! [*She knocks off the end of a coconut
with the machete, preparing a rum-coco.*]

SHANNON: Now fun is fun, Miss Fellowes, but an accusation
like that—

MISS FELLOWES: I *priced* them in *pharmacies,* because I
suspected that—

SHANNON: Miss Fellowes, I am a gentleman, and as a gentleman I can't be insulted like this. I mean I can't accept insults of that kind even from a member of a tour that I am
conducting. And, Miss Fellowes, I think you might also remember, you might try to remember, that you're speaking to
an ordained minister of the Church.

MISS FELLOWES: *De*-frocked! But still trying to pass himself off as a minister!

MAXINE: How about a rum-coco? We give a complimentary
rum-coco to all our guests here. [*Her offer is apparently un-
heard. She shrugs and drinks the rum-coco herself.*]

SHANNON: —Miss Fellowes? In every party there is always one individual that's discontented, that is not satisfied with all I do to make the tour more . . . unique—to make it different from the ordinary, to give it a personal thing, the Shannon touch.

MISS FELLOWES: The gyp touch, the touch of a defrocked minister.

SHANNON: Miss Fellowes, don't, don't, don't . . . do what . . . you're doing! [*He is on the verge of hysteria, he makes some incoherent sounds, gesticulates with clenched fits, then stumbles wildly across the verandah and leans panting for breath against a post.*] Don't! Break! *Human! Pride!*

VOICE FROM DOWN THE HILL [*a very Texan accent*]: Judy? They're taking our luggage!

MISS FELLOWES [*shouting down the hill*]: Girls! Girls! Don't let those boys touch your luggage. Don't let them bring your luggage in this dump!

GIRL'S VOICE [*from below*]: Judy! We can't stop them!

MAXINE: Those kids don't understand English.

MISS FELLOWES [*wild with rage*]: Will you please tell those boys to take that luggage back down to the bus? [*She calls to the party below again.*] Girls! Hold onto your luggage, don't let them take it away! We're going to drive back to A-cap-ul-co! *You hear?*

GIRL'S VOICE: Judy, they want a swim, first!

MISS FELLOWES: I'll be right back. [*She rushes off, shouting at the Mexican boys.*] You! Boys! Muchachos! *You carry that luggage back down!*

[*The voices continue, fading.* SHANNON *moves brokenly across the verandah.* MAXINE *shakes her head.*]

MAXINE: Shannon, give 'em the bus key and let 'em go.

SHANNON: And me do what?

MAXINE: Stay here.

SHANNON: In Fred's old bedroom—yeah, in Fred's old bedroom.

MAXINE: You could do worse.

SHANNON: Could I? Well, then, I'll do worse, I'll . . . do worse.

MAXINE: Aw now, baby.

SHANNON: If I could do worse, I'll do worse. . . . [*He grips the section of railing by the verandah steps and stares with wide, lost eyes. His chest heaves like a spent runner's and he is bathed in sweat.*]

MAXINE: Give me that ignition key. I'll take it down to the driver while you bathe and rest and have a rum-coco, baby.

[SHANNON *simply shakes his head slightly. Harsh bird cries sound in the rain forest. Voices are heard on the path.*]

HANNAH: Nonno, you've lost your sun glasses.

NONNO: No. Took them off. No sun.

[HANNAH *appears at the top of the path, pushing her grandfather,* NONNO, *in a wheelchair. He is a very old man but has a powerful voice for his age and always seems to be shouting something of importance.* NONNO *is a poet and a showman. There is a good kind of pride and he has it, carrying it like a banner wherever he goes. He is immaculately dressed—a linen suit, white as his thick poet's hair; a black string tie; and he is holding a black cane with a gold crook.*]

NONNO: Which way is the sea?

HANNAH: Right down below the hill, Nonno. [*He turns in

the wheelchair and raises a hand to shield his eyes.] We can't
see it from here. [*The old man is deaf, and she shouts to make
him hear.*]

NONNO: I can feel it and smell it. [*A murmur of wind
sweeps through the rain forest.*] It's the cradle of life. [*He is
shouting, too.*] Life began in the sea.

MAXINE: These two with your party?

SHANNON: No.

MAXINE: They look like a pair of loonies.

SHANNON: Shut up.

[SHANNON *looks at* HANNAH *and* NONNO *steadily, with a relief of tension almost like that of someone going under
hypnosis. The old man still squints down the path, blindly,
but* HANNAH *is facing the verandah with a proud person's
hope of acceptance when it is desperately needed.*]

HANNAH: How do you do.

MAXINE: Hello.

HANNAH: Have you ever tried pushing a gentleman in a
wheelchair uphill through a rain forest?

MAXINE: Nope, and I wouldn't even try it *downhill.*

HANNAH: Well, now that we've made it, I don't regret the
effort. What a view for a painter! [*She looks about her, panting, digging into her shoulder-bag for a handkerchief, aware
that her face is flushed and sweating.*] They told me in town
that this was the ideal place for a painter, and they weren't
—*whew*—exaggerating!

SHANNON: You've got a scratch on your forehead.

HANNAH: Oh, is that what I felt.

SHANNON: Better put iodine on it.

HANNAH: Yes, I'll attend to that—*whew*—later, thank you.

MAXINE: Anything I can do for you?

HANNAH: I'm looking for the manager of the hotel.

MAXINE: Me—speaking.

HANNAH: Oh, *you're* the manager, *good!* How do you do, I'm Hannah Jelkes, Mrs. . . .

MAXINE: Faulk, Maxine Faulk. What can I do for you folks? [*Her tone indicates no desire to do anything for them.*]

HANNAH [*turning quickly to her grandfather*]: Nonno, the manager is a *lady* from the *States.*

[NONNO *lifts a branch of wild orchids from his lap, ceremonially, with the instinctive gallantry of his kind.*]

NONNO [*shouting*]: Give the lady these—botanical curiosities!—you picked on the way up.

HANNAH: I believe they're wild orchids, isn't that what they are?

SHANNON: Laelia tibicina.

HANNAH: Oh!

NONNO: But tell her, Hannah, tell her to keep them in the icebox till after dark, they draw bees in the sun! [*He rubs a sting on his chin with a rueful chuckle.*]

MAXINE: Are you all looking for rooms here?

HANNAH: Yes, we are, but we've come without reservations.

MAXINE: Well, honey, the Costa Verde is closed in September—except for a few special guests, so. . . .

SHANNON: They're special guests, for God's sake.

MAXINE: I thought you said they didn't come with your party.

HANNAH: Please let us be special guests.

MAXINE: *Watch out!*

[NONNO *has started struggling out of the wheelchair.* SHANNON *rushes over to keep him from falling.* HANNAH *has started toward him, too, then seeing that* SHANNON *has caught him, she turns back to* MAXINE.]

HANNAH: In twenty-five years of travel this is the first time we've ever arrived at a place without advance reservations.

MAXINE: Honey, that old man ought to be in a hospital.

HANNAH: Oh, no, no, he just sprained his ankle a little in Taxco this morning. He just needs a good night's rest, he'll be on his feet tomorrow. His recuperative powers are absolutely amazing for someone who is ninety-seven years *young*.

SHANNON: Easy, Grampa. Hang on. [*He is supporting the old man up to the verandah.*] Two steps. One! Two! Now you've made it, Grampa.

[NONNO *keeps chuckling breathlessly as* SHANNON *gets him onto the verandah and into a wicker rocker.*]

HANNAH [*breaking in quickly*]: I can't tell you how much I appreciate your taking us in here now. It's—providential.

MAXINE: Well, I can't send that old man back down the hill—right now—but like I told you the Costa Verde's practically closed in September. I just take in a few folks as a special accommodation and we operate on a special basis this month.

NONNO [*cutting in abruptly and loudly*]: Hannah, tell the lady that my perambulator is temporary. I will soon be ready

to crawl and then to toddle and before long I will be leaping
around here like an—old—mountain—goat, ha-ha-ha-ha. . . .

HANNAH: Yes, I explained that, Grandfather.

NONNO: I don't like being on wheels.

HANNAH: Yes, my grandfather feels that the decline of the
western world began with the invention of the wheel. [*She
laughs heartily, but* MAXINE's *look is unresponsive.*]

NONNO: And tell the manager . . . the, uh, lady . . . that I
know some hotels don't want to take dogs, cats or monkeys
and some don't even solicit the patronage of infants in their
late nineties who arrive in perambulators with flowers instead
of rattles . . . [*He chuckles with a sort of fearful, slightly
mad quality.* HANNAH *perhaps has the impulse to clap a hand
over his mouth at this moment but must stand there smiling
and smiling and smiling.*] . . . and a brandy flask instead of a
teething ring, but tell her that these, uh, concessions to man's
seventh age are only temporary, and. . . .

HANNAH: Nonno, I told her the wheelchair's because of a
sprained ankle, Nonno!

SHANNON [*to himself*]: Fantastic.

NONNO: And after my siesta, I'll wheel it back down the hill,
I'll kick it back down the hill, right into the sea, and tell her.
. . .

HANNAH: Yes? What, Nonno? [*She has stopped smiling now.
Her tone and her look are frankly desperate.*] What shall I
tell her now, Nonno?

NONNO: Tell her that if she'll forgive my disgraceful lon-
gevity and this . . . temporary decrepitude . . . I will present
her with the last signed . . . compitty [*he means* "copy"] of
my first volume of verse, published in . . . when, Hannah?

HANNAH [*hopelessly*]: The day that President Ulysses S.
Grant was inaugurated, Nonno.

NONNO: *Morning Trumpet!* Where is it—you have it, give it to her right now.

HANNAH: Later, a little later! [*Then she turns to* MAXINE *and* SHANNON.] My grandfather is the poet Jonathan Coffin. He is ninety-seven years *young* and will be ninety-eight years *young* the fifth of next month, October.

MAXINE: Old folks are remarkable, yep. The office phone's ringing—excuse me, I'll be right back. [*She goes around the verandah.*]

NONNO: Did I talk too much?

HANNAH [*quietly, to* SHANNON]: I'm afraid that he did. I don't think she's going to take us.

SHANNON: She'll take you. Don't worry about it.

HANNAH: Nobody would take us in town, and if we don't get in here, I would have to wheel him back down through the rain forest, and then *what,* then *where?* There would just be the road, and no direction to move in, except out to sea—and I doubt that we could make it divide before us.

SHANNON: That won't be necessary. I have a little influence with the patrona.

HANNAH: Oh, then, do use it, please. Her eyes said *no* in big blue capital letters.

[SHANNON *pours some water from a pitcher on the verandah and hands it to the old man.*]

NONNO: What is this—libation?

SHANNON: Some icewater, Grampa.

HANNAH: Oh, that's kind of you. Thank you. I'd better give him a couple of salt tablets to wash down with it. [*Briskly she removes a bottle from her shoulder-bag.*] Won't you have some? I see you're perspiring, too. You have to be careful not

to become dehydrated in the hot seasons under the Tropic of
Cancer.

SHANNON [*pouring another glass of water*]: Are you a little
financially dehydrated, too?

HANNAH: That's right. Bone-dry, and I think the patrona
suspects it. It's a logical assumption, since I pushed him up
here myself, and the patrona has the look of a very logical
woman. I am sure she knows that we couldn't afford to hire
the taxi driver to help us up here.

MAXINE [*calling from the back*]: Pancho?

HANNAH: A woman's practicality when she's managing
something is harder than a man's for another woman to
cope with, so if you have influence with her, please do use
it. Please try to convince her that my grandfather will be
on his feet tomorrow, if not tonight, and with any luck
whatsoever, the money situation will be solved just as quickly.
Oh, here she comes back, do help us!

[*Involuntarily,* HANNAH *seizes hold of* SHANNON'S *wrist as*
MAXINE *stalks back onto the verandah, still shouting for*
PANCHO. *The Mexican boy reappears, sucking a juicy
peeled mango—its juice running down his chin onto his
throat.*]

MAXINE: Pancho, run down to the beach and tell Herr
Fahrenkopf that the German Embassy's waiting on the phone
for him. [PANCHO *stares at her blankly until she repeats the
order in Spanish.*] Dile a Herr Fahrenkopf que la embajada
alemana lo llama al teléfono. Corre, corre! [PANCHO *starts
indolently down the path, still sucking noisily on the mango.*]
I said *run!* Corre, corre! [*He goes into a leisurely loping pace
and disappears through the foliage.*]

HANNAH: What graceful people they are!

MAXINE: Yeah, they're graceful like cats, and just as dependable, too.

HANNAH: Shall we, uh, . . . *register* now?

MAXINE: You all can register later but I'll have to collect six dollars from you first if you want to put your names in the pot for supper. That's how I've got to operate here out of season.

HANNAH: Six? Dollars?

MAXINE: Yeah, three each. In season we operate on the continental plan but out of season like this we change to the modified American plan.

HANNAH: Oh, what is the, uh . . . modification of it? [*She gives* SHANNON *a quick glance of appeal as she stalls for time, but his attention has turned inward as the bus horn blows down the hill.*]

MAXINE: Just two meals are included instead of all three.

HANNAH [*moving closer to* SHANNON *and raising her voice*]: Breakfast and dinner?

MAXINE: A continental breakfast and a cold lunch.

SHANNON [*aside*]: Yeah, very cold—cracked ice—if you crack it yourself.

HANNAH [*reflectively*]: Not dinner.

MAXINE: No! Not dinner.

HANNAH: Oh, I see, uh, but . . . we, uh, operate on a special basis ourselves. I'd better explain it to you.

MAXINE: How do you mean "operate,"—on what "basis"?

HANNAH: Here's our card. I think you may have heard of us. [*She presents the card to* MAXINE.] We've had a good many write-ups. My grandfather is the oldest living and practicing poet. *And* he gives recitations. I . . . paint . . . water colors and I'm a "quick sketch artist." We travel together. We pay our way as we go by my grandfather's recitations and the sale of my water colors and quick character sketches in charcoal or pastel.

SHANNON [*to himself*]: I have fever.

HANNAH: I usually pass among the tables at lunch and dinner in a hotel. I wear an artist's smock—picturesquely dabbed with paint—wide Byronic collar and flowing silk tie. I don't push myself on people. I just display my work and smile at them sweetly and if they invite me to do so sit down to make a quick character sketch in pastel or charcoal. If not? Smile sweetly and go on.

SHANNON: What does Grandpa do?

HANNAH: We pass among the tables together slowly. I introduce him as the world's oldest living and practicing poet. If invited, he gives a recitation of a poem. Unfortunately all of his poems were written a long time ago. But do you know, he has started a new poem? For the first time in twenty years he's started another poem!

SHANNON: Hasn't finished it yet?

HANNAH: He still has inspiration, but his power of concentration has weakened a little, of course.

MAXINE: Right now he's not concentrating.

SHANNON: Grandpa's catchin' forty winks. Grampa? Let's hit the sack.

MAXINE: Now wait a minute. I'm going to call a taxi for these folks to take them back to town.

HANNAH: Please don't do that. We tried every hotel in town and they wouldn't take us. I'm afraid I have to place myself at your . . . mercy.

[*With infinite gentleness* SHANNON *has roused the old man and is leading him into one of the cubicles back of the*

*verandah. Distant cries of bathers are heard from the
beach. The afternoon light is fading very fast now as the
sun has dropped behind an island hilltop out to sea.*]

MAXINE: Looks like you're in for one night. Just one.

HANNAH: Thank you.

MAXINE: The old man's in number 4. You take 3. Where's
your luggage—no luggage?

HANNAH: I hid it behind some palmettos at the foot of
the path.

SHANNON [*shouting to* PANCHO]: Bring up her luggage. Tu,
flojo . . . las maletas . . . baja las palmas. Vamos! [*The
Mexican boys rush down the path.*] Maxine honey, would
you cash a postdated check for me?

MAXINE [*shrewdly*]: Yeah—mañana, maybe.

SHANNON: Thanks—generosity is the cornerstone of your
nature.

[MAXINE *utters her one-note bark of a laugh as she marches
around the corner of the verandah.*]

HANNAH: I'm dreadfully afraid my grandfather had a
slight stroke in those high passes through the sierras. [*She
says this with the coolness of someone saying that it may
rain before nightfall. An instant later, a long, long sigh of
wind sweeps the hillside. The bathers are heard shouting
below.*]

SHANNON: Very old people get these little "cerebral accidents," as they call them. They're not regular strokes, they're
just little cerebral . . . incidents. The symptoms clear up so
quickly that sometimes the old people don't even know
they've had them.

[*They exchange this quiet talk without looking at each
other. The Mexican boys crash back through the bushes*

at the top of the path, bearing some pieces of ancient luggage fantastically plastered with hotel and travel stickers indicating a vast range of wandering. The boys deposit the luggage near the steps.]

SHANNON: How many times have you been around the world?

HANNAH: Almost as many times as the world's been around the sun, and I feel as if I had gone the whole way on foot.

SHANNON [*picking up her luggage*]: What's your cell number?

HANNAH [*smiling faintly*]: I believe she said it was cell number 3.

SHANNON: She probably gave you the one with the leaky roof. [*He carries the bags into the cubicle.* MAXINE *is visible to the audience only as she appears outside the door to her office on the wing of the verandah.*] But you won't find out till it rains and then it'll be too late to do much about it but swim out of it. [HANNAH *laughs wanly. Her fatigue is now very plain.* SHANNON *comes back out with her luggage.*] Yep, she gave you the one with the leaky roof so you take mine and. . . .

HANNAH: Oh, no, no, Mr. Shannon, I'll find a dry spot if it rains.

MAXINE [*from around the corner of the verandah*]: Shannon!

[*A bit of pantomime occurs between* HANNAH *and* SHANNON. *He wants to put her luggage in cubicle number 5. She catches hold of his arm, indicating by gesture toward the back that it is necessary to avoid displeasing the proprietor.* MAXINE *shouts his name louder.* SHANNON *surrenders to* HANNAH's *pleading and puts her luggage back in the leaky cubicle number 3.*]

HANNAH: Thank you so much, Mr. Shannon. [*She dis-*

appears behind the mosquito netting. MAXINE *advances to the
verandah angle as* SHANNON *starts toward his own cubicle.*]

MAXINE [*mimicking* HANNAH'S *voice*]: "Thank you so much,
Mr. Shannon."

SHANNON: Don't be bitchy. Some people say thank you
sincerely. [*He goes past her and down the steps from the end
of the verandah.*] I'm going down for a swim now.

MAXINE: The water's blood temperature this time of day.

SHANNON: Yeah, well, I have a fever so it'll seem cooler
to me. [*He crosses rapidly to the jungle path leading to the
beach.*]

MAXINE [*following him*]: Wait for me, I'll. . . .

[*She means she will go down with him, but he ignores her
call and disappears into the foliage.* MAXINE *shrugs angrily
and goes back onto the verandah. She faces out, gripping
the railing tightly and glaring into the blaze of the sunset
as if it were a personal enemy. Then the ocean breathes a
long cooling breath up the hill, as* NONNO'S *voice is heard
from his cubicle.*]

NONNO:

     How calmly does the orange branch
     Observe the sky begin to blanch,
     Without a cry, without a prayer,
     With no expression of despair. . . .

[*And from a beach cantina in the distance a marimba band
is heard playing a popular song of that summer of 1940,
"Palabras de Mujer"—which means "Words of Women."*]

SLOW DIM OUT AND SLOW CURTAIN

Act Two

Several hours later: near sunset.
The scene is bathed in a deep
golden, almost coppery light;
the heavy tropical foliage gleams with wetness from a recent
rain.

MAXINE *comes around the turn of the verandah. To the*
formalities of evening she has made the concession of chang-
ing from levis to clean white cotton pants, and from a blue
work shirt to a pink one. She is about to set up the folding
cardtables for the evening meal which is served on the
verandah. All the while she is talking, she is setting up tables,
etc.

MAXINE: Miss Jelkes?

[HANNAH *lifts the mosquito net over the door of cubicle*
number 3.]

HANNAH: Yes, Mrs. Faulk?

MAXINE: Can I speak to you while I set up these tables
for supper?

HANNAH: Of course, you may. I wanted to speak to you,
too. [*She comes out. She is now wearing her artist's smock.*]

MAXINE: Good.

HANNAH: I just wanted to ask you if there's a tub-bath
Grandfather could use. A shower is fine for me—I prefer a
shower to a tub—but for my grandfather there is some danger
of falling down in a shower and at his age, although he says
he is made out of India rubber, a broken hipbone would be
a very serious matter, so I. . . .

44

MAXINE: What I wanted to say is I called up the Casa de Huéspedes about you and your Grampa, and I can get you in there.

HANNAH: Oh, but we don't want to *move!*

MAXINE: The Costa Verde isn't the right place for you. Y'see, we cater to folks that like to rough it a little, and—well, frankly, we cater to younger people.

[HANNAH *has started unfolding a cardtable.*]

HANNAH: Oh yes . . . uh . . . well . . . the, uh, Casa de Huéspedes, that means a, uh, sort of a rooming house, Mrs. Faulk?

MAXINE: Boarding house. They feed you, they'll even feed you on credit.

HANNAH: Where is it located?

MAXINE: It has a central location. You could get a doctor there quick if the old man took sick on you. You got to think about that.

HANNAH: Yes, I—[*She nods gravely, more to herself than* MAXINE.]—I *have* thought about that, but. . . .

MAXINE: What are you doing?

HANNAH: Making myself useful.

MAXINE: Don't do that. I don't accept help from guests here.

[HANNAH *hesitates, but goes on setting the tables.*]

HANNAH: Oh, please, let me. Knife and fork on one side, spoon on the . . . ? [*Her voice dies out.*]

MAXINE: Just put the plates on the napkins so they don't blow away.

HANNAH: Yes, it is getting breezy on the verandah. [*She continues setting the table.*]

MAXINE: Hurricane winds are already hitting up coast.

HANNAH: We've been through several typhoons in the Orient. Sometimes *outside* disturbances like that are an almost welcome distraction from *inside* disturbances, aren't they? [*This is said almost to herself. She finishes putting the plates on the paper napkins.*] When do you want us to leave here, Mrs. Faulk?

MAXINE: The boys'll move you in my station wagon tomorrow—no charge for the service.

HANNAH: That is very kind of you. [MAXINE *starts away.*] Mrs. Faulk?

MAXINE [*turning back to her with obvious reluctance*]: Huh?

HANNAH: Do you know jade?

MAXINE: Jade?

HANNAH: Yes.

MAXINE: Why?

HANNAH: I have a small but interesting collection of jade pieces. I asked if you know jade because in jade it's the craftsmanship, the carving of the jade, that's most important about it. [*She has removed a jade ornament from her blouse.*] This one, for instance—a miracle of carving. Tiny as it is, it has two figures carved on it—the legendary Prince Ahk and Princess Angh, and a heron flying above them. The artist that carved it probably received for this miraculously delicate workmanship, well, I would say perhaps the price of a month's supply of rice for his family, but the merchant who employed him sold it, I would guess, for at least three hundred pounds sterling to an English lady who got tired of it and gave it to me, perhaps because I painted her not as she was at that

time but as I could see she must have looked in her youth.
Can you see the carving?

MAXINE: Yeah, honey, but I'm not operating a hock shop
here, I'm trying to run a hotel.

HANNAH: I know, but couldn't you just accept it as security
for a few days' stay here?

MAXINE: You're completely broke, are you?

HANNAH: Yes, we are—completely.

MAXINE: You say that like you're proud of it.

HANNAH: I'm not proud of it or ashamed of it either. It
just happens to be what's happened to us, which has never
happened before in all our travels.

MAXINE [*grudgingly*]: You're telling the truth, I reckon,
but I told you the truth, too, when I told you, when you
came here, that I had just lost my husband and he'd left
me in such a financial hole that if living didn't mean more
to me than money, I'd might as well have been dropped in
the ocean with him.

HANNAH: Ocean?

MAXINE [*peacefully philosophical about it*]: I carried out
his burial instructions exactly. Yep, my husband, Fred Faulk,
was the greatest game fisherman on the West Coast of Mexico—he'd racked up unbeatable records in sailfish, tarpon,
kingfish, barracuda—and on his deathbed, last week, he requested to be dropped in the sea, yeah, right out there in
that bay, not even sewed up in canvas, just in his fisherman
outfit. So now old Freddie the Fisherman is feeding the fish
—fishes' revenge on old Freddie. How about that, I ask you?

HANNAH [*regarding* MAXINE *sharply*]: I doubt that he regrets
it.

MAXINE: I do. It gives me the shivers.

[*She is distracted by the German party singing a marching song on the path up from the beach.* SHANNON *appears at the top of the path, a wet beachrobe clinging to him.* MAXINE'S *whole concentration shifts abruptly to him. She freezes and blazes with it like an exposed power line. For a moment the "hot light" is concentrated on her tense, furious figure.* HANNAH *provides a visual counterpoint. She clenches her eyes shut for a moment, and when they open, it is on a look of stoical despair of the refuge she has unsuccessfully fought for. Then* SHANNON *approaches the verandah and the scene is his.*]

SHANNON: Here they come up, your conquerors of the world, Maxine honey, singing "Horst Wessel." [*He chuckles fiercely, and starts toward the verandah steps.*]

MAXINE: Shannon, wash that sand off you before you come on the verandah.

[*The Germans are heard singing the "Horst Wessel" marching song. Soon they appear, trooping up from the beach like an animated canvas by Rubens. They are all nearly nude, pinked and bronzed by the sun. The women have decked themselves with garlands of pale green seaweed, glistening wet, and the Munich-opera bridegroom is blowing on a great conch shell. His father-in-law, the tank manufacturer, has his portable radio, which is still transmitting a shortwave broadcast about the Battle of Britain, now at its climax.*]

HILDA [*capering, astride her rubber horse*]: Horsey, horsey, horsey!

HERR FAHRENKOPF [*ecstatically*]: London is burning, the heart of London's on fire! [WOLFGANG *turns a handspring onto the verandah and walks on his hands a few paces, then tumbles over with a great whoop.* MAXINE *laughs delightedly with the Germans.*] Beer, beer, beer!

FRAU FAHRENKOPF: Tonight champagne!

[*The euphoric horseplay and shouting continue as they*

gambol around the turn of the verandah. SHANNON *has come onto the porch.* MAXINE'S *laughter dies out a little sadly, with envy.*]

SHANNON: You're turning this place into the Mexican Berchtesgaden, Maxine honey?

MAXINE: I told you to wash that sand off. [*Shouts for beer from the Germans draw her around the verandah corner.*]

HANNAH: Mr. Shannon, do you happen to know the Casa de Huéspedes, or anything about it, I mean? [SHANNON *stares at her somewhat blankly*.] We are, uh, thinking of . . . *moving* there tomorrow. Do you, uh, recommend it?

SHANNON: I recommend it along with the Black Hole of Calcutta and the Siberian salt mines.

HANNAH [*nodding reflectively*]: I suspected as much. Mr. Shannon, in your touring party, do you think there might be anyone interested in my water colors? Or in my character sketches?

SHANNON: I doubt it. I doubt that they're corny enough to please my ladies. *Oh-oh! Great Caesar's ghost. . . .*

[*This exclamation is prompted by the shrill, approaching call of his name.* CHARLOTTE *appears from the rear, coming from the hotel annex, and rushes like a teen-age Medea toward the verandah.* SHANNON *ducks into his cubicle, slamming the door so quickly that a corner of the mosquito netting is caught and sticks out, flirtatiously.* CHARLOTTE *rushes onto the verandah.*]

CHARLOTTE: *Larry!*

HANNAH: Are you looking for someone, dear?

CHARLOTTE: Yeah, the man conducting our tour, Larry Shannon.

HANNAH: Oh, Mr. Shannon. I think he went down to the beach.

CHARLOTTE: I just now saw him coming up from the beach. [*She is tense and trembling, and her eyes keep darting up and down the verandah.*]

HANNAH: Oh. Well. . . . But. . . .

CHARLOTTE: Larry? Larry! [*Her shouts startle the rain-forest birds into a clamorous moment.*]

HANNAH: Would you like to leave a message for him, dear?

CHARLOTTE: No. I'm staying right here till he comes out of wherever he's hiding.

HANNAH: Why don't you just sit down, dear. I'm an artist, a painter. I was just sorting out my water colors and sketches in this portfolio, and look what I've come across. [*She selects a sketch and holds it up.*]

SHANNON [*from inside his cubicle*]: Oh, God!

CHARLOTTE [*darting to the cubicle*]: Larry, let me in there!

[*She beats on the door of the cubicle as HERR FAHRENKOPF comes around the verandah with his portable radio. He is bug-eyed with excitement over the news broadcast in German.*]

HANNAH: Guten abend.

[*HERR FAHRENKOPF jerks his head with a toothy grin, raising a hand for silence. HANNAH nods agreeably and approaches him with her portfolio of drawings. He maintains the grin as she displays one picture after another. HANNAH is un-certain whether the grin is for the pictures or the news broadcast. He stares at the pictures, jerking his head from time to time. It is rather like the pantomime of showing lantern slides.*]

CHARLOTTE [*suddenly crying out again*]: Larry, open this door and let me in! I know you're in there, Larry!

HERR FAHRENKOPF: Silence, please, for one moment! This is a recording of Der Führer addressing the Reichstag just . . . [*He glances at his wristwatch.*] . . . eight hours ago, today, transmitted by Deutsches Nachrichtenbüro to Mexico City. Please! Quiet, bitte!

[*A human voice like a mad dog's bark emerges from the static momentarily.* CHARLOTTE *goes on pounding on* SHANNON'S *door.* HANNAH *suggests in pantomime that they go to the back verandah, but* HERR FAHRENKOPF *despairs of hearing the broadcast. As he rises to leave, the light catches his polished glasses so that he appears for a moment to have electric light bulbs in his forehead. Then he ducks his head in a genial little bow and goes out beyond the verandah, where he performs some muscle-flexing movements of a formalized nature, like the preliminary stances of Japanese Suma wrestlers.*]

HANNAH: May I show you my work on the other verandah?

[HANNAH *had started to follow* HERR FAHRENKOPF *with her portfolio, but the sketches fall out, and she stops to gather them from the floor with the sad, preoccupied air of a lovely child picking flowers.*]

[SHANNON'S *head slowly, furtively, appears through the window of his cubicle. He draws quickly back as* CHARLOTTE *darts that way, stepping on* HANNAH'S *spilt sketches.* HANNAH *utters a soft cry of protest, which is drowned by* CHARLOTTE'S *renewed clamor.*]

CHARLOTTE: Larry, Larry, Judy's looking for me. Let me come in, Larry, before she finds me here!

SHANNON: You can't come in. Stop shouting and I'll come out.

CHARLOTTE: All right, come out.

SHANNON: Stand back from the door so I *can*.

[*She moves a little aside and he emerges from his cubicle like a man entering a place of execution. He leans against the wall, mopping the sweat off his face with a handkerchief.*]

SHANNON: How does Miss Fellowes know what happened that night? Did you tell her?

CHARLOTTE: I didn't tell her, she guessed.

SHANNON: Guessing isn't knowing. If she is just guessing, that means she doesn't know—I mean if you're not lying, if you didn't tell her.

[HANNAH *has finished picking up her drawings and moves quietly over to the far side of the verandah.*]

CHARLOTTE: Don't talk to me like that.

SHANNON: Don't complicate my life now, please, for God's sake, don't complicate my life now.

CHARLOTTE: Why have you changed like this?

SHANNON: I have a fever. Don't complicate my . . . fever.

CHARLOTTE: You act like you hated me now.

SHANNON: You're going to get me kicked out of Blake Tours, Charlotte.

CHARLOTTE: Judy is, not me.

SHANNON: Why did you sing "I Love You Truly" at me?

CHARLOTTE: Because I do love you truly!

SHANNON: Honey girl, don't you know that nothing worse could happen to a girl in your, your . . . unstable condition . . .

than to get emotionally mixed up with a man in ~~my unstable~~ condition, huh?

CHARLOTTE: No, no, no, I—

SHANNON [*cutting through*]: Two unstable conditions can set a whole world on fire, can blow it up, past repair, and that is just as true between two people as it's true between. . . .

CHARLOTTE: All I know is you've got to marry me, Larry, after what happened between us in Mexico City!

SHANNON: A man in my condition can't marry, it isn't decent or legal. He's lucky if he can even hold onto his job. [*He keeps catching hold of her hands and plucking them off his shoulders.*] I'm almost out of my mind, can't you see that, honey?

CHARLOTTE: I don't believe you don't love me.

SHANNON: Honey, it's almost impossible for anybody to believe they're not loved by someone they believe they love, but, honey, I love *nobody*. I'm like that, it isn't my fault. When I brought you home that night I told you goodnight in the hall, just kissed you on the cheek like the little girl that you are, but the instant I opened my door, you rushed into my room and I couldn't get you out of it, not even when I, oh God, tried to scare you out of it by, oh God, don't you remember?

[MISS FELLOWES' *voice is heard from back of the hotel calling,* "Charlotte!"]

CHARLOTTE: Yes, I remember that after making love to me, you hit me, Larry, you struck me in the face, and you twisted my arm to make me kneel on the floor and pray with you for forgiveness.

SHANNON: I do that, I do that always when I, when . . . I don't have a dime left in my nervous emotional bank account —I can't write a check on it, now.

CHARLOTTE: Larry, let me help you!

MISS FELLOWES [approaching]: Charlotte, Charlotte, Charlie!

CHARLOTTE: Help me and let me help you!

SHANNON: The helpless can't help the helpless!

CHARLOTTE: Let me in, Judy's coming!

SHANNON: Let me go. Go away!

[He thrusts her violently back and rushes into his cubicle, slamming and bolting the door—though the gauze netting is left sticking out. As MISS FELLOWES charges onto the verandah, CHARLOTTE runs into the next cubicle, and HANNAH moves over from where she has been watching and meets her in the center.]

MISS FELLOWES: Shannon, Shannon! Where are you?

HANNAH: I think Mr. Shannon has gone down to the beach.

MISS FELLOWES: Was Charlotte Goodall with him? A young blonde girl in our party—was she with him?

HANNAH: No, nobody was with him, he was completely alone.

MISS FELLOWES: I heard a door slam.

HANNAH: That was mine.

MISS FELLOWES [pointing to the door with the gauze sticking out]: Is this yours?

HANNAH: Yes, mine. I rushed out to catch the sunset.

[At this moment MISS FELLOWES hears CHARLOTTE sobbing in HANNAH's cubicle. She throws the door open.]

MISS FELLOWES: Charlotte! Come out of there, Charlie! [She has seized CHARLOTTE by the wrist.] What's your word worth—nothing? You promised you'd stay away from him! [CHARLOTTE *frees her arm, sobbing bitterly.* MISS FELLOWES *seizes her again, tighter, and starts dragging her away.*] I have talked to your father about this man by long distance and he's getting out a warrant for his arrest, if he dare try coming back to the States after this!

CHARLOTTE: I don't care.

MISS FELLOWES: I do! I'm responsible for you.

CHARLOTTE: I don't want to go back to Texas!

MISS FELLOWES: Yes, you do! And you will!

[*She takes* CHARLOTTE *firmly by the arm and drags her away behind the hotel.* HANNAH *comes out of her cubicle, where she had gone when* MISS FELLOWES *pulled* CHARLOTTE *out of it.*]

SHANNON [*from his cubicle*]: Ah, God. . . .

[HANNAH *crosses to his cubicle and knocks by the door.*]

HANNAH: The coast is clear now, Mr. Shannon.

[SHANNON *does not answer or appear. She sets down her portfolio to pick up* NONNO'S *white linen suit, which she had pressed and hung on the verandah. She crosses to his cubicle with it, and calls in.*]

HANNAH: Nonno? It's almost time for supper! There's going to be a lovely, stormy sunset in a few minutes.

NONNO [*from within*]: Coming!

HANNAH: So is Christmas, Nonno.

NONNO: So is the Fourth of July!

HANNAH: We're past the Fourth of July. Hallowe'en comes next and then Thanksgiving. I hope you'll come forth sooner.

[*She lifts the gauze net over his cubicle door.*] Here's your suit, I've pressed it. [*She enters the cubicle.*]

NONNO: It's mighty dark in here, Hannah.

HANNAH: I'll turn the light on for you.

[SHANNON *comes out of his cubicle, like the survivor of a plane crash, bringing out with him several pieces of his clerical garb. The black heavy silk bib is loosely fastened about his panting, sweating chest. He hangs over it a heavy gold cross with an amethyst center and attempts to fasten on a starched round collar. Now* HANNAH *comes back out of* NONNO'S *cubicle, adjusting the flowing silk tie which goes with her "artist" costume. For a moment they both face front, adjusting their two outfits. They are like two actors in a play which is about to fold on the road, preparing gravely for a performance which may be the last one.*]

HANNAH [*glancing at* SHANNON]: Are you planning to conduct church services of some kind here tonight, Mr. Shannon?

SHANNON: Goddamit, please help me with this! [*He means the round collar.*]

HANNAH [*crossing behind him*]: If you're not going to conduct a church service, why get into that uncomfortable outfit?

SHANNON: Because I've been accused of being defrocked and of lying about it, that's why. I want to show the ladies that I'm still a clocked—*frocked!*—minister of the. . . .

HANNAH: Isn't that lovely gold cross enough to convince the ladies?

SHANNON: No, they know I redeemed it from a Mexico City pawnshop, and they suspect that that's where I got it in the first place.

HANNAH: Hold still just a minute. [*She is behind him, trying to fasten the collar.*] There now, let's hope it stays on.

The buttonhole is so frayed I'm afraid that it won't hold the button. [*Her fear is instantly confirmed: the button pops out.*]

SHANNON: Where'd it go?

HANNAH: Here, right under. . . .

[*She picks it up.* SHANNON *rips the collar off, crumples it and hurls it off the verandah. Then he falls into the hammock, panting and twisting.* HANNAH *quietly opens her sketch pad and begins to sketch him. He doesn't at first notice what she is doing.*]

HANNAH [*as she sketches*]: How long have you been inactive in the, uh, Church, Mr. Shannon?

SHANNON: What's that got to do with the price of rice in China?

HANNAH [*gently*]: Nothing.

SHANNON: What's it got to do with the price of coffee beans in Brazil?

HANNAH: I retract the question. With apologies.

SHANNON: To answer your question politely, I have been inactive in the Church for all but one year since I was ordained a minister of the Church.

HANNAH [*sketching rapidly and moving forward a bit to see his face better*]: Well, that's quite a sabbatical, Mr. Shannon.

SHANNON: Yeah, that's . . . quite a . . . sabbatical.

[NONNO'S *voice is heard from his cubicle repeating a line of poetry several times.*]

SHANNON: Is your grandfather talking to himself in there?

HANNAH: No, he composes out loud. He has to commit his

lines to memory because he can't see to write them or read
them.

SHANNON: Sounds like he's stuck on one line.

HANNAH: Yes. I'm afraid his memory is failing. Memory
failure is his greatest dread. [*She says this almost coolly, as if
it didn't matter.*]

SHANNON: Are you drawing me?

HANNAH: Trying to. You're a very difficult subject. When
the Mexican painter Siqueiros did his portrait of the American
poet Hart Crane he had to paint him with closed eyes because he couldn't paint his eyes open—there was too much
suffering in them and he couldn't paint it.

SHANNON: Sorry, but I'm not going to close my eyes for
you. I'm hypnotizing myself—at least trying to—by looking at
the light on the orange tree . . . leaves.

HANNAH: That's all right. I can paint your eyes open.

SHANNON: I had one parish one year and then I wasn't defrocked but I was . . . locked out of my church.

HANNAH: Oh . . . Why did they lock you out of it?

SHANNON: Fornication and heresy . . . in the same week.

HANNAH [*sketching rapidly*]: What were the circumstances
of the . . . uh . . . first offense?

SHANNON: Yeah, the fornication came first, preceded the
heresy by several days. A very young Sunday-school teacher
asked to see me privately in my study. A pretty little thing—
no chance in the world—only child, and both of her parents
were spinsters, almost identical spinsters wearing clothes of
the opposite sexes. Fooling some of the people some of the
time but not me—none of the time. . . . [*He is pacing the
verandah with gathering agitation, and the all-inclusive mock-*

ery that his guilt produces.] Well, she declared herself to me—wildly.

HANNAH: A declaration of love?

SHANNON: Don't make *fun* of me, honey!

HANNAH: I wasn't.

SHANNON: The natural, or unnatural, attraction of one . . . lunatic for . . . another . . . that's all it was. I was the goddamnedest prig in those days that even you could imagine. I said, let's kneel down together and pray and we did, we knelt down, but all of a sudden the kneeling position turned to a reclining position on the rug of my study and . . . When we got up? I struck her. Yes, I did, I struck her in the face and called her a damned little tramp. So she ran home. I heard the next day she'd cut herself with her father's straightblade razor. Yeah, the paternal spinster shaved.

HANNAH: Fatally?

SHANNON: Just broke the skin surface enough to bleed a little, but it made a scandal.

HANNAH: Yes, I can imagine that it . . . provoked some comment.

SHANNON: That it did, it did that. [*He pauses a moment in his fierce pacing as if the recollection still appalled him.*] So the next Sunday when I climbed into the pulpit and looked down over all of those smug, disapproving, accusing faces uplifted, I had an impulse to shake them—so I shook them. I had a prepared sermon—meek, apologetic—I threw it away, tossed it into the chancel. Look here, I said, I shouted, I'm tired of conducting services in praise and worship of a senile delinquent—yeah, that's what I said, I shouted! All your Western theologies, the whole mythology of them, are based on the concept of God as a *senile delinquent* and, by God, I will not and cannot continue to conduct services in praise and worship of this, this . . . this. . . . .

HANNAH [*quietly*]: Senile delinquent?

SHANNON: Yeah, this angry, petulant old man. I mean he's represented like a bad-tempered childish old, old, sick, peevish man—I mean like the sort of old man in a nursing home that's putting together a jigsaw puzzle and can't put it together and gets furious at it and kicks over the table. Yes, I tell you they *do* that, all our theologies do it—accuse God of being a cruel, senile delinquent, blaming the world and brutally punishing all he created for his own faults in construction, and then, ha-ha, yeah—a thunderstorm broke that Sunday. . . .

HANNAH: You mean *outside* the church?

SHANNON: Yep, it was wilder than I was! And out they slithered, they slithered out of their pews to their shiny black cockroach sedans, ha-ha, and I shouted after them, hell, I even followed them halfway out of the church, shouting after them as they. . . . [*He stops with a gasp for breath.*]

HANNAH: Slithered out?

SHANNON: I shouted after them, go on, go home and close your house windows, all your windows and doors, against the truth about God!

HANNAH: Oh, my heavens. Which is just what they did— poor things.

SHANNON: Miss Jelkes honey, Pleasant Valley, Virginia, was an exclusive suburb of a large city and these poor things were not poor—materially speaking.

HANNAH [*smiling a bit*]: What was the, uh, upshot of it?

SHANNON: Upshot of it? Well, I wasn't defrocked. I was just locked out of the church in Pleasant Valley, Virginia, and put in a nice little private asylum to recuperate from a complete nervous breakdown as they preferred to regard it, and then, and then I . . . I entered my present line—tours of God's world conducted by a minister of God with a cross and a round collar to prove it. Collecting evidence!

HANNAH: Evidence of what, Mr. Shannon?

SHANNON [*a touch shyly now*]: My personal idea of God, not as a senile delinquent, but as a. . . .

HANNAH: Incomplete sentence.

SHANNON: It's going to storm tonight—a terrific electric storm. Then you will see the Reverend T. Lawrence Shannon's conception of God Almighty paying a visit to the world he created. I want to go back to the Church and preach the gospel of God as Lightning and Thunder . . . and also stray dogs vivisected and . . . and . . . and. . . . [*He points out suddenly toward the sea.*] That's him! There he is now! [*He is pointing out at a blaze, a majestic apocalypse of gold light, shafting the sky as the sun drops into the Pacific.*] His oblivious majesty—and *here I am* on this . . . dilapidated verandah of a cheap hotel, out of season, in a country caught and destroyed in its flesh and corrupted in its spirit by its gold-hungry Conquistadors that bore the flag of the Inquisition along with the Cross of Christ. Yes . . . and. . . . [*There is a pause.*]

HANNAH: Mr. Shannon . . . ?

SHANNON: Yes . . . ?

HANNAH [*smiling a little*]: I have a strong feeling you will go back to the Church with this evidence you've been collecting, but when you do and it's a black Sunday morning, look out over the congregation, over the smug, complacent faces for a few old, very old faces, looking up at you, as you begin your sermon, with eyes like a piercing cry for something to still look up to, something to still believe in. And then I think you'll not shout what you say you shouted that black Sunday in Pleasant Valley, Virginia. I think you will throw away the violent, furious sermon, you'll toss *it* into the chancel, and talk about . . . no, maybe talk about . . . nothing . . . just. . . .

SHANNON: What?

HANNAH: Lead them beside still waters because you know how badly they need the still waters, Mr. Shannon.

[*There is a moment of silence between them.*]

SHANNON: Lemme see that thing. [*He seizes the sketch pad from her and is visibly impressed by what he sees. There is another moment which is prolonged to* HANNAH'S *embarrassment.*]

HANNAH: Where did you say the patrona put your party of ladies?

SHANNON: She had her . . . Mexican concubines put their luggage in the annex.

HANNAH: Where is the annex?

SHANNON: Right down the hill back of here, but all of my ladies except the teen-age Medea and the older Medea have gone out in a glass-bottomed boat to observe the . . . submarine marvels.

HANNAH: Well, when they come back to the annex they're going to observe my water colors with some marvelous submarine prices marked on the mattings.

SHANNON: By God, you're a hustler, aren't you, you're a fantastic cool hustler.

HANNAH: Yes, like *you*, Mr. Shannon. [*She gently removes her sketch pad from his grasp.*] Oh, Mr. Shannon, if Nonno, Grandfather, comes out of his cell number 4 before I get back, will you please look out for him for me? I won't be longer than three shakes of a lively sheep's tail. [*She snatches up her portfolio and goes briskly off the verandah.*]

SHANNON: Fantastic, absolutely fantastic.

[*There is a windy sound in the rain forest and a flicker of gold light like a silent scattering of gold coins on the verandah; then the sound of shouting voices. The*

Mexican boys appear with a wildly agitated creature—a captive iguana tied up in a shirt. They crouch down by the cactus clumps that are growing below the verandah and hitch the iguana to a post with a piece of rope. MAXINE *is attracted by the commotion and appears on the verandah above them.*]

PEDRO: Tenemos fiesta!*

PANCHO: Comeremos bien.

PEDRO: Dámela, dámela! Yo la ataré.

PANCHO: *Yo* la cojí—*yo* la ataré!

PEDRO: Lo que vas a *hacer* es dejarla escapar.

MAXINE: Ammarla fuerte! Ole, ole! No la dejes escapar. Déjala moverse! [*to* SHANNON] They caught an iguana.

SHANNON: I've noticed they did that, Maxine.

[*She is holding her drink deliberately close to him. The Germans have heard the commotion and crowd onto the verandah.* FRAU FAHRENKOPF *rushes over to* MAXINE.]

FRAU FAHRENKOPF: What is this? What's going on? A snake? Did they catch a snake?

MAXINE: No. *Lizard.*

FRAU FAHRENKOPF [*with exaggerated revulsion*]: Ouuu . . . lizard! [*She strikes a grotesque attitude of terror as if she were threatened by Jack the Ripper.*]

SHANNON [*to* MAXINE]: You like iguana meat, don't you?

FRAU FAHRENKOPF: Eat? *Eat?* A big *lizard?*

---

* We're going to have a feast! / We'll eat good. / Give it to me! I'll tie it up. / *I* caught it—*I'll* tie it up! / You'll only let it get away. / Tie it up tight! Ole, ole! Don't let it get away. Give it enough room!

MAXINE: Yep, they're mighty good eating—taste like white meat of chicken.

[FRAU FAHRENKOPF *rushes back to her family. They talk excitedly in German about the iguana.*]

SHANNON: If you mean Mexican chicken, that's no recommendation. Mexican chickens are scavengers and they taste like what they scavenge.

MAXINE: Naw, I mean Texas chicken.

SHANNON [*dreamily*]: Texas . . . chicken. . . .

[*He paces restlessly down the verandah.* MAXINE *divides her attention between his tall, lean figure, that seems incapable of stillness, and the wriggling bodies of the Mexican boys lying on their stomachs half under the verandah—as if she were mentally comparing two opposite attractions to her simple, sensual nature.* SHANNON *turns at the end of the verandah and sees her eyes fixed on him.*]

SHANNON: What is the sex of this iguana, Maxine?

MAXINE: Hah, who cares about the sex of an iguana . . . [*He passes close by her.*] . . . except another . . . iguana?

SHANNON: Haven't you heard the limerick about iguanas? [*He removes her drink from her hand and it seems as if he might drink it, but he only sniffs it, with an expression of repugnance. She chuckles.*]

> There was a young gaucho named Bruno
> Who said about love, This I do know:
> Women are fine, and sheep are divine,
> But iguanas are—*Número Uno!*

[*On "Número Uno"* SHANNON *empties* MAXINE'S *drink over the railing, deliberately onto the humped, wriggling posterior of* PEDRO, *who springs up with angry protests.*]

PEDRO: Me cago . . . hijo de la . . .

SHANNON: Qué? Qué?

MAXINE: Vete!

[SHANNON *laughs viciously. The iguana escapes and both boys rush shouting after it. One of them dives on it and recaptures it at the edge of the jungle.*]

PANCHO: La iguana se escapó.

MAXINE: Cójela, cójela! La cojiste? Si no la cojes, te morderá el culo. La cojiste?

PEDRO: La cojí.*

[*The boys wriggle back under the verandah with the iguana.*]

MAXINE [*returning to* SHANNON]: I thought you were gonna break down and take a drink, Reverend.

SHANNON: Just the odor of liquor makes me feel nauseated.

MAXINE: You couldn't smell it if you got it *in* you. [*She touches his sweating forehead. He brushes her hand off like an insect.*] Hah! [*She crosses over to the liquor cart, and he looks after her with a sadistic grin.*]

SHANNON: Maxine honey, whoever told you that you look good in tight pants was not a sincere friend of yours.

[*He turns away. At the same instant, a crash and a hoarse, startled outcry are heard from* NONNO'S *cubicle.*]

MAXINE: I knew it, I *knew* it! The old man's took a fall!

[SHANNON *rushes into the cubicle, followed by* MAXINE.]

[*The light has been gradually, steadily dimming during the incident of the iguana's escape. There is, in effect, a division*

---

* The iguana's escaped. / Get it, get it! Have you got it? If you don't, it'll bite your behind. Have you got it? / He's got it.

of scenes here, though it is accomplished without a black-out or curtain. As SHANNON *and* MAXINE *enter* NONNO'S *cubicle,* HERR FAHRENKOPF *appears on the now twilit verandah. He turns on an outsize light fixture that is suspended from overhead, a full pearly-moon of a light globe that gives an unearthly luster to the scene. The great pearly globe is decorated by night insects, large but gossamer moths that have immolated themselves on its surface: the light through their wings gives them an opalescent color, a touch of fantasy.*

[*Now* SHANNON *leads the old poet out of his cubicle, onto the facing verandah. The old man is impeccably dressed in snow-white linen with a black string tie. His leonine mane of hair gleams like silver as he passes under the globe.*]

NONNO: No bones broke, I'm made out of India rubber!

SHANNON: A traveler-born falls down many times in his travels.

NONNO: Hannah? [*His vision and other senses have so far deteriorated that he thinks he is being led out by* HANNAH.] I'm pretty sure I'm going to finish it here.

SHANNON [*shouting, gently*]: I've got the same feeling, Grampa.

[MAXINE *follows them out of the cubicle.*]

NONNO: I've never been surer of anything in my life.

SHANNON [*gently and wryly*]: I've never been surer of anything in mine either.

[HERR FAHRENKOPF *has been listening with an expression of entrancement to his portable radio, held close to his ear, the sound unrealistically low. Now he turns it off and makes an excited speech.*]

HERR FAHRENKOPF: The London fires have spread all the way from the heart of London to the Channel coast! Goering,

Field Marshall Goering, calls it "the new phase of conquest!"
Superfirebombs! Each night!

[NONNO *catches only the excited tone of this announcement
and interprets it as a request for a recitation. He strikes the
floor with his cane, throws back his silver-maned head and
begins the delivery in a grand, declamatory style.*]

NONNO:
> Youth must be wanton, youth must be quick,
> Dance to the candle while lasteth the wick,
>
> Youth must be foolish and. . . .

[NONNO *falters on the line, a look of confusion and fear on
his face. The Germans are amused.* WOLFGANG *goes up to*
NONNO *and shouts into his face.*]

WOLFGANG: Sir? What is your age? How old?

[HANNAH, *who has just returned to the verandah, rushes up
to her grandfather and answers for him.*]

HANNAH: He is ninety-seven years *young!*

HERR FAHRENKOPF: How old?

HANNAH: Ninety-seven—almost a *century young!*

[HERR FAHRENKOPF *repeats this information to his beaming
wife and* HILDA *in German.*]

NONNO [*cutting in on the Germans*]:
> Youth must be foolish and mirthful and blind,
> Gaze not before and glance not behind,
>
> Mark not. . . .

[*He falters again.*]

HANNAH [*prompting him, holding tightly onto his arm*]:
> Mark not the shadow that darkens the way—

[*They recite the next lines together.*]
      Regret not the glitter of any lost day,

      But laugh with no reason except the red wine,
      For youth must be youthful and foolish and blind!

[*The Germans are loudly amused.* WOLFGANG *applauds directly in the old poet's face.* NONNO *makes a little unsteady bow, leaning forward precariously on his cane.* SHANNON *takes a firm hold of his arm as* HANNAH *turns to the Germans, opening her portfolio of sketches and addressing* WOLFGANG.]

HANNAH: Am I right in thinking you are on your honeymoon? [*There is no response, and she repeats the question in German while* FRAU FAHRENKOPF *laughs and nods vehemently.*] Habe ich recht das Sie auf Ihrer Hochzeitsreise sind? Was für eine hübsche junge Braut! Ich mache Pastell-Skizzen . . . darf ich, würden Sie mir erlauben . . . ? Würden Sie, bitte . . . bitte. . . .

[HERR FAHRENKOPF *bursts into a Nazi marching song and leads his party to the champagne bucket on the table at the left.* SHANNON *has steered* NONNO *to the other table.*]

NONNO [*exhilarated*]: Hannah! What was the *take?*

HANNAH [*embarrassed*]: Grandfather, sit down, please stop shouting!

NONNO: Hah? Did they cross your palm with silver or paper, Hannah?

HANNAH [*almost desperately*]: Nonno! No more shouting! Sit down at the table. It's time to *eat!*

SHANNON: Chow time, Grampa.

NONNO [*confused but still shouting*]: How much did they come across with?

HANNAH: Nonno! *Please!*

NONNO: Did they, did you . . . sell 'em a . . . water color?

HANNAH: No sale, Grandfather!

MAXINE: Hah!

[HANNAH *turns to* SHANNON, *her usual composure shattered, or nearly so.*]

HANNAH: He won't sit down or stop shouting.

NONNO [*blinking and beaming with the grotesque suggestion of an old coquette*]: Hah? How rich did we strike it, Hannah?

SHANNON: *You* sit down, Miss Jelkes. [*He says it with gentle authority, to which she yields. He takes hold of the old man's forearm and places in his hand a crumpled Mexican bill.*] Sir? Sir? [*He is shouting.*] Five! Dollars! I'm putting it in your pocket.

HANNAH: We can't accept . . . gratuities, Mr. Shannon.

SHANNON: Hell, I gave him five pesos.

NONNO: Mighty good for one poem!

SHANNON: Sir? Sir? The *pecuniary rewards* of a *poem* are *grossly inferior* to its *merits, always!*

[*He is being fiercely, almost mockingly tender with the old man—a thing we are when the pathos of the old, the ancient, the dying is such a wound to our own (savagely beleaguered) nerves and sensibilities that this outside demand on us is beyond our collateral, our emotional reserve. This is as true of* HANNAH *as it is of* SHANNON, *of course. They have both overdrawn their reserves at this point of the encounter between them.*]

NONNO: Hah? Yes. . . . [*He is worn out now, but still shouting.*] We're going to clean up in this place!

SHANNON: You bet you're going to clean up here!

[MAXINE *utters her one-note bark of a laugh.* SHANNON *throws a hard roll at her. She wanders amiably back toward the German table.*]

NONNO [*tottering, panting, hanging onto* SHANNON'S *arm, thinking it is* HANNAH'S]: Is the, the . . . dining room . . . crowded? [*He looks blindly about with wild surmise.*]

SHANNON: Yep, it's filled to capacity! There's a big crowd at the door! [*His voice doesn't penetrate the old man's deafness.*]

NONNO: If there's a cocktail lounge, Hannah, we ought to . . . work that . . . first. Strike while the iron is hot, ho, ho, while it's hot. . . . [*This is like a delirium—only as strong a woman as* HANNAH *could remain outwardly impassive.*]

HANNAH: He thinks you're me, Mr. Shannon. Help him into a chair. Please stay with him a minute, I. . . .

[*She moves away from the table and breathes as if she has just been dragged up half-drowned from the sea.* SHANNON *eases the old man into a chair. Almost at once* NONNO'S *feverish vitality collapses and he starts drifting back toward half sleep.*]

SHANNON [*crossing to* HANNAH]: What're you breathing like that for?

HANNAH: Some people take a drink, some take a pill. I just take a few deep breaths.

SHANNON: You're making too much out of this. It's a natural thing in a man as old as Grampa.

HANNAH: I know, I know. He's had more than one of these little "cerebral accidents" as you call them, and all in the last few months. He was amazing till lately. I had to show his passport to prove that he was the oldest living and practicing poet on earth. We did well, we made expenses and *more!* But . . . when I saw he was failing, I tried to persuade him to go back to Nantucket, but he conducts our tours. He said, "No, *Mexico!*" So here we are on this windy hilltop like a pair of scarecrows. . . . The bus from Mexico City broke down at an altitude of 15,000 feet above sea level. That's when I think the latest cerebral incident happened. It isn't so much the loss of hearing and sight but the . . . dimming out of the mind that I can't bear, because until lately, just lately, his mind was amazingly clear. But yesterday? In Taxco? I spent nearly all we had left on the wheelchair for him and still he insisted that we go on with the trip till we got to the sea, the . . . cradle of life as he calls it. . . . [*She suddenly notices* NONNO, *sunk in his chair as if lifeless. She draws a sharp breath, and goes quietly to him.*]

SHANNON [*to the Mexican boys*]: Servicio! Aquí! [*The force of his order proves effective: they serve the fish course.*]

HANNAH: What a kind man you are. I don't know how to thank you, Mr. Shannon. I'm going to wake him up now. Nonno! [*She claps her hands quietly at his ear. The old man rouses with a confused, breathless chuckle.*] Nonno, linen napkins. [*She removes a napkin from the pocket of her smock.*] I always carry one with me, you see, in case we run into paper napkins as sometimes happens, you see. . . .

NONNO: Wonderful place here. . . . I hope it is à la carte, Hannah, I want a very light supper so I won't get sleepy. I'm going to work after supper. I'm going to finish it here.

HANNAH: Nonno? We've made a friend here. Nonno, this is the Reverend Mr. Shannon.

NONNO [*struggling out of his confusion*]: Reverend?

HANNAH [*shouting to him*]: Mr. Shannon's an Episcopal clergyman, Nonno.

NONNO: A man of God?

HANNAH: A man of God, on vacation.

NONNO: Hannah, tell him I'm too old to baptize and too young to bury but on the market for marriage to a rich widow, fat, fair and forty.

[NONNO *is delighted by all of his own little jokes. One can
see him exchanging these pleasantries with the rocking-chair
brigades of summer hotels at the turn of the century—and
with professors' wives at little colleges in New England. But
now it has become somewhat grotesque in a touching way,
this desire to please, this playful manner, these venerable
jokes.* SHANNON *goes along with it. The old man touches
something in him which is outside of his concern with himself. This part of the scene, which is played in a "scherzo"
mood, has an accompanying windy obligato on the hilltop—
all through it we hear the wind from the sea gradually rising,
sweeping up the hill through the rain forest, and there are
fitful glimmers of lightning in the sky.*]

NONNO: But very few ladies ever go past forty if you believe
'em, ho, ho! Ask him to . . . give the blessing. Mexican food
needs blessing.

SHANNON: Sir, you give the blessing. I'll be right with you.
[*He has broken one of his shoelaces.*]

NONNO: Tell him I will oblige him on one condition.

SHANNON: What condition, sir?

NONNO: That you'll keep my daughter company when I retire
after dinner. I go to bed with the chickens and get up with the
roosters, ho, ho! So you're a man of God. A benedict or a
bachelor?

SHANNON: Bachelor, sir. No sane and civilized woman would
have me, Mr. Coffin.

NONNO: What did he say, Hannah?

HANNAH [*embarrassed*]: Nonno, give the blessing.

NONNO [*not hearing this*]: I call her my daughter, but she's
my daughter's daughter. We've been in charge of each other
since she lost both her parents in the very first automobile crash
on the island of Nantucket.

HANNAH: Nonno, give the blessing.

NONNO: She isn't a modern flapper, she isn't modern and she—doesn't flap, but she was brought up to be a wonderful wife and mother. But . . . I'm a selfish old man so I've kept her all to myself.

HANNAH [*shouting into his ear*]: Nonno, Nonno, the blessing!

NONNO [*rising with an effort*]: Yes, the blessing. Bless this food to our use, and ourselves to Thy service. Amen. [*He totters back into his chair.*]

SHANNON: Amen.

[NONNO's *mind starts drifting, his head drooping forward. He murmurs to himself.*]

SHANNON: How good is the old man's poetry?

HANNAH: My grandfather was a fairly well-known minor poet before the First World War and for a little while after.

SHANNON: In the minor league, huh?

HANNAH: Yes, a minor league poet with a major league spirit. I'm proud to be his granddaughter. . . . [*She draws a pack of cigarettes from her pocket, then replaces it immediately without taking a cigarette.*]

NONNO [*very confused*]: Hannah, it's too hot for . . . hot cereals this . . . morning. . . . [*He shakes his head several times with a rueful chuckle.*]

HANNAH: He's not quite back, you see, he thinks it's morning. [*She says this as if making an embarrassing admission, with a quick, frightened smile at SHANNON.*]

SHANNON: Fantastic—fantastic.

HANNAH: That word "fantastic" seems to be your favorite word, Mr. Shannon.

SHANNON [*looking out gloomily from the verandah*]: Yeah, well, you know we—live on two levels, Miss Jelkes, the realistic level and the fantastic level, and which is the real one, really. . . .

HANNAH: I would say both, Mr. Shannon.

SHANNON: But when you live on the fantastic level as I have lately but have got to operate on the realistic level, that's when you're spooked, that's the spook. . . . [*This is said as if it were a private reflection.*] I thought I'd shake the spook here but conditions have changed here. I didn't know the patrona had turned to a widow, a sort of bright widow spider. [*He chuckles almost like* NONNO.]

[MAXINE *has pushed one of those gay little brass-and-glass liquor carts around the corner of the verandah. It is laden with an ice bucket, coconuts and a variety of liquors. She hums gaily to herself as she pushes the cart close to the table.*]

MAXINE: Cocktails, anybody?

HANNAH: No, thank you, Mrs. Faulk, I don't think we care for any.

SHANNON: People don't drink cocktails between the fish and the entrée, Maxine honey.

MAXINE: Grampa needs a toddy to wake him up. Old folks need a toddy to pick 'em up. [*She shouts into the old man's ear.*] Grampa! How about a toddy? [*Her hips are thrust out at* SHANNON.]

SHANNON: Maxine, your ass—excuse me, Miss Jelkes—your hips, Maxine, are too fat for this verandah.

MAXINE: Hah! Mexicans like 'em, if I can judge by the pokes and pinches I get in the busses to town. And so do the Germans. Ev'ry time I go near Herr Fahrenkopf he gives me a pinch or a goose.

SHANNON: Then go near him again for another goose.

MAXINE: Hah! I'm mixing Grampa a Manhattan with two cherries in it so he'll live through dinner.

SHANNON: Go on back to your Nazis, I'll mix the Manhattan for him. [*He goes to the liquor cart.*]

MAXINE [*to* HANNAH]: How about you, honey, a little soda with lime juice?

HANNAH: Nothing for me, thank you.

SHANNON: Don't make nervous people more nervous, Maxine.

MAXINE: You better let me mix that toddy for Grampa, you're making a mess of it, Shannon.

[*With a snort of fury, he thrusts the liquor cart like a battering ram at her belly. Some of the bottles fall off it; she thrusts it right back at him.*]

HANNAH: Mrs. Faulk, Mr. Shannon, this is childish, please stop it!

[*The Germans are attracted by the disturbance. They cluster around, laughing delightedly.* SHANNON *and* MAXINE *seize opposite ends of the rolling liquor cart and thrust it toward each other, both grinning fiercely as gladiators in mortal combat. The Germans shriek with laughter and chatter in German.*]

HANNAH: Mr. Shannon, stop it! [*She appeals to the Germans.*] *Bitte!* Nehmen Sie die Spirituosen weg. Bitte, nehmen Sie die weg.

[SHANNON *has wrested the cart from* MAXINE *and pushed it at the Germans. They scream delightedly. The cart crashes into the wall of the verandah.* SHANNON *leaps down the steps and runs into the foliage. Birds scream in the rain forest. Then sudden quiet returns to the verandah as the Germans go back to their own table.*]

MAXINE: Crazy, black Irish Protestant son of a . . . Protestant!

HANNAH: Mrs. Faulk, he's putting up a struggle not to drink.

MAXINE: Don't interfere. You're an interfering woman.

HANNAH: Mr. Shannon is dangerously . . . disturbed.

MAXINE: I know how to handle him, honey—you just met him today. Here's Grampa's Manhattan cocktail with two cherries in it.

HANNAH: Please don't call him Grampa.

MAXINE: Shannon calls him Grampa.

HANNAH [*taking the drink*]: He doesn't make it sound condescending, but you *do*. My grandfather is a gentleman in the true sense of the word, he is a <u>*gentle man*</u>.

MAXINE: What are you?

HANNAH: I am his granddaughter.

MAXINE: Is that all you are?

HANNAH: I think it's enough to be.

MAXINE: Yeah, but you're also a deadbeat, using that dying old man for a front to get in places without the cash to pay even one day in advance. Why, you're dragging him around with you like Mexican beggars carry around a sick baby to put the touch on the tourists.

HANNAH: I told you I had no money.

MAXINE: Yes, and I told you that I was a widow—recent. In such a financial hole they might as well have buried me with my husband.

[SHANNON *reappears from the jungle foliage but remains unnoticed by* HANNAH *and* MAXINE.]

HANNAH [*with forced calm*]: Tomorrow morning, at day-break, I will go in town. I will set up my easel in the plaza and peddle my water colors and sketch tourists. I am not a weak person, my failure here isn't typical of me.

MAXINE: I'm not a weak person either.

HANNAH: No. By no means, no. Your strength is awe-inspiring.

MAXINE: You're goddam right about that, but how do you think you'll get to Acapulco without the cabfare or even the busfare there?

HANNAH: I will go on shanks' mare, Mrs. Faulk—islanders are good walkers. And if you doubt my word for it, if you really think I came here as a deadbeat, then I will put my grandfather back in his wheelchair and push him back down this hill to the road and all the way back into town.

MAXINE: Ten miles, with a storm coming up?

HANNAH: Yes, I would—I will. [*She is dominating* MAXINE *in this exchange. Both stand beside the table.* NONNO'S *head is drooping back into sleep.*]

MAXINE: I wouldn't let you.

HANNAH: But you've made it clear that you don't want us to stay here for one night even.

MAXINE: The storm would blow that old man out of his wheelchair like a dead leaf.

HANNAH: He would prefer that to staying where he's not welcome, and I would prefer it for him, and for myself, Mrs. Faulk. [*She turns to the Mexican boys.*] Where is his wheel-chair? Where is my grandfather's wheelchair?

[*This exchange has roused the old man. He struggles up from his chair, confused, strikes the floor with his cane and starts declaiming a poem.*]

NONNO:
>Love's an old remembered song
>A drunken fiddler plays,
>Stumbling crazily along
>Crooked alleyways.
>When his heart is mad with music
>He will play the—

HANNAH: Nonno, not now, Nonno! He thought someone asked for a poem. [*She gets him back into the chair.* HANNAH *and* MAXINE *are still unaware of* SHANNON.]

MAXINE: Calm down, honey.

HANNAH: I'm perfectly calm, Mrs. Faulk.

MAXINE: I'm *not*. That's the trouble.

HANNAH: I understand that, Mrs. Faulk. You lost your husband just lately. I think you probably miss him more than you know.

MAXINE: No, the trouble is Shannon.

HANNAH: You mean his nervous state and his . . . ?

MAXINE: No, I just mean Shannon. I want you to lay off him, honey. You're not for Shannon and Shannon isn't for you.

HANNAH: Mrs. Faulk, I'm a New England spinster who is pushing forty.

MAXINE: I got the vibrations between you—I'm very good at catching vibrations between people—and there sure was a vibration between you and Shannon the moment you got here. That, just that, believe me, nothing but that has made this . . . misunderstanding between us. So if you just don't mess with Shannon, you and your Grampa can stay on here as long as you want to, honey.

HANNAH: Oh, Mrs. Faulk, do I look like a *vamp?*

MAXINE: They come in all types. I've had all types of them here.

[SHANNON *comes over to the table*.]

SHANNON: Maxine, I told you don't make nervous people more nervous, but you wouldn't listen.

MAXINE: What you need is a drink.

SHANNON: Let me decide about that.

HANNAH: Won't you sit down with us, Mr. Shannon, and eat something? Please. You'll feel better.

SHANNON: I'm not hungry right now.

HANNAH: Well, just sit down with us, won't you?

[SHANNON *sits down with* HANNAH.]

MAXINE [*warningly to* HANNAH]: O.K. O.K. . . .

NONNO [*rousing a bit and mumbling*]: Wonderful . . . wonderful place here.

[MAXINE *retires from the table and wheels the liquor cart over to the German party*.]

SHANNON: Would you have gone through with it?

HANNAH: Haven't you ever played poker, Mr. Shannon?

SHANNON: You mean you were bluffing?

HANNAH: Let's say I was drawing to an inside straight. [*The wind rises and sweeps up the hill like a great waking sigh from the ocean*.] It *is* going to storm. I hope your ladies aren't still out in that, that . . . glass-bottomed boat, observing the, uh, submarine . . . marvels.

SHANNON: That's because you don't know these ladies. However, they're back from the boat trip. They're down at the cantina, dancing together to the jukebox and hatching new plots to get me kicked out of Blake Tours.

HANNAH: What would you do if you. . . .

SHANNON: Got the sack? Go back to the Church or take the long swim to China. [HANNAH *removes a crumpled pack of cigarettes from her pocket. She discovers only two left in the pack and decides to save them for later. She returns the pack to her pocket.*] May I have one of your cigarettes, Miss Jelkes? [*She offers him the pack. He takes it from her and crumples it and throws it off the verandah.*] Never smoke those, they're made out of tobacco from cigarette stubs that beggars pick up off sidewalks and out of gutters in Mexico City. [*He produces a tin of English cigarettes.*] Have these—Benson and Hedges, imported, in an airtight tin, my luxury in my life.

HANNAH: Why—thank you, I will, since you have thrown mine away.

SHANNON: I'm going to tell you something about yourself. You are a lady, a *real* one and a *great* one.

HANNAH: What have I done to merit that compliment from you?

SHANNON: It isn't a compliment, it's just a report on what I've noticed about you at a time when it's hard for me to notice anything outside myself. You took out those Mexican cigarettes, you found you just had two left, you can't afford to buy a new pack of even that cheap brand, so you put them away for later. Right?

HANNAH: Mercilessly accurate, Mr. Shannon.

SHANNON: But when I asked you for one, you offered it to me without a sign of reluctance.

HANNAH: Aren't you making a big point out of a small matter?

SHANNON: Just the opposite, honey, I'm making a small point out of a very large matter. [SHANNON *has put a cigarette in his lips but has no matches.* HANNAH *has some and she lights his cigarette for him.*] How'd you learn how to light a match in the wind?

HANNAH: Oh, I've learned lots of useful little things like that. I wish I'd learned some *big* ones.

SHANNON: Such as what?

HANNAH: How to help you, Mr. Shannon. . . .

SHANNON: Now I know why I came here!

HANNAH: To meet someone who can light a match in the wind?

SHANNON [*looking down at the table, his voice choking*]: To meet someone who wants to *help me,* Miss Jelkes. . . . [*He makes a quick, embarrassed turn in the chair, as if to avoid her seeing that he has tears in his eyes. She regards him steadily and tenderly, as she would her grandfather.*]

HANNAH: Has it been so long since anyone has wanted to help you, or have you just. . . .

SHANNON: Have I—what?

HANNAH: Just been so much involved with a struggle in yourself that you haven't noticed when people have wanted to help you, the little they can? I know people torture each other many times like devils, but sometimes they do see and know each other, you know, and then, if they're decent, they do want to help each other all that they can. Now will you please help *me?* Take care of Nonno while I remove my water colors from the annex verandah because the storm is coming up by leaps and bounds now.

[*He gives a quick, jerky nod, dropping his face briefly into the cup of his hands. She murmurs "Thank you" and springs up, starting along the verandah. Halfway across, as the storm closes in upon the hilltop with a thunderclap and a sound of rain coming,* HANNAH *turns to look back at the table.* SHANNON *has risen and gone around the table to* NONNO.]

SHANNON: Grampa? Nonno? Let's get up before the rain hits us, Grampa.

NONNO: What? What?

[SHANNON *gets the old man out of his chair and shepherds him to the back of the verandah as* HANNAH *rushes toward the annex. The Mexican boys hastily clear the table, fold it up and lean it against the wall.* SHANNON *and* NONNO *turn and face toward the storm, like brave men facing a firing squad.* MAXINE *is excitedly giving orders to the boys.*]

MAXINE: Pronto, pronto, muchachos! Pronto, pronto!* Llevaros todas las cosas! Pronto, pronto! Recoje los platos! Apúrate con el mantel!

PEDRO: Nos estamos dando prisa!

PANCHO: Que el chubasco lave los platos!

[*The German party look on the storm as a Wagnerian climax. They rise from their table as the boys come to clear it, and start singing exultantly. The storm, with its white convulsions of light, is like a giant white bird attacking the hilltop of the Costa Verde.* HANNAH *reappears with her water colors clutched against her chest.*]

SHANNON: Got them?

HANNAH: Yes, just in time. Here is your God, Mr. Shannon.

SHANNON [*quietly*]: Yes, I see him, I hear him, I know him. And if he doesn't know that I know him, let him strike me dead with a bolt of his lightning.

---

* Hurry, hurry, boys! Pick everything up! Get the plates! Hurry with the table cloth! / We *are* hurrying! / Let the storm wash the plates!

[He moves away from the wall to the edge of the verandah as a fine silver sheet of rain descends off the sloping roof, catching the light and dimming the figures behind it. Now everything is silver, delicately lustrous. SHANNON extends his hands under the rainfall, turning them in it as if to cool them. Then he cups them to catch the water in his palms and bathes his forehead with it. The rainfall increases. The sound of the marimba band at the beach cantina is brought up the hill by the wind. SHANNON lowers his hands from his burning forehead and stretches them out through the rain's silver sheet as if he were reaching for something outside and beyond himself. Then nothing is visible but these reaching-out hands. A pure white flash of lightning reveals HANNAH and NONNO against the wall, behind SHANNON, and the electric globe suspended from the roof goes out, the power extinguished by the storm. A clear shaft of light stays on SHANNON'S reaching-out hands till the stage curtain has fallen, slowly.]*

INTERMISSION

---

* Note: In staging, the plastic elements should be restrained so that they don't take precedence over the more important human values. It should not seem like an "effect curtain." The faint, windy music of the marimba band from the cantina should continue as the house-lights are brought up for the intermission.

Act Three

The verandah, several hours later. Cubicles number 3, 4, and 5 are dimly lighted within. We see HANNAH *in number 3, and* NONNO *in number 4.* SHANNON, *who has taken off his shirt, is seated at a table on the verandah, writing a letter to his Bishop. All but this table have been folded and stacked against the wall and* MAXINE *is putting the hammock back up which had been taken down for dinner. The electric power is still off and the cubicles are lighted by oil lamps. The sky has cleared completely, the moon is making for full and it bathes the scene in an almost garish silver which is intensified by the wetness from the recent rainstorm. Everything is drenched—there are pools of silver here and there on the floor of the verandah. At one side a smudge-pot is burning to repel the mosquitoes, which are particularly vicious after a tropical downpour when the wind is exhausted.*

SHANNON *is working feverishly on the letter to the Bishop, now and then slapping at a mosquito on his bare torso. He is shiny with perspiration, still breathing like a spent runner, muttering to himself as he writes and sometimes suddenly drawing a loud deep breath and simultaneously throwing back his head to stare up wildly at the night sky.* HANNAH *is seated on a straight-back chair behind the mosquito netting in her cubicle— very straight herself, holding a small book in her hands but looking steadily over it at* SHANNON, *like a guardian angel. Her hair has been let down.* NONNO *can be seen in his cubicle rocking back and forth on the edge of the narrow bed as he goes over and over the lines of his first new poem in "twenty-some years"—which he knows is his last one.*

Now and then the sound of distant music drifts up from the beach cantina.

MAXINE: Workin' on your sermon for next Sunday, Rev'-rend?

SHANNON: I'm writing a very important letter, Maxine. [*He means don't disturb me.*]

MAXINE: Who to, Shannon?

SHANNON: The Dean of the Divinity School at Sewanee. [MAXINE *repeats* "Sewanee" *to herself, tolerantly.*] Yes, and I'd appreciate it very much, Maxine honey, if you'd get Pedro or Pancho to drive into town with it tonight so it will go out first thing in the morning.

MAXINE: The kids took off in the station wagon already— for some cold beers and hot whores at the cantina.

SHANNON: "Fred's dead"—he's lucky. . . .

MAXINE: Don't misunderstand me about Fred, baby. I miss him, but we'd not only stopped sleeping together, we'd stopped talking together except in grunts—no quarrels, no misunderstandings, but if we exchanged two grunts in the course of a day, it was a long conversation we'd had that day between us.

SHANNON: Fred knew when I was spooked—wouldn't have to tell him. He'd just look at me and say, "Well, Shannon, you're spooked."

MAXINE: Yeah, well, Fred and me'd reached the point of just grunting.

SHANNON: Maybe he thought you'd turned into a pig, Maxine.

MAXINE: Hah! You know damn well that Fred respected me, Shannon, like I did Fred. We just, well, you know . . . age difference. . . .

SHANNON: Well, you've got Pedro and Pancho.

MAXINE: Employees. They don't respect me enough. When you let employees get too free with you, personally, they stop respecting you, Shannon. And it's, well, it's . . . humiliating —not to be . . . respected.

SHANNON: Then take more bus trips to town for the Mexican pokes and the pinches, or get Herr Fahrenkopf to "respect" you, honey.

MAXINE: Hah! You kill me. I been thinking lately of selling out here and going back to the States, to Texas, and operat-

ing a tourist camp outside some live town like Houston or
Dallas, on a highway, and renting out cabins to business execu-
tives wanting a comfortable little intimate little place to give a
little after-hours dictation to their cute little secretaries that
can't type or write shorthand. Complimentary rum-cocos—
bathrooms with bidets. I'll introduce the bidet to the States.

SHANNON: Does everything have to wind up on that level
with you, Maxine?

MAXINE: Yes and no, baby. I know the difference between
loving someone and just sleeping with someone—even I know
about that. [*He starts to rise.*] We've both reached a point
where we've got to settle for something that works for us in
our lives—even if it isn't on the highest kind of level.

SHANNON: I don't want to rot.

MAXINE: You wouldn't. I wouldn't let you! I know your
psychological history. I remember one of your conversations
on this verandah with Fred. You was explaining to him how
your problems first started. You told him that Mama, your
Mama, used to send you to bed before you was ready to sleep
—so you practiced the little boy's vice, you amused yourself
with yourself. And once she caught you at it and whaled your
backside with the back side of a hairbrush because she said
she had to punish you for it because it made God mad as
much as it did Mama, and she had to punish you for it so
God wouldn't punish you for it harder than she would.

SHANNON: I was talking to Fred.

MAXINE: Yeah, but I heard it, all of it. You said you loved
God and Mama and so you quit it to please them, but it was
your secret pleasure and you harbored a secret resentment
against Mama and God for making you give it up. And so
you got back at God by preaching atheistical sermons and
you got back at Mama by starting to lay young girls.

SHANNON: I have never delivered an atheistical sermon,
and never would or could when I go back to the Church.

MAXINE: You're not going back to no Church. Did you mention the charge of statutory rape to the Divinity Dean?

SHANNON [*thrusting his chair back so vehemently that it
topples over*]: Why don't you *let up* on me? You haven't let up

on me since I got here this morning! *Let up on me!* Will you please *let up* on me?

MAXINE [*smiling serenely into his rage.*]: Aw baby. . . .

SHANNON: What do you mean by "aw baby"? What do you want out of me, Maxine honey?

MAXINE: Just to do this. [*She runs her fingers through his hair. He thrusts her hand away.*]

SHANNON: Ah, God. [*Words fail him. He shakes his head with a slight, helpless laugh and goes down the steps from the verandah.*]

MAXINE: The Chinaman in the kitchen says, "No sweat." . . . "No sweat." He says that's all his philosophy. All the Chinese philosophy in three words, "Mei yoo guanchi"— which is Chinese for "No sweat." . . . With your record and a charge of statutory rape hanging over you in Texas, how could you go to a church except to the Holy Rollers with some lively young female rollers and a bushel of hay on the church floor?

SHANNON: I'll drive into town in the bus to post this letter tonight. [*He has started toward the path. There are sounds below. He divides the masking foliage with his hands and looks down the hill.*]

MAXINE [*descending the steps from the verandah*]: Watch out for the spook, he's out there.

SHANNON: My ladies are up to something. They're all down there on the road, around the bus.

MAXINE: They're running out on you, Shannon.

[*She comes up beside him. He draws back and she looks down the hill. The light in number 3 cubicle comes on and HANNAH rises from the little table that she had cleared for letter-writing. She removes her Kabuki robe from a hook and puts it on as an actor puts on a costume in his dressing room. NONNO's cubicle is also lighted dimly. He sits on the edge of his cot, rocking slightly back and forth, uttering an indistinguishable mumble of lines from his poem.*]

MAXINE: Yeah. There's a little fat man down there that looks like Jake Latta to me. Yep, that's Jake, that's Latta. I reckon Blake Tours has sent him here to take over your party, Shannon. [SHANNON *looks out over the jungle and lights a cigarette with jerky fingers.*] Well, let him do it. No sweat! He's coming up here now. Want me to handle it for you?

SHANNON: I'll handle it for myself. You keep out of it, please.

[*He speaks with a desperate composure.* HANNAH *stands just behind the curtain of her cubicle, motionless as a painted figure, during the scene that follows.* JAKE LATTA *comes puffing up the verandah steps, beaming genially.*]

LATTA: Hi there, Larry.

SHANNON: Hello, Jake. [*He folds his letter into an envelope.*] Mrs. Faulk honey, this goes air special.

MAXINE: First you'd better address it.

SHANNON: Oh!

[SHANNON *laughs and snatches the letter back, fumbling in his pocket for an address book, his fingers shaking uncontrollably.* LATTA *winks at* MAXINE. *She smiles tolerantly.*]

LATTA: How's our boy doin', Maxine?

MAXINE: He'd feel better if I could get him to take a drink.

LATTA: Can't you get a drink down him?

MAXINE: Nope, not even a rum-coco.

LATTA: Let's have a rum-coco, Larry.

SHANNON: You have a rum-coco, Jake. I have a party of ladies to take care of. And I've discovered that situations come up in this business that call for cold, sober judgment. How about you? Haven't you ever made that discovery, Jake? What're you doing here? Are you here with a party?

LATTA: I'm here to pick up your party, Larry boy.

SHANNON: That's interesting! On whose authority, Jake?

LATTA: Blake Tours wired me in Cuernavaca to pick up your party here and put them together with mine cause you'd had this little nervous upset of yours and. . . .

SHANNON: Show me the wire! Huh?

LATTA: The bus driver says you took the ignition key to the bus.

SHANNON: That's right. I have the ignition key to the bus and I have this party and neither the bus or the party will pull out of here till I say so.

LATTA: Larry, you're a sick boy. Don't give me trouble.

SHANNON: What jail did they bail you out of, you fat zero?

LATTA: Let's have the bus key, Larry.

SHANNON: Where did they dig you up? You've got no party in Cuernavaca, you haven't been out with a party since 'thirty-seven.

LATTA: Just give me the bus key, Larry.

SHANNON: In a pig's—snout!—like yours!

LATTA: Where is the reverend's bedroom, Mrs. Faulk?

SHANNON: The bus key is in my pocket. [*He slaps his pants pocket fiercely.*] Here, right here, in my pocket! Want it? Try and get it, Fatso!

LATTA: What language for a reverend to use, Mrs. Faulk. . . .

SHANNON [*holding up the key*]: See it? [*He thrusts it back into his pocket.*] Now go back wherever you crawled from. My party of ladies is staying here three more days because several of them are in no condition to travel and neither—neither am I.

LATTA: They're getting in the bus now.

SHANNON: How are you going to start it?

LATTA: Larry, don't make me call the bus driver up here to hold you down while I get that key away from you. You want to see the wire from Blake Tours? Here. [*He produces the wire.*] Read it.

SHANNON: You sent that wire to yourself.

LATTA: From Houston?

SHANNON: You had it sent you from Houston. What's that

prove? Why, Blake Tours was nothing, *nothing!*—till they got
me. You think they'd let me go?—Ho, ho! Latta, it's caught
up with you, Latta, all the whores and tequila have hit your
brain now, Latta. [LATTA *shouts down the hill for the bus
driver.*] Don't you realize what I mean to Blake Tours?
Haven't you seen the brochure in which they mention, they
brag, that special parties are conducted by the Reverend T.
Lawrence Shannon, D.D., noted world traveler, lecturer, son
of a minister and grandson of a bishop, and the direct de-
scendant of two colonial governors? [MISS FELLOWES *appears
at the verandah steps.*] Miss Fellowes has read the brochure,
she's memorized the brochure. She knows what it says about
me.

MISS FELLOWES [*to* LATTA]: Have you got the bus key?

LATTA: Bus driver's going to get it away from him, lady.
[*He lights a cigar with dirty, shaky fingers.*]

SHANNON: Ha-ha-ha-ha-ha! [*His laughter shakes him back
against the verandah wall.*]

LATTA: He's gone. [*He touches his forehead.*]

SHANNON: Why, those ladies . . . have had . . . some of
them, most of them if not all of them . . . for the first time
in their lives the advantage of contact, social contact, with
a gentleman born and bred, whom under no other circumstances they could have possibly met . . . let alone be given
the chance to insult and accuse and. . . .

MISS FELLOWES: Shannon! The girls are in the bus and we
want to go now, so give up that key. Now!

[HANK, *the bus driver, appears at the top of the path,
whistling casually: he is not noticed at first.*]

SHANNON: If I didn't have a decent sense of responsibility to
these parties I take out, I would gladly turn over your party—
because I don't like your party—to this degenerate here, this
Jake Latta of the gutter-rat Lattas. Yes, I would—I would
surrender the bus key in my pocket, even to Latta, but I am
not that irresponsible, no, I'm not, to the parties that I take
out, regardless of the party's treatment of me. I still feel
responsible for them till I get them back wherever I picked
them up. [HANK *comes onto the verandah.*] Hi, Hank. Are you
friend or foe?

HANK: Larry, I got to get that ignition key now so we can get moving down there.

SHANNON: Oh! Then *foe!* I'm disappointed, Hank. I thought you were friend, not foe. [HANK *puts a wrestler's armlock on* SHANNON *and* LATTA *removes the bus key from his pocket.* HANNAH *raises a hand to her eyes.*] O.K., O.K., you've got the bus key. By force. I feel exonerated now of all responsibility. Take the bus and the ladies in it and go. Hey, Jake, did you know they had lesbians in Texas—without the dikes the plains of Texas would be engulfed by the Gulf. [*He nods his head violently toward* MISS FELLOWES, *who springs forward and slaps him.*] Thank you, Miss Fellowes. Latta, hold on a minute. I will not be stranded here. I've had unusual expenses on this trip. Right now I don't have my fare back to Houston or even to Mexico City. Now if there's any truth in your statement that Blake Tours have really authorized you to take over my party, then I am sure they have . . . [*He draws a breath, almost gasping.*] . . . I'm sure they must have given you something in the . . . the nature of . . . *severance* pay? Or at least enough to get me back to the States?

LATTA: I got no money for you.

SHANNON: I hate to question your word, but. . . .

LATTA: We'll drive you back to Mexico City. You can sit up front with the driver.

SHANNON: *You* would do that, Latta. *I'd* find it *humiliating.* Now! Give me my severance pay!

LATTA: Blake Tours is having to refund those ladies half the price of the tour. That's your severance pay. And Miss Fellowes tells me you got plenty of money out of this young girl you seduced in. . . .

SHANNON: Miss Fellowes, did you really make such a . . . ?

MISS FELLOWES: When Charlotte returned that night, she'd cashed two traveler's checks.

SHANNON: After I had spent all my own cash.

MISS FELLOWES: On what? Whores in the filthy places you took her through?

SHANNON: Miss Charlotte cashed two ten-dollar traveler's checks because I had spent all the cash I had on me. And I've never had to, I've certainly never desired to, have relations with whores.

MISS FELLOWES: You took her through ghastly places, such as. . . .

SHANNON: I showed her what she wanted me to show her. Ask her! I showed her San Juan de Letran, I showed her Tenampa and some other places not listed in the Blake Tours brochure. I showed her more than the floating gardens at Xochimilco, Maximilian's Palace, and the mad Empress Carlotta's little homesick chapel, Our Lady of Guadalupe, the monument to Juarez, the relics of the Aztec civilization, the sword of Cortez, the headdress of Montezuma. I showed her what she told me she wanted to see. Where is she? Where is Miss . . . oh, down there with the ladies. [*He leans over the rail and shouts down.*] Charlotte! Charlotte! [MISS FELLOWES *seizes his arm and thrusts him away from the verandah rail.*]

MISS FELLOWES: Don't you dare!

SHANNON: Dare what?

MISS FELLOWES: Call her, speak to her, go near her, you, you . . . *filthy!*

[MAXINE *reappears at the corner of the verandah, with the ceremonial rapidity of a cuckoo bursting from a clock to announce the hour. She just stands there with an incongruous grin, her big eyes unblinking, as if they were painted on her round beaming face.* HANNAH *holds a gold-lacquered Japanese fan motionless but open in one hand; the other hand touches the netting at the cubicle door as if she were checking an impulse to rush to* SHANNON'S *defense. Her attitude has the style of a Kabuki dancer's pose.* SHANNON'S *manner becomes courtly again.*]

SHANNON: Oh, all right, I won't. I only wanted her to confirm my story that I took her out that night at her request, not at my . . . suggestion. All that I did was offer my services to her when *she* told *me* she'd like to see things not listed in the brochure, not usually witnessed by ordinary tourists such as. . . .

MISS FELLOWES: Your hotel bedroom? Later? That too? She came back *flea*-bitten!

SHANNON: Oh, now, don't exaggerate, please. Nobody ever got any fleas off Shannon.

MISS FELLOWES: Her clothes had to be fumigated!

SHANNON: I understand your annoyance, but you are going too far when you try to make out that I gave Charlotte fleas. I don't deny that. . . .

MISS FELLOWES: Wait till they get my *report!*

SHANNON: I don't deny that it's possible to get fleabites on a tour of inspection of what lies under the public surface of cities, off the grand boulevards, away from the nightclubs, even away from Diego Rivera's murals, but. . . .

MISS FELLOWES: Oh, preach that in a pulpit, Reverend Shannon *de*-frocked!

SHANNON [*ominously*]: You've said that once too often. [*He seizes her arm.*] This time before witnesses. Miss Jelkes? Miss Jelkes!

[HANNAH *opens the curtain of her cubicle.*]

HANNAH: Yes, Mr. Shannon, what is it?

SHANNON: You heard what this. . . .

MISS FELLOWES: Shannon! Take your hand off my arm!

SHANNON: Miss Jelkes, just tell me, did you hear what she . . . [*His voice stops oddly with a choked sobbing sound. He runs at the wall and pounds it with his fists.*]

MISS FELLOWES: I spent this entire afternoon and over twenty dollars checking up on this impostor, with long-distance phone calls.

HANNAH: Not impostor—you mustn't say things like that.

MISS FELLOWES: You were locked out of your church!—for atheism and seducing of girls!

SHANNON [*turning about*]: In front of God and witnesses, you are lying, lying!

LATTA: Miss Fellowes, I want you to know that Blake Tours was deceived about this character's background and Blake Tours will see that he is blacklisted from now on at every travel agency in the States.

SHANNON: How about Africa, Asia, Australia? The whole world, Latta, God's world, has been the range of my travels. I haven't stuck to the schedules of the brochures and I've always allowed the ones that were willing to see, to *see!*—the underworlds of all places, and if they had hearts to be touched, feelings to feel with, I gave them a priceless chance to feel and be touched. And none will ever forget it, none of them, ever, never! [*The passion of his speech imposes a little stillness.*]

LATTA: Go on, lie back in your hammock, that's all you're good for, Shannon. [*He goes to the top of the path and shouts down the hill.*] O.K., let's get cracking. Get that luggage strapped on top of the bus, we're moving! [*He starts down the hill with* MISS FELLOWES.]

NONNO [*incongruously, from his cubicle*]:

> How calmly does the orange branch
> Observe the sky begin to blanch. . . .

[SHANNON *sucks in his breath with an abrupt, fierce sound. He rushes off the verandah and down the path toward the road.* HANNAH *calls after him, with a restraining gesture.* MAXINE *appears on the verandah. Then a great commotion commences below the hill, with shrieks of outrage and squeals of shocked laughter.*]

MAXINE [*rushing to the path*]: Shannon! Shannon! Get back up here, get back up here. Pedro, Pancho, traerme a Shannon. Que está haciendo allí? Oh, my God! Stop him, for God's sake, somebody stop him!

[SHANNON *returns, panting and spent. He is followed by* MAXINE.]

MAXINE: Shannon, go in your room and stay there until that party's gone.

SHANNON: Don't give me orders.

MAXINE: You do what I tell you to do or I'll have you removed—you know where.

SHANNON: Don't push me, don't pull at me, Maxine.

MAXINE: All right, do as I say.

SHANNON: Shannon obeys only Shannon.

MAXINE: You'll sing a different tune if they put you where they put you in 'thirty-six. Remember 'thirty-six, Shannon?

SHANNON: O.K., Maxine, just . . . let me breathe alone, please. I won't go but I will lie in the . . . hammock.

MAXINE: Go into Fred's room where I can watch you.

SHANNON: Later, Maxine, not yet.

MAXINE: Why do you always come here to crack up, Shannon?

SHANNON: It's the hammock, Maxine, the hammock by the rain forest.

MAXINE: Shannon, go in your room and stay there until I get back. Oh, my God, the money. They haven't paid the mother-grabbin' bill. I got to go back down there and collect their goddam bill before they. . . . Pancho, vigílalo, entiendes? [*She rushes back down the hill, shouting "Hey! Just a minute down there!"*]

SHANNON: What did I do? [*He shakes his head, stunned.*] I don't know what I did.

[HANNAH *opens the screen of her cubicle but doesn't come out. She is softly lighted so that she looks, again, like a medieval sculpture of a saint. Her pale gold hair catches the soft light. She has let it down and still holds the silver-backed brush with which she was brushing it.*]

SHANNON: God almighty, I . . . what did I do? I don't know what I did. [*He turns to the Mexican boys who have come back up the path.*] Qué hice? Qué hice?

[*There is breathless, spasmodic laughter from the boys as* PANCHO *informs him that he pissed on the ladies' luggage.*]

PANCHO: Tú measte en las maletas de las señoras!

[SHANNON *tries to laugh with the boys, while they bend double with amusement.* SHANNON'S *laughter dies out in little choked spasms. Down the hill,* MAXINE'S *voice is raised in angry altercation with* JAKE LATTA. MISS FELLOWES' *voice is lifted and then there is a general rhubarb to which is added the roar of the bus motor.*]

SHANNON: There go my ladies, ha, ha! There go my . . . [*He turns about to meet* HANNAH'S *grave, compassionate gaze. He tries to laugh again. She shakes her head with a slight restraining gesture and drops the curtain so that her softly luminous figure is seen as through a mist.*] . . . ladies, the last of my—ha, ha!—ladies. [*He bends far over the verandah rail, then straightens violently and with an animal outcry begins to pull at the chain suspending the gold cross about his neck.* PANCHO *watches indifferently as the chain cuts the back of* SHANNON'S *neck.* HANNAH *rushes out to him.*]

HANNAH: Mr. Shannon, stop that! You're cutting yourself doing that. That isn't necessary, so stop it! [*to* PANCHO] Agárrale las manos! [PANCHO *makes a halfhearted effort to comply, but* SHANNON *kicks at him and goes on with the furious self-laceration.*] Shannon, let me do it, let me take it off you. Can I take it off you? [*He drops his arms. She struggles with the clasp of the chain but her fingers are too shaky to work it.*]

SHANNON: No, no, it won't come off, I'll have to break it off me.

HANNAH: No, no, wait—I've got it. [*She has now removed it.*]

SHANNON: Thanks. Keep it. Goodbye! [*He starts toward the path down to the beach.*]

HANNAH: Where are you going? What are you going to do?

SHANNON: I'm going swimming. I'm going to swim out to China!

HANNAH: No, no, not tonight, Shannon! Tomorrow . . . tomorrow, Shannon!

[*But he divides the trumpet-flowered bushes and passes through them.* HANNAH *rushes after him, screaming for*

"Mrs. Faulk." MAXINE *can be heard shouting for the Mexican boys.*]

MAXINE: Muchachos, cojerlo! Atarlo! Está loco. Traerlo aquí. Catch him, he's crazy. Bring him back and tie him up!

[*In a few moments* SHANNON *is hauled back through the bushes and onto the verandah by* MAXINE *and the boys. They rope him into the hammock. His struggle is probably not much of a real struggle—histrionics mostly. But* HANNAH *stands wringing her hands by the steps as* SHANNON, *gasping for breath, is tied up.*]

HANNAH: The ropes are too tight on his chest!

MAXINE: No, they're not. He's acting, acting. He likes it! I know this black Irish bastard like nobody ever knowed him, so you keep out of it, honey. He cracks up like this so regular that you can set a calendar by it. Every eighteen months he does it, and twice he's done it here and I've had to pay for his medical care. Now I'm going to call in town to get a doctor to come out here and give him a knockout injection, and if he's not better tomorrow he's going into the Casa de Locos again like he did the last time he cracked up on me!

[*There is a moment of silence.*]

SHANNON: Miss Jelkes?

HANNAH: Yes.

SHANNON: Where are you?

HANNAH: I'm right here behind you. Can I do anything for you?

SHANNON: Sit here where I can see you. Don't stop talking. I have to fight this panic.

[*There is a pause. She moves a chair beside his hammock. The Germans troop up from the beach. They are delighted by the drama that* SHANNON *has provided. In their scanty swimsuits they parade onto the verandah and gather about* SHANNON'S *captive figure as if they were looking at a funny animal in a zoo. Their talk is in German except when they speak directly to* SHANNON *or* HANNAH. *Their heavily handsome figures gleam with oily wetness and they keep chuckling lubriciously.*]

HANNAH: Please! Will you be so kind as to leave him alone?

[*They pretend not to understand her.* FRAU FAHRENKOPF *bends over* SHANNON *in his hammock and speaks to him loudly and slowly in English.*]

FRAU FAHRENKOPF: Is this true you make pee-pee all over the suitcases of the ladies from Texas? Hah? Hah? You run down there to the bus and right in front of the ladies you pees all over the luggage of the ladies from Texas?

[HANNAH'S *indignant protest is drowned in the Rabelaisian laughter of the Germans.*]

HERR FAHRENKOPF: Thees is vunderbar, vunderbar! Hah? Thees is a epic gesture! Hah? Thees is the way to demonstrate to ladies that you are a American *gentleman!* Hah?

[*He turns to the others and makes a ribald comment. The two women shriek with amusement,* HILDA *falling back into the arms of* WOLFGANG, *who catches her with his hands over her almost nude breasts.*]

HANNAH [*calling out*]: Mrs. Faulk! Mrs. Faulk! [*She rushes to the verandah angle as* MAXINE *appears there.*] Will you please ask these people to leave him alone. They're tormenting him like an animal in a trap.

[*The Germans are already trooping around the verandah, laughing and capering gaily.*]

SHANNON [*suddenly, in a great shout*]: Regression to infantilism, ha, ha, regression to infantilism . . . The infantile protest, ha, ha, ha, the infantile expression of rage at Mama and rage at God and rage at the goddam crib, and rage at the everything, rage at the . . . everything. . . . Regression to infantilism. . . .

[*Now all have left but* HANNAH *and* SHANNON.]

SHANNON: Untie me.

HANNAH: Not yet.

SHANNON: I can't stand being tied up.

HANNAH: You'll have to stand it a while.

SHANNON: It makes me panicky.

HANNAH: I know.

SHANNON: A man can die of panic.

HANNAH: Not if he enjoys it as much as you, Mr. Shannon.

[*She goes into her cubicle directly behind his hammock. The cubicle is lighted and we see her removing a small teapot and a tin of tea from her suitcase on the cot, then a little alcohol burner. She comes back out with these articles.*]

SHANNON: What did you mean by that insulting remark?

HANNAH: What remark, Mr. Shannon?

SHANNON: That I enjoy it.

HANNAH: Oh . . . that.

SHANNON: Yes. That.

HANNAH: That wasn't meant as an insult, just an observation. I don't judge people, I draw them. That's all I do, just draw them, but in order to draw them I have to observe them, don't I?

SHANNON: And you've observed, you think you've observed, that I like being tied in this hammock, trussed up in it like a hog being hauled off to the slaughterhouse, Miss Jelkes.

HANNAH: Who wouldn't like to suffer and atone for the sins of himself and the world if it could be done in a hammock with ropes instead of nails, on a hill that's so much lovelier than Golgotha, the Place of the Skull, Mr. Shannon? There's something almost voluptuous in the way that you twist and groan in that hammock—no nails, no blood, no death. Isn't that a comparatively comfortable, almost voluptuous kind of crucifixion to suffer for the guilt of the world, Mr. Shannon?

[*She strikes a match to light the alcohol burner. A pure blue jet of flame springs up to cast a flickering, rather unearthly glow on their section of the verandah. The glow is delicately refracted by the subtle, faded colors of her robe—a robe given to her by a Kabuki actor who posed for her in Japan.*]

SHANNON: Why have you turned against me all of a sudden, when I need you the most?

HANNAH: I haven't turned against you at all, Mr. Shannon. I'm just attempting to give you a character sketch of yourself, in words instead of pastel crayons or charcoal.

SHANNON: You're certainly suddenly very sure of some New England spinsterish attitudes that I didn't know you had in you. I thought that you were an *emancipated* Puritan, Miss Jelkes.

HANNAH: Who is . . . ever . . . completely?

SHANNON: I thought you were sexless but you've suddenly turned into a woman. Know how I know that? Because you, not me—not me—are taking pleasure in my tied-up condition. All women, whether they face it or not, want to see a man in a tied-up situation. They work at it all their lives, to get a man in a tied-up situation. Their lives are fulfilled, they're satisfied at last, when they get a man, or as many men as they can, in the tied-up situation. [HANNAH *leaves the alcohol burner and teapot and moves to the railing where she grips a verandah post and draws a few deep breaths.*] You don't like this observation of you? The shoe's too tight for comfort when it's on your own foot, Miss Jelkes? Some deep breaths again—feeling panic?

HANNAH [*recovering and returning to the burner*]: I'd like to untie you right now, but let me wait till you've passed through your present disturbance. You're still indulging yourself in your . . . your Passion Play performance. I can't help observing this self-indulgence in you.

SHANNON: What rotten indulgence?

HANNAH: Well, your busload of ladies from the Female College in Texas. I don't like those ladies any more than you do, but after all, they did save up all year to make this Mexican tour, to stay in stuffy hotels and eat the food they're used to. They want to be at home away from home, but you . . . you indulged yourself, Mr. Shannon. You did conduct the tour as if it was just for you, for your own pleasure.

SHANNON: Hell, what pleasure—going through hell all the way?

HANNAH: Yes, but comforted, now and then, weren't you,

by the little musical prodigy under the wing of the college vocal instructor?

SHANNON: Funny, ha-ha funny! Nantucket spinsters have their wry humor, don't they?

HANNAH: Yes, they do. They have to.

SHANNON [*becoming progressively quieter under the cool influence of her voice behind him*]: I can't see what you're up to, Miss Jelkes honey, but I'd almost swear you're making a pot of tea over there.

HANNAH: That is just what I'm doing.

SHANNON: Does this strike you as the right time for a tea party?

HANNAH: This isn't plain tea, this is poppyseed tea.

SHANNON: Are you a slave to the poppy?

HANNAH: It's a mild, sedative drink that helps you get through nights that are hard for you to get through and I'm making it for my grandfather and myself as well as for you, Mr. Shannon. Because, for all three of us, this won't be an easy night to get through. Can't you hear him in his cell number 4, mumbling over and over and over the lines of his new poem? It's like a blind man climbing a staircase that goes to nowhere, that just falls off into space, and I hate to say what it is. . . . [*She draws a few deep breaths behind him.*]

SHANNON: Put some hemlock in his poppyseed tea tonight so he won't wake up tomorrow for the removal to the Casa de Huéspedes. Do that act of mercy. Put in the hemlock and I will consecrate it, turn it to God's blood. Hell, if you'll get me out of his hammock I'll serve it to him myself, I'll be your accomplice in this act of mercy. I'll say, "Take and drink this, the blood of our—"

HANNAH: Stop it! Stop being childishly cruel! I can't stand for a person that I respect to talk and behave like a small, cruel boy, Mr. Shannon.

SHANNON: What've you found to respect in me, Miss . . . Thin-Standing-Up-Female-Buddha?

HANNAH: I respect a person that has had to fight and howl for his decency and his—

SHANNON: *What* decency?

HANNAH: Yes, for his decency and his bit of goodness, much more than I respect the lucky ones that just had theirs handed out to them at birth and never afterwards snatched away from them by . . . unbearable . . . torments, I. . . .

SHANNON: You *respect* me?

HANNAH: I do.

SHANNON: But you just said that I'm taking pleasure in a . . . voluptuous crucifixion without nails. A . . . what? . . . painless atonement for the—

HANNAH [*cutting in*]: Yes, but I think—

SHANNON: Untie me!

HANNAH: Soon, soon. Be patient.

SHANNON: Now!

HANNAH: Not quite yet, Mr. Shannon. Not till I'm reasonably sure that you won't swim out to China, because, you see, I think you think of the . . . "the long swim to China" as another painless atonement. I mean I don't think you think you'd be intercepted by sharks and barracudas before you got far past the barrier reef. And I'm afraid you *would be*. It's as simple as that, if that is simple.

SHANNON: What's simple?

HANNAH: Nothing, except for simpletons, Mr. Shannon.

SHANNON: Do you believe in people being tied up?

HANNAH: Only when they might take the long swim to China.

SHANNON: All right, Miss Thin-Standing-Up-Female-Buddha, just light a Benson & Hedges cigarette for me and put it in my mouth and take it out when you hear me choking on it—if that doesn't seem to you like another bit of voluptuous self-crucifixion.

HANNAH [*looking about the verandah*]: I will, but . . . where did I put them?

SHANNON: I have a pack of my own in my pocket.

HANNAH: Which pocket?

SHANNON: I don't know which pocket, you'll have to frisk me for it. [*She pats his jacket pocket.*]

HANNAH: They're not in your coat pocket.

SHANNON: Then look for them in my pants' pockets.

[*She hesitates to put her hand in his pants' pockets, for a moment.* HANNAH *has always had a sort of fastidiousness, a reluctance, toward intimate physical contact. But after the momentary fastidious hesitation, she puts her hands in his pants' pocket and draws out the cigarette pack.*]

SHANNON: Now light it for me and put it in my mouth.

[*She complies with these directions. Almost at once he chokes and the cigarette is expelled.*]

HANNAH: You've dropped it on you—where is it?

SHANNON [*twisting and lunging about in the hammock*]: It's under me, under me, burning. Untie me, for God's sake, will you—it's burning me through my pants!

HANNAH: Raise your hips so I can—

SHANNON: I can't, the ropes are too tight. Untie me, un-tieeeee meeeeee!

HANNAH: I've found it, I've got it!

[*But* SHANNON'S *shout has brought* MAXINE *out of her office. She rushes onto the verandah and sits on* SHANNON'S *legs.*]

MAXINE: Now hear this, you crazy black Irish mick, you! You Protestant black Irish looney, I've called up Lopez, Doc Lopez. Remember him—the man in the dirty white jacket that come here the last time you cracked up here? And hauled you off to the Casa de Locos? Where they threw you into that cell with nothing in it but a bucket and straw and a water pipe? That you crawled up the water pipe? And dropped head-down on the floor and got a concussion? Yeah, and I told him you were back here to crack up again and if you didn't quiet down here tonight you should be hauled out in the morning.

SHANNON [*cutting in, with the honking sound of a panicky goose*]: Off, off, off, off, off!

HANNAH: Oh, Mrs. Faulk, Mr. Shannon won't quiet down till he's left alone in the hammock.

MAXINE: Then why don't *you* leave him alone?

HANNAH: I'm not sitting on him and he . . . has to be cared for by someone.

MAXINE: And the someone is *you?*

HANNAH: A long time ago, Mrs. Faulk, I had experience with someone in Mr. Shannon's condition, so I know how necessary it is to let them be quiet for a while.

MAXINE: He wasn't quiet, he was shouting.

HANNAH: He will quiet down again. I'm preparing a sedative tea for him, Mrs. Faulk.

MAXINE: Yeah, I see. Put it out. Nobody cooks here but the Chinaman in the kitchen.

HANNAH: This is just a little alcohol burner, a spirit lamp, Mrs. Faulk.

MAXINE: I know what it is. It goes out! [*She blows out the flame under the burner.*]

SHANNON: Maxine honey? [*He speaks quietly now.*] Stop persecuting this lady. You can't intimidate her. A bitch is no match for a lady except in a brass bed, honey, and sometimes not even there.

[*The Germans are heard shouting for beer—a case of it to take down to the beach.*]

WOLFGANG: Eine Kiste Carta Blanca.

FRAU FAHRENKOPF: Wir haben genug gehabt . . . vielleicht nicht.

HERR FAHRENKOPF: Nein! Niemals genug.

HILDA: Mutter du bist dick . . . aber wir sind es nicht.

SHANNON: Maxine, you're neglecting your duties as a beer-hall waitress. [*His tone is deceptively gentle.*] They want a case of Carta Blanca to carry down to the beach, so give it to 'em . . . and tonight, when the moon's gone down, if you'll let me out of this hammock, I'll try to imagine you as a . . . as a nymph in her teens.

MAXINE: A fat lot of good you'd be in your present condition.

SHANNON: Don't be a sexual snob at your age, honey.

MAXINE: Hah! [*But the unflattering offer has pleased her realistically modest soul, so she goes back to the Germans.*]

SHANNON: Now let me try a bit of your poppyseed tea, Miss Jelkes.

HANNAH: I ran out of sugar, but I had some ginger, some sugared ginger. [*She pours a cup of tea and sips it.*] Oh, it's not well brewed yet, but try to drink some now and the— [*She lights the burner again.*]—the second cup will be better. [*She crouches by the hammock and presses the cup to his lips. He raises his head to sip it, but he gags and chokes.*]

SHANNON: *Caesar's ghost!*—it could be chased by the witches' brew from Macbeth.

HANNAH: Yes, I know, it's still bitter.

[*The Germans appear on the wing of the verandah and go trooping down to the beach, for a beer festival and a moonlight swim. Even in the relative dark they have a luminous color, an almost phosphorescent pink and gold color of skin. They carry with them a case of Carta Blanca beer and the fantastically painted rubber horse. On their faces are smiles of euphoria as they move like a dream-image, starting to sing a marching song as they go.*]

SHANNON: Fiends out of hell with the . . . voices of . . . angels.

HANNAH: Yes, they call it "the logic of contradictions," Mr. Shannon.

SHANNON [*lunging suddenly forward and undoing the loosened ropes*]: Out! Free! Unassisted!

HANNAH: Yes, I never doubted that you could get loose, Mr. Shannon.

SHANNON: Thanks for your help, anyhow.

HANNAH: Where are you going?

[*He has crossed to the liquor cart.*]

SHANNON: Not far. To the liquor cart to make myself a rum-coco.

HANNAH: Oh. . . .

SHANNON [*at the liquor cart*]: Coconut? Check. Machete? Check. Rum? Double check! Ice? The ice bucket's empty. O.K., it's a night for warm drinks. Miss Jelkes? Would you care to have your complimentary rum-coco?

HANNAH: No thank you, Mr. Shannon.

SHANNON: You don't mind me having mine?

HANNAH: Not at all, Mr. Shannon.

SHANNON: You don't disapprove of this weakness, this self-indulgence?

HANNAH: Liquor isn't your problem, Mr. Shannon.

SHANNON: What is my problem, Miss Jelkes?

HANNAH: The oldest one in the world—the need to believe in something or in someone—almost anyone—almost anything . . . something.

SHANNON: Your voice sounds hopeless about it.

HANNAH: No, I'm not hopeless about it. In fact, I've discovered something to believe in.

SHANNON: Something like . . . God?

HANNAH: No.

SHANNON: What?

HANNAH: Broken gates between people so they can reach each other, even if it's just for one night only.

SHANNON: One night stands, huh?

HANNAH: One night . . . communication between them on a

verandah outside their . . . separate cubicles, Mr. Shannon.

SHANNON: You don't mean physically, do you?

HANNAH: No.

SHANNON: I didn't think so. Then what?

HANNAH: A little understanding exchanged between them, a wanting to help each other through nights like this.

SHANNON: Who was the someone you told the widow you'd helped long ago to get through a crack-up like this one I'm going through?

HANNAH: Oh . . . that. Myself.

SHANNON: You?

HANNAH: Yes. I can help you because I've been through what you are going through now. I had something like your spook—I just had a different name for him. I called him the blue devil, and . . . oh . . . we had quite a battle, quite a contest between us.

SHANNON: Which you obviously won.

HANNAH: I couldn't afford to lose.

SHANNON: How'd you beat your blue devil?

HANNAH: I showed him that I could endure him and I made him respect my endurance.

SHANNON: How?

HANNAH: Just by, just by . . . enduring. Endurance is something that spooks and blue devils respect. And they respect all the tricks that panicky people use to outlast and outwit their panic.

SHANNON: Like poppyseed tea?

HANNAH: Poppyseed tea or rum-cocos or just a few deep breaths. Anything, everything, that we take to give them the slip, and so to keep on going.

SHANNON: To where?

HANNAH: To somewhere like this, perhaps. This verandah over the rain forest and the still-water beach, after long, difficult travels. And I don't mean just travels about the world, the earth's surface. I mean . . . subterranean travels, the . . . the journeys that the spooked and bedeviled people are forced to take through the . . . the *unlighted* sides of their natures.

SHANNON: Don't tell me you have a dark side to your nature. [*He says this sardonically.*]

HANNAH: I'm sure I don't have to tell a man as experienced and knowledgeable as you, Mr. Shannon, that everything has its shadowy side?

[*She glances up at him and observes that she doesn't have his attention. He is gazing tensely at something off the verandah. It is the kind of abstraction, not vague but fiercely concentrated, that occurs in madness. She turns to look where he's looking. She closes her eyes for a moment and draws a deep breath, then goes on speaking in a voice like a hypnotist's, as if the words didn't matter, since he is not listening to her so much as to the tone and the cadence of her voice.*]

HANNAH: Everything in the whole solar system has a shadowy side to it except the sun itself—the sun is the single exception. You're not listening, are you?

SHANNON [*as if replying to her*]: The spook is in the rain forest. [*He suddenly hurls his coconut shell with great violence off the verandah, creating a commotion among the jungle birds.*] Good shot—it caught him right on the kisser and his teeth flew out like popcorn from a popper.

HANNAH: Has he gone off—to the dentist?

SHANNON: He's retreated a little way away for a little while, but when I buzz for my breakfast tomorrow, he'll bring it in to me with a grin that'll curdle the milk in the coffee and he'll stink like a . . . a gringo drunk in a Mexican jail who's slept all night in his vomit.

HANNAH: If you wake up before I'm out, I'll bring your coffee in to you . . . if you call me.

SHANNON [*his attention returns to her*]: No, you'll be gone, God help me.

HANNAH: Maybe and maybe not. I might think of something tomorrow to placate the widow.

SHANNON: The widow's implacable, honey.

HANNAH: I think I'll think of something because I have to. I can't let Nonno be moved to the Casa de Huéspedes, Mr. Shannon. Not any more than I could let you take the long swim out to China. You know that. Not if I can prevent it, and when I have to be resourceful, I can be very resourceful.

SHANNON: How'd you get over your crack-up?

HANNAH: I never cracked up, I couldn't afford to. Of course, I nearly did once. I was young once, Mr. Shannon, but I was one of those people who can be young without really having their youth, and not to have your youth when you are young is naturally very disturbing. But I was lucky. My work, this occupational therapy that I gave myself—painting and doing quick character sketches—made me look out of myself, not in, and gradually, at the far end of the tunnel that I was struggling out of I began to see this faint, very faint gray light—the light of the world outside me—and I kept climbing toward it. I had to.

SHANNON: Did it stay a gray light?

HANNAH: No, no, it turned white.

SHANNON: Only white, never gold?

HANNAH: No, it stayed only white, but white is a very good light to see at the end of a long black tunnel you thought would be never-ending, that only God or Death could put a stop to, especially when you . . . since I was . . . far from sure about God.

SHANNON: You're still unsure about him?

HANNAH: Not as unsure as I was. You see, in my profession I have to look hard and close at human faces in order to catch something in them before they get restless and call out, "Waiter, the check, we're leaving." Of course sometimes, a few times, I just see blobs of wet dough that pass for human faces, with bits of jelly for eyes. Then I cue in Nonno to give a recitation, because I can't draw such faces. But those aren't the usual faces, I don't think they're even real. Most times I *do* see something, and I can catch it—I *can*, like I caught something in your face when I sketched you this afternoon with your eyes open. Are you still listening to me? [*He crouches beside her chair, looking up at her intently.*] In Shanghai, Shannon, there is a place that's called the House for the Dying —the old and penniless dying, whose younger, penniless living children and grandchildren take them there for them to get through with their dying on pallets, on straw mats. The first time I went there it shocked me, I ran away from it. But I came back later and I saw that their children and grandchildren and the custodians of the place had put little comforts beside their death-pallets, little flowers and opium candies and religious emblems. That made me able to stay to draw their dying faces. Sometimes only their eyes were still alive, but, Mr. Shannon, those eyes of the penniless dying with those last little comforts beside them, I tell you, Mr. Shannon, those eyes looked up with their last dim life left in them as clear as the stars in the Southern Cross, Mr. Shannon. And now . . . now I am going to say something to you that will sound like something that only the spinster granddaughter of a minor romantic poet is likely to say. . . . Nothing I've ever seen has seemed as beautiful to me, not even the view from this verandah between the sky and the still-water beach, and lately . . . lately my grandfather's eyes have looked up at me like that. . . . [*She rises abruptly and crosses to the front of the verandah.*] Tell me, what is that sound I keep hearing down there?

SHANNON: There's a marimba band at the cantina on the beach.

HANNAH: I don't mean that, I mean that scraping, scuffling sound that I keep hearing under the verandah.

SHANNON: Oh, that. The Mexican boys that work here have caught an iguana and tied it up under the verandah, hitched it to a post, and naturally of course it's trying to scramble away. But it's got to the end of its rope, and get any further it cannot. Ha-ha—that's it. [*He quotes from* NONNO's *poem:* "And still the orange," etc.] Do you have any life of your own—besides your water colors and sketches and your travels with Grampa?

HANNAH: We make a home for each other, my grandfather and I. Do you know what I mean by a home? I don't mean a regular home. I mean I don't mean what other people mean when they speak of a home, because I don't regard a home as a . . . well, as a place, a building . . . a house . . . of wood,

bricks, stone. I think of a home as being a thing that two people have between them in which each can . . . well, nest—
rest—live in, emotionally speaking. Does that make any sense
to you, Mr. Shannon?

SHANNON: Yeah, complete. But. . . .

HANNAH: Another incomplete sentence.

SHANNON: We better leave it that way. I might've said something to hurt you.

HANNAH: I'm not thin skinned, Mr. Shannon.

SHANNON: No, well, then, I'll say it. . . . [*He moves to the
liquor cart.*] When a bird builds a nest to rest in and live in, it
doesn't build it in a . . . a falling-down tree.

HANNAH: I'm not a bird, Mr. Shannon.

SHANNON: I was making an analogy, Miss Jelkes.

HANNAH: I thought you were making yourself another rum-
coco, Mr. Shannon.

SHANNON: Both. When a bird builds a nest, it builds it with
an eye for the . . . the relative permanence of the location,
and also for the purpose of mating and propagating its species.

HANNAH: I still say that I'm not a bird, Mr. Shannon, I'm a
human being and when a member of that fantastic species
builds a nest in the heart of another, the question of permanence isn't the first or even the last thing that's considered . . .
necessarily? . . . always? Nonno and I have been continually
reminded of the impermanence of things lately. We go back to
a hotel where we've been many times before and it isn't there
any more. It's been demolished and there's one of those glassy,
brassy new ones. Or if the old one's still there, the manager
or the Maitre D who always welcomed us back so cordially
before has been replaced by someone new who looks at us
with suspicion.

SHANNON: Yeah, but you still had each other.

HANNAH: Yes. We did.

SHANNON: But when the old gentleman goes?

HANNAH: Yes?

SHANNON: What will you do? Stop?

HANNAH: Stop or go on . . . probably go on.

SHANNON: Alone? Checking into hotels alone, eating alone at tables for one in a corner, the tables waiters call aces.

HANNAH: Thank you for your sympathy, Mr. Shannon, but in my profession I'm obliged to make quick contacts with strangers who turn to friends very quickly.

SHANNON: Customers aren't friends.

HANNAH: They turn to friends, if they're friendly.

SHANNON: Yeah, but how will it seem to be traveling alone after so many years of traveling with. . . .

HANNAH: I will know how it feels when I feel it—and don't say alone as if nobody had ever gone on alone. For instance, you.

SHANNON: I've always traveled with trainloads, planeloads and busloads of tourists.

HANNAH: That doesn't mean you're still not really alone.

SHANNON: I never fail to make an intimate connection with someone in my parties.

HANNAH: Yes, the youngest young lady, and I was on the verandah this afternoon when the latest of these young ladies gave a demonstration of how lonely the intimate connection has always been for you. The episode in the cold, inhuman hotel room, Mr. Shannon, for which you despise the lady almost as much as you despise yourself. Afterwards you are so polite to the lady that I'm sure it must chill her to the bone, the scrupulous little attentions that you pay her in return for your little enjoyment of her. The gentleman-of-Virginia act that you put on for her, your noblesse oblige treatment of her . . . Oh no, Mr. Shannon, don't kid yourself that you ever travel with someone. You have always traveled alone except for your spook, as you call it. He's your traveling companion. Nothing, nobody else has traveled with you.

SHANNON: Thank you for your sympathy, Miss Jelkes.

HANNAH: You're welcome, Mr. Shannon. And now I think I had better warm up the poppyseed tea for Nonno. Only a good night's sleep could make it possible for him to go on from here tomorrow.

SHANNON: Yes, well, if the conversation is over—I think I'll go down for a swim now.

HANNAH: To China?

SHANNON: No, not to China, just to the little island out here with the sleepy bar on it . . . called the Cantina Serena.

HANNAH: Why?

SHANNON: Because I'm not a nice drunk and I was about to ask you a not nice question.

HANNAH: Ask it. There's no set limit on questions here tonight.

SHANNON: And no set limit on answers?

HANNAH: None I can think of between you and me, Mr. Shannon.

SHANNON: That I will take you up on.

HANNAH: Do.

SHANNON: It's a bargain.

HANNAH: Only do lie back down in the hammock and drink a full cup of the poppyseed tea this time. It's warmer now and the sugared ginger will make it easier to get down.

SHANNON: All right. The question is this: have you never had in your life any kind of a lovelife? [HANNAH *stiffens for a moment.*] I thought you said there was no limit set on questions.

HANNAH: We'll make a bargain—I will answer your question *after* you've had a full cup of the poppyseed tea so you'll be able to get the good night's sleep you need, too. It's fairly warm now and the sugared ginger's made it much more— [*She sips the cup.*]—palatable.

SHANNON: You think I'm going to drift into dreamland so you can welch on the bargain? [*He accepts the cup from her.*]

HANNAH: I'm not a welcher on bargains. Drink it all. All. *All!*

SHANNON [*with a disgusted grimace as he drains the cup*]:
Great Caesar's ghost. [*He tosses the cup off the verandah and
falls into the hammock, chuckling.*] The oriental idea of a
Mickey Finn, huh? Sit down where I can see you, Miss Jelkes
honey. [*She sits down in a straight-back chair, some distance
from the hammock.*] Where I can see you! I don't have an
x-ray eye in the back of my head, Miss Jelkes. [*She moves the
chair alongside the hammock.*] Further, further, up further.
[*She complies.*] There now. Answer the question now, Miss
Jelkes honey.

HANNAH: Would you mind repeating the question.

SHANNON [*slowly, with emphasis*]: Have you never had in
all of your life and your travels any experience, any encounter,
with what Larry-the-crackpot Shannon thinks of as a lovelife?

HANNAH: There are . . . worse things than chastity, Mr.
Shannon.

SHANNON: Yeah, lunacy and death are both a little worse,
maybe! But chastity isn't a thing that a beautiful woman or an
attractive man falls into like a booby trap or an overgrown
gopher hole, is it? [*There is a pause.*] I still think you are
welching on the bargain and I. . . . [*He starts out of the hammock.*]

HANNAH: Mr. Shannon, this night is just as hard for me to
get through as it is for you to get through. But it's you that
are welching on the bargain, you're not staying in the hammock. Lie back down in the hammock. Now. Yes. Yes, I have
had two experiences, well, encounters, with. . . .

SHANNON: *Two*, did you say?

HANNAH: Yes, I said two. And I wasn't exaggerating and
don't you say "fantastic" before I've told you both stories.
When I was sixteen, your favorite age, Mr. Shannon, each
Saturday afternoon my grandfather Nonno would give me
thirty cents, my allowance, my pay for my secretarial and
housekeeping duties. Twenty-five cents for admission to the
Saturday matinee at the Nantucket movie theatre and five
cents extra for a bag of popcorn, Mr. Shannon. I'd sit at the
almost empty back of the movie theatre so that the popcorn
munching wouldn't disturb the other movie patrons. Well . . .

one afternoon a young man sat down beside me and pushed his . . . knee against mine and . . . I moved over two seats but he moved over beside me and continued this . . . pressure! I jumped up and screamed, Mr. Shannon. He was arrested for molesting a minor.

SHANNON: Is he still in the Nantucket jail?

HANNAH: No. I got him out. I told the police that it was a Clara Bow picture—it *was* a Clara Bow picture—and I was just overexcited.

SHANNON: Fantastic.

HANNAH: Yes, very! The second experience is much more recent, only two years ago, when Nonno and I were operating at the Raffles Hotel in Singapore, and doing very well there, making expenses and more. One evening in the Palm Court of the Raffles we met this middle-aged, sort of nondescript Australian salesman. You know—plump, bald-spotted, with a bad attempt at speaking with an upper-class accent and terribly overfriendly. He was alone and looked lonely. Grandfather said him a poem and I did a quick character sketch that was shamelessly flattering of him. He paid me more than my usual asking price and gave my grandfather five Malayan dollars, yes, and he even purchased one of my water colors. Then it was Nonno's bedtime. The Aussie salesman asked me out in a sampan with him. Well, he'd been so generous . . . I accepted. I did, I accepted. Grandfather went up to bed and I went out in the sampan with this ladies' underwear salesman. I noticed that he became more and more. . . .

SHANNON: What?

HANNAH: Well . . . *agitated* . . . as the afterglow of the sunset faded out on the water. [*She laughs with a delicate sadness.*] Well, finally, eventually, he leaned toward me . . . we were vis-à-vis in the sampan . . . and he looked intensely, passionately into my eyes. [*She laughs again.*] And he said to me: "Miss Jelkes? Will you do me a favor? Will you do something for me?" "What?" said I. "Well," said he, "if I turn my back, if I look the other way, will you take off some piece of your clothes and let me hold it, just hold it?"

SHANNON: Fantastic!

HANNAH: Then he said, "It will just take a few seconds." "Just a few seconds for what?" I asked him. [*She gives the same laugh again.*] He didn't say for what, but. . . .

SHANNON: His satisfaction?

HANNAH: Yes.

SHANNON: What did you do—in a situation like that?

HANNAH: I . . . gratified his request, I did! And he kept his promise. He did keep his back turned till I said ready and threw him . . . the part of my clothes.

SHANNON: What did he do with it?

HANNAH: He didn't move, except to seize the article he'd requested. I looked the other way while his satisfaction took place.

SHANNON: Watch out for commercial travelers in the Far East. Is that the moral, Miss Jelkes honey?

HANNAH: Oh, no, the moral is oriental. Accept whatever situation you cannot improve.

SHANNON: "When it's inevitable, lean back and enjoy it"—is that it?

HANNAH: He'd bought a water color. The incident was embarrassing, not violent. I left and returned unmolested. Oh, and the funniest part of all is that when we got back to the Raffles Hotel, he took the piece of apparel out of his pocket like a bashful boy producing an apple for his schoolteacher and tried to slip it into my hand in the elevator. I wouldn't accept it. I whispered, "Oh, please keep it, Mr. Willoughby!" He'd paid the asking price for my water color and somehow the little experience had been rather touching, I mean it was so *lonely*, out there in the sampan with violet streaks in the sky and this little middle-aged Australian making sounds like he was dying of asthma! And the planet Venus coming serenely out of a fair-weather cloud, over the Straits of Malacca. . . .

SHANNON: And that experience . . . you call that a. . . .

HANNAH: A love experience? Yes. I do call it one.

[*He regards her with incredulity, peering into her face so closely that she is embarrassed and becomes defensive.*]

SHANNON: That, that . . . sad, dirty little episode, you call it a . . . ?

HANNAH [*cutting in sharply*]: Sad it certainly was—for the odd little man—but why do you call it "dirty"?

SHANNON: How did you feel when you went into your bedroom?

HANNAH: Confused, I . . . a little confused, I suppose. . . . I'd known about loneliness—but not that degree or . . . depth of it.

SHANNON: You mean it didn't *disgust* you?

HANNAH: Nothing human disgusts me unless it's unkind, violent. And I told you how gentle he was—apologetic, shy, and really very, well, *delicate* about it. However, I do grant you it was on the rather fantastic level.

SHANNON: You're. . . .

HANNAH: I am *what?* "Fantastic?"

[*While they have been talking,* NONNO's *voice has been heard now and then, mumbling, from his cubicle. Suddenly it becomes loud and clear.*]

NONNO:
          And finally the broken stem,
          The plummeting to earth and then. . . .

[*His voice subsides to its mumble.* SHANNON, *standing behind* HANNAH, *places his hand on her throat.*]

HANNAH: What is that for? Are you about to strangle me, Mr. Shannon?

SHANNON: You can't stand to be touched?

HANNAH: Save it for the widow. It isn't for me.

SHANNON: Yes, you're right. [*He removes his hand.*] I could do it with Mrs. Faulk, the inconsolable widow, but I couldn't with you.

HANNAH [*dryly and lightly*]: Spinster's loss, widow's gain, Mr. Shannon.

SHANNON: Or widow's loss, spinster's gain. Anyhow it sounds

like some old parlor game in a Virginia or Nantucket Island parlor. But . . . I wonder something. . . .

HANNAH: What do you wonder?

SHANNON: If we couldn't . . . *travel* together, I mean just *travel* together?

HANNAH: Could we? In your opinion?

SHANNON: Why not, I don't see why not.

HANNAH: I think the impracticality of the idea will appear much clearer to you in the morning, Mr. Shannon. [*She folds her dimly gold-lacquered fan and rises from her chair.*] Morning can always be counted on to bring us back to a more realistic level. . . . Good night, Mr. Shannon. I have to pack before I'm too tired to.

SHANNON: Don't leave me out here alone yet.

HANNAH: I have to pack now so I can get up at daybreak and try my luck in the plaza.

SHANNON: You won't sell a water color or sketch in that blazing hot plaza tomorrow. Miss Jelkes honey, I don't think you're operating on the realistic level.

HANNAH: Would I be if I thought we could travel together?

SHANNON: I still don't see why we couldn't.

HANNAH: Mr. Shannon, you're not well enough to travel anywhere with anybody right now. Does that sound cruel of me?

SHANNON: You mean that I'm stuck here for good? Winding up with the . . . inconsolable widow?

HANNAH: We all wind up with something or with someone, and if it's someone instead of just something, we're lucky, perhaps . . . unusually lucky. [*She starts to enter her cubicle, then turns to him again in the doorway.*] Oh, and tomorrow. . . . [*She touches her forehead as if a little confused as well as exhausted.*]

SHANNON: What about tomorrow?

HANNAH [*with difficulty*]: I think it might be better, tomorrow, if we avoid showing any particular interest in each other, because Mrs. Faulk is a morbidly jealous woman.

SHANNON: *Is* she?

HANNAH: Yes, she seems to have misunderstood our . . . sympathetic interest in each other. So I think we'd better avoid any more long talks on the verandah. I mean till she's thoroughly reassured it might be better if we just say good morning or good night to each other.

SHANNON: We don't even have to say that.

HANNAH: I will, but you don't have to answer.

SHANNON [*savagely*]: How about wall-tappings between us by way of communication? You know, like convicts in separate cells communicate with each other by tapping on the walls of the cells? One tap: I'm here. Two taps: are you there? Three taps: yes, I am. Four taps: that's good, we're together. *Christ!* . . . Here, take this. [*He snatches the gold cross from his pocket.*] Take my gold cross and hock it, it's 22-carat gold.

HANNAH: What do you, what are you . . . ?

SHANNON: There's a fine amethyst in it, it'll pay your travel expenses back to the States.

HANNAH: Mr. Shannon, you're making no sense at all now.

SHANNON: Neither are you, Miss Jelkes, talking about tomorrow, and. . . .

HANNAH: All I was saying was. . . .

SHANNON: You won't *be* here tomorrow! Had you forgotten you won't be here tomorrow?

HANNAH [*with a slight, shocked laugh*]: Yes, I *had,* I'd *forgotten!*

SHANNON: The widow wants you out and out you'll go, even if you sell your water colors like hotcakes to the pariah dogs in the plaza. [*He stares at her, shaking his head hopelessly.*]

HANNAH: I suppose you're right, Mr. Shannon. I must be too tired to think or I've contracted your fever. . . . It had actually slipped my mind for a moment that—

NONNO [*abruptly, from his cubicle*]: Hannah!

HANNAH [*rushing to his door*]: Yes, what is it, Nonno? [*He doesn't hear her and repeats her name louder.*] Here I am, I'm here.

NONNO: Don't come in yet, but stay where I can call you.

HANNAH: Yes, I'll *hear* you, Nonno. [*She turns toward* SHANNON, *drawing a deep breath.*]

SHANNON: Listen, if you don't take this gold cross that I never want on me again, I'm going to pitch it off the verandah at the spook in the rain forest. [*He raises an arm to throw it, but she catches his arm to restrain him.*]

HANNAH: All right, Mr. Shannon, I'll take it, I'll hold it for you.

SHANNON: Hock it, honey, you've got to.

HANNAH: Well, if I do, I'll mail the pawn ticket to you so you can redeem it, because you'll want it again, when you've gotten over your fever. [*She moves blindly down the verandah and starts to enter the wrong cubicle.*]

SHANNON: That isn't your cell, you went past it. [*His voice is gentle again.*]

HANNAH: I did, I'm sorry. I've never been this tired in all my life. [*She turns to face him again. He stares into her face. She looks blindly out, past him.*] Never! [*There is a slight pause.*] What did you say is making that constant, dry, scuffling sound beneath the verandah?

SHANNON: I told you.

HANNAH: I didn't hear you.

SHANNON: I'll get my flashlight, I'll show you. [*He lurches rapidly into his cubicle and back out with a flashlight.*] It's an iguana. I'll show you. . . . See? The iguana? At the end of its rope? Trying to go on past the end of its goddam rope? Like you! Like *me*! Like Grampa with his last poem!

[*In the pause which follows singing is heard from the beach.*]

HANNAH: What is a—what—iguana?

SHANNON: It's a kind of lizard—a big one, a giant one. The Mexican kids caught it and tied it up.

HANNAH: Why did they tie it up?

SHANNON: Because that's what they do. They tie them up and fatten them up and then eat them up, when they're ready for eating. They're a delicacy. Taste like white meat of chicken. At least the Mexicans think so. And also the kids, the Mexican kids, have a lot of fun with them, poking out their eyes with sticks and burning their tails with matches. You know? Fun? Like that?

HANNAH: Mr. Shannon, please go down and cut it loose!

SHANNON: I can't do that.

HANNAH: Why can't you?

SHANNON: Mrs. Faulk wants to eat it. I've got to please Mrs. Faulk, I am at her mercy. I am at her disposal.

HANNAH: I don't understand. I mean I don't understand how anyone could eat a big lizard.

SHANNON: Don't be so critical. If you got hungry enough you'd eat it too. You'd be surprised what people will eat if hungry. There's a lot of hungry people still in the world. Many have died of starvation, but a lot are still living and hungry, believe you me, if you will take my word for it. Why, when I was conducting a party of—*ladies?*—yes, ladies . . . through a country that shall be nameless but in this world, we were passing by rubberneck bus along a tropical coast when we saw a great mound of . . . well, the smell was unpleasant. One of my ladies said, "Oh, Larry, what is that?" My name being Lawrence, the most familiar ladies sometimes call me Larry. I didn't use the four-letter word for what the great mound was. I didn't think it was necessary to say it. Then she noticed, and I noticed too, a pair of very old natives of this nameless country, practically naked except for a few filthy rags, creeping and crawling about this mound of . . . and . . . occasionally stopping to pick something out of it, and pop it into their mouths. What? Bits of undigested . . . food particles, Miss Jelkes. [*There is silence for a moment. She makes a gagging sound in her throat and rushes the length of the verandah to the wooden steps and disappears for a while.* SHANNON *continues, to himself and the moon.*] Now why did I tell her that? Because it's true? That's no reason to tell her, because it's true.

Yeah. Because it's true was a good reason not to tell her. Except . . . I think I first *faced* it in that nameless country. The gradual, rapid, natural, unnatural—predestined, accidental— cracking up and going to pieces of young Mr. T. Lawrence Shannon, yes, still *young* Mr. T. Lawrence Shannon, by which rapid-slow process . . . his final tour of ladies through tropical countries. . . . Why did I say "tropical"? Hell! Yes! It's always been tropical countries I took ladies through. Does that, does that—huh?—signify something, I wonder? Maybe. Fast decay is a thing of hot climates, steamy, hot, wet climates, and I run back to them like a . . . . Incomplete sentence. . . . Always seducing a lady or two, or three or four or five ladies in the party, but really ravaging her first by pointing out to her the—what?—horrors? Yes, horrors!—of the tropical country being conducted a tour through. My . . . brain's going out now, like a failing—power. . . . So I stay here, I reckon, and live off la patrona for the rest of my life. Well, she's old enough to predecease me. She could check out of here first, and I imagine that after a couple of years of having to satisfy her I might be prepared for the shock of her passing on. . . . Cruelty . . . pity. What is it? . . . Don't know, all I know is. . . .

HANNAH [*from below the verandah*]: You're talking to yourself.

SHANNON: No. To you. I knew you could hear me out there, but not being able to see you I could say it easier, you know . . . ?

NONNO:
    A chronicle no longer gold,
    A bargaining with mist and mould. . . .

HANNAH [*coming back onto the verandah*]: I took a closer look at the iguana down there.

SHANNON: You did? How did you like it? Charming? Attractive?

HANNAH: No, it's not an attractive creature. Nevertheless I think it should be cut loose.

SHANNON: Iguanas have been known to bite their tails off when they're tied up by their tails.

HANNAH: This one is tied by its throat. It can't bite its own head off to escape from the end of the rope, Mr. Shannon. Can you look at me and tell me truthfully that you don't know it's able to feel pain and panic?

SHANNON: You mean it's one of God's creatures?

HANNAH: If you want to put it that way, yes, it is. Mr. Shannon, will you please cut it loose, set it free? Because if you don't, I will.

SHANNON: Can you look at *me* and tell *me* truthfully that this reptilian creature, tied up down there, doesn't mostly disturb you because of its parallel situation to your Grampa's dying-out effort to finish one last poem, Miss Jelkes?

HANNAH: Yes, I. . . .

SHANNON: Never mind completing that sentence. We'll play God tonight like kids play house with old broken crates and boxes. All right? Now Shannon is going to go down there with his machete and cut the damn lizard loose so it can run back to its bushes because God won't do it and we are going to play God here.

HANNAH: I knew you'd do that. And I thank you.

[SHANNON *goes down the two steps from the verandah with the machete. He crouches beside the cactus that hides the iguana and cuts the rope with a quick, hard stroke of the machete. He turns to look after its flight, as the low, excited mumble in cubicle 3 grows louder. Then* NONNO'S *voice turns to a sudden shout.*]

NONNO: *Hannah! Hannah!* [*She rushes to him, as he wheels himself out of his cubicle onto the verandah.*]

HANNAH: Grandfather! What is it?

NONNO: I! believe! it! is! *finished!* Quick, before I forget it—pencil, paper! Quick! please! Ready?

HANNAH: Yes. All ready, Grandfather.

NONNO [*in a loud, exalted voice*]:

> How calmly does the orange branch
> Observe the sky begin to blanch
> Without a cry, without a prayer,
> With no betrayal of despair.

Sometime while night obscures the tree
The zenith of its life will be
Gone past forever, and from thence
A second history will commence.

A chronicle no longer gold,
A bargaining with mist and mould,
And finally the broken stem
The plummeting to earth; and then

An intercourse not well designed
For beings of a golden kind
Whose native green must arch above
The earth's obscene, corrupting love.

And still the ripe fruit and the branch
Observe the sky begin to blanch
Without a cry, without a prayer,
With no betrayal of despair.

O Courage, could you not as well
Select a second place to dwell,
Not only in that golden tree
But in the frightened heart of me?

Have you got it?

HANNAH: Yes!

NONNO: All of it?

HANNAH: Every word of it.

NONNO: It is *finished*?

HANNAH: Yes.

NONNO: Oh! God! Finally finished?

HANNAH: Yes, finally finished. [*She is crying. The singing voices flow up from the beach.*]

NONNO: After waiting so long!

HANNAH: Yes, we waited so long.

NONNO: And it's good! It is *good*?

HANNAH: It's—it's. . . .

NONNO: What?

HANNAH: Beautiful, Grandfather! [*She springs up, a fist to her mouth.*] Oh, Grandfather, I am so happy for you. Thank you for writing such a lovely poem! It was worth the long wait. Can you sleep now, Grandfather?

NONNO: You'll have it typewritten tomorrow?

HANNAH: Yes. I'll have it typed up and send it off to *Harper's.*

NONNO: Hah? I didn't hear that, Hannah.

HANNAH [*shouting*]: I'll have it typed up tomorrow, and mail it to *Harper's* tomorrow! They've been waiting for it a long time, too! You know!

NONNO: Yes, I'd like to pray now.

HANNAH: Good night. Sleep now, Grandfather. You've finished your loveliest poem.

NONNO [*faintly, drifting off*]: Yes, thanks and praise . . .

[MAXINE *comes around the front of the verandah, followed by* PEDRO *playing a harmonica softly. She is prepared for a night swim, a vividly striped towel thrown over her shoulders. It is apparent that the night's progress has mellowed her spirit: her face wears a faint smile which is suggestive of those cool, impersonal, all-comprehending smiles on the carved heads of Egyptian or Oriental deities. Bearing a rumcoco, she approaches the hammock, discovers it empty, the ropes on the floor, and calls softly to* PEDRO.]

MAXINE: Shannon ha escapado! [PEDRO *goes on playing dreamily. She throws back her head and shouts.*] SHANNON! [*The call is echoed by the hill beyond.* PEDRO *advances a few steps and points under the verandah.*]

PEDRO: Miré. Allé 'hasta Shannon.

[SHANNON *comes into view from below the verandah, the severed rope and machete dangling from his hands.*]

MAXINE: What are you doing down there, Shannon?

SHANNON: I cut loose one of God's creatures at the end of the rope.

[HANNAH, *who has stood motionless with closed eyes behind*

the wicker chair, goes quietly toward the cubicles and out of the moon's glare.]

MAXINE [*tolerantly*]: What'd you do that for, Shannon.

SHANNON: So that one of God's creatures could scramble home safe and free. . . . A little act of grace, Maxine.

MAXINE [*smiling a bit more definitely*]: C'mon up here, Shannon. I want to talk to you.

SHANNON [*starting to climb onto the verandah, as* MAXINE *rattles the ice in the coconut shell*]: What d'ya want to talk about, Widow Faulk?

MAXINE: Let's go down and swim in that liquid moonlight.

SHANNON: Where did you pick up that poetic expression?

[MAXINE *glances back at* PEDRO *and dismisses him with,* "Vamos." *He leaves with a shrug, the harmonica fading out.*]

MAXINE: Shannon, I want you to stay with me.

SHANNON [*taking the rum-coco from her*]: You want a drinking companion?

MAXINE: No, I just want you to stay here, because I'm alone here now and I need somebody to help me manage the place.

[HANNAH *strikes a match for a cigarette.*]

SHANNON [*looking toward her*]: I want to remember that face. I won't see it again.

MAXINE: Let's go down to the beach.

SHANNON: I can make it down the hill, but not back up.

MAXINE: I'll get you back up the hill. [*They have started off now, toward the path down through the rain forest.*] I've got five more years, maybe ten, to make this place attractive to the male clientele, the middle-aged ones at least. And you can take care of the women that are with them. That's what you can do, you know that, Shannon.

[*He chuckles happily. They are now on the path,* MAXINE *half-leading, half-supporting him. Their voices fade as* HANNAH *goes into* NONNO'S *cubicle and comes back with a*

*shawl, her cigarette left inside. She pauses between the door
and the wicker chair and speaks to herself and the sky.*]

HANNAH: Oh, God, can't we stop now? Finally? Please let
us. It's so quiet here, now.

[*She starts to put the shawl about* NONNO, *but at the same
moment his head drops to the side. With a soft intake of
breath, she extends a hand before his mouth to see if he is
still breathing. He isn't. In a panicky moment, she looks right
and left for someone to call to. There's no one. Then she
bends to press her head to the crown of* NONNO'S *and the
curtain starts to descend.*]

THE END

About the Author

Tennessee Williams (Thomas Lanier Williams) was born in Columbus, Mississippi on March 26, 1914, and lived there until he was twelve, when his family moved to St. Louis. His education at the University of Missouri (1931-33) was interrupted for financial reasons, but he later (1938) received his B.A. from the University of Iowa. Tennessee Williams started writing and publishing poetry when very young, while simultaneouly holding a variety of jobs—starting with a clerical position in the shoe company that also employed his father. His first real recognition came in 1940 when he received a Rockefeller fellowship and his first play, *Battle of Angels*, was produced by the Theatre Guild in Boston. His first financial break, which enabled him to give full attention to his writing, came with an offer from MGM, which he accepted, abandoning his job as a movie usher. After six months of work in Hollywood, he devoted his time to writing *The Glass Menagerie*, the initial success which established him as one of the leading American playwrights.

Since that time, his plays have been made into movies, produced on TV, turned into operas and ballets—*A Streetcar Named Desire, Summer and Smoke, The Night of the Iguana, Cat on a Hot Tin Roof*, and *The Glass Menagerie*, to name just a few. In May of 1969 Tennessee Williams was awarded the Gold Medal for Literature by the American Academy of Arts and Letters and the National Institute of Arts and Letters. He died on February 25, 1983.

He is the author of the following works: *Baby Doll, Battle of Angels, Camino Real, Cat on a Hot Tin Roof* (winner of the Pulitzer Prize and Drama Critics' Award), *Dragon Country* (short plays, including *In the Bar of a Tokyo Hotel*), *The Eccentricities of a Nightingale, Eight Mortal Ladies Possessed* (stories), *The Glass Menagerie, Hard Candy* (stories), *In the Winter of Cities* (poems), *Kingdom of Earth (The Seven Descents of Myrtle), The Knightly Quest* (stories), *Memoirs* (autobiography), *The Milk Train Doesn't Stop Here Anymore, Moise and the World of Reason* (novel), *The Night of the Iguana* (winner of the Drama Critics' Award), *One Arm & Other Stories, Orpheus Descending, Out Cry, Period of Adjustment, The Roman Spring of Mrs. Stone* (novel), *The Rose Tattoo, Small Craft Warnings, A Streetcar Named Desire* (winner of the Pulitzer Prize and Drama Critics' Award), *Suddenly Last Summer, Summer and Smoke, Sweet Bird of Youth, 27 Wagons Full of Cotton,* and *The Two-Character Play.*